Praise for

WHEN BOOKS WENT TO WAR

"Heartwarming war stories aren't easy to come by ... *When Books Went to War* winds up feeling like the bibliophile's equivalent of *It's a Wonderful Life*." — Janet Maslin, *New York Times*

"[*When Books Went to War*] packs a wallop. Whether or not you're a book lover, you'll be moved by the impeccably researched tale. Manning not only illuminates a dusty slice of World War II history that most of us know nothing about but also reminds us, in the digital era of movies and TV, just how powerfully literature once figured in people's lives. Grade: **A**." — *Entertainment Weekly*

"Ably resurrects the important story of the ASE program ... Not only a readable, accessible addition to World War II, literature; it's also a book that will be enjoyed by lovers of books about books." — *Boston Globe*

"Inspirational and optimistic ... Will appeal to bibliophiles, World War II enthusiasts, and anyone interested in the stories of the so-called Greatest Generation. It will also appeal to anyone who likes a story with a happy ending." — *Christian Science Monitor*

"★★★★ [out of four] ... Crisply written and compelling ... Both a tribute to the civilizing influence of books and a careful account of what it took — a lot — to ensure that U.S. fighting men had the right stuff to read ... Manning's portrait of this seemingly prosaic slice of the war effort is more than colorful; it's also a cultural history that does much to explain modern America." — *USA Today*

"This is the beautiful story of a great, nearly forgotten chapter in our history. In addition to sending men, bombers, and rifles overseas to win World War II, America sent books — filling the bored hours that separate war's terrors, helping give purpose to the fight, and shaping the taste of generations. What a wonderful thing." — Nathaniel Fick, author of *One Bullet Away*

"Fascinating ... The idea that 'books were intertwined with the values at stake in the war' is central to Manning's study." — *Smithsonian*

"The Armed Services Editions ... helped to rescue *The Great Gatsby* from the remaindered bin and to propel Betty Smith's *A Tree Grows in Brooklyn* into the ranks of modern classics ... *When Books Went to War* doggedly documents the years of bureaucratic maneuvering that resulted in the creation and deployment of the ASEs."
— Maureen Corrigan, *Washington Post*

"Recuperat[es] a fascinating story ... Goes far towards recovering a lost aspect of [the] war." — *Times Literary Supplement*

"Fascinating ... Her eye for zesty quotes — Manning makes excellent use of soldiers' letters—is spot on." — *Newsday*

"Well-written, carefully researched, and drawing upon primary sources and news articles, this book brings to life a little-known part of World War II culture ... Highly readable and extremely appealing."
— *Library Journal*

"Delightful ... Engrossing ... Manning's entertaining account will have readers nostalgic for that seemingly distant era when books were high priority." — *Publishers Weekly*

"Intriguing ... A fresh perspective on the trials of war and the power of books." — *Kirkus Reviews*

"Thoroughly engaging, enlightening, and often uplifting ... I was enthralled and moved."
— Tim O'Brien, author of *The Things They Carried*

"Every avid reader loves a book about books. Molly Guptill Manning's *When Books Went to War* is that and more: a thrilling and concise history of World War II featuring the written word."
— Megan Marshall, Pulitzer Prize–winning author of *Margaret Fuller*

WHEN BOOKS
WENT TO WAR

WHEN BOOKS WENT TO WAR

*The Stories That Helped Us
Win World War II*

Molly Guptill Manning

MARINER BOOKS
An Imprint of HarperCollins*Publishers*
Boston   New York

First Mariner Books edition 2015

Copyright © 2014 by Molly Guptill Manning

All rights reserved.

marinerbooks.com

Library of Congress Cataloging-in-Publication Data
Manning, Molly Guptill, date.
When books went to war : the stories that helped us win World War II /
Molly Guptill Manning.
pages cm
Includes bibliographical references and index.
ISBN 978-0-544-53502-2 (hardback) — ISBN 978-0-544-57040-5 (trade paper) —
ISBN 978-0-544-53517-6 (ebook)
1. World War, 1939–1945 — United States — Literature and the war.
2. Books and reading — United States — History — 20th century.
3. Publishers and publishing — United States — History — 20th century.
4. American literature — 20th century — History and criticism.
5. War in literature. I. Title.
Z1003.2.M36 2014
028'.90973 — dc23
2014033571

Book design by Brian Moore

Printed in the United States of America
22 23 24 25 26 LBC 12 11 10 9 8

Illustration credits appear on page 267.

For my husband, Christopher Manning

Books cannot be killed by fire.

People die, but books never die. No man and no force can put thought in a concentration camp forever. No man and no force can take from the world the books that embody man's eternal fight against tyranny. In this war, we know, books are weapons.

Franklin D. Roosevelt

BOOKS ARE WEAPONS IN THE WAR OF IDEAS

Contents

Introduction

"Were you ever so upset emotionally that you had to tell some-one about it, to sit down and write it out?" a Marine asked in a letter to the author Betty Smith. "That is how I feel now," he confided.

"You see I am . . . 20 year[s] old . . . but I feel twice that age. I went through hell in two years of combat overseas . . . I just wanted you to understand that despite my youth I have seen a little bit of suffering."

At the time this Marine wrote his letter, malaria ravaged his body and he was hospitalized and confined to bed rest. Yet he credited the illness with saving his life. During his time in sick-bay, he was given an Armed Services Edition of Smith's *A Tree Grows in Brooklyn*. "I have read it twice and am halfway through it again," and "every time I read it, I feel more deeply than I did before," he said.

"Ever since the first time I struggled through knee deep mud . . . carrying a stretcher from which my buddie's life dripped away in precious blood and I was powerless to help him, I have felt hard and cynical against this world and have felt sure that I was no longer capable of loving anything or anybody," he wrote. He went through the war with a "dead heart . . . and dulled mind," believing he had lost the ability to feel.

It was only as he read *A Tree Grows in Brooklyn* that some-thing inside him began to stir. "I can't explain the emotional re-action that took place, I only know that it happened and that this heart of mine turned over and became alive again. A surge of confidence has swept through me and I feel that maybe a fellow has a fighting chance in this world after all. I'll never be able to explain to you the gratitude and love that fill my heart in appreciation of what your book means to me." It brought laughter and joy, and also tears. Although it "was unusual for a supposedly battle-hardened marine to do such an effeminate thing as weep over a piece of fiction, . . . I'm not ashamed," he said. His tears proved he was human.

"I don't think I would have been able to sleep this night," he wrote in closing, "unless I bared my heart to the person who caused it to live again."

The American forces serving in World War II were composed primarily of citizen soldiers — people who had no notion of going to war until Pearl Harbor was attacked. Many volunteered and others were drafted, and together these unprepared and unknowing souls faced a daunting combination of hurried training at bare-bones facilities, and days and weeks of transport, boredom, and fear. They experienced horrors and unimaginable scenes of violence and destruction for which no training could fully prepare them, and, for many, recuperation in hospitals spread around the world. They were constantly reminded of their proximity to death. As one soldier remarked, it was not uncommon to "have breakfast with a man and at supper time he has been buried."

The war took a tremendous physical and psychological toll on the men who fought it. The infantrymen plodded through endless mud, advanced as snipers fired at them, and slumbered in the comfort of rain-filled foxholes — sometimes to the lullaby of squealing mortars in the distance and buzzing insects swarming about them. They always seemed to be wet, dirty, muddy, uncomfortable, and exhausted. They marched and fought through searing heat and bitter cold, faced disease — malaria, typhus, and infections of all kinds — and bore the brunt of the enemy's bullets and bombs. It is understandable why they referred to themselves as the "God-damned infantry."

The pilots and crews of the B-17 Flying Fortresses, B-24 Liberators, B-25 Mitchells, B-26 Marauders, and B-29 Superfortresses faced a different series of perils: flying a steady course as flak pierced holes in their planes, engaging in sudden aerial battles, and witnessing crew members suffer or die from injuries incurred midflight. Their limbs became painfully numb as they endured subzero temperatures during long journeys in unheated aircraft, and the relief they experienced upon safe return was often accompanied by the devastation of learning that others did not complete the trip back. Many planes crash-landed, ran out of fuel, or just plain crashed. The B-24s and B-26s did not earn the monikers Flying Coffin and Widow-Maker for nothing.

Those in the Navy had their own set of problems. The initial thrill of sailing the seas and seeing the world from a gleaming ship was chilled by the isolation of days and weeks spent outside the sight of land. "Loneliness" and "boredom" took on new meanings. Meanwhile, the constant threat of lurking submarines and the mere sight or muffled din of an approaching enemy plane rattled the nerves of even the bravest sailor. There was no disguising cruisers or destroyers on the open sea. When the "music" started, they were like ducks in a shooting gallery.

The days were grinding, the stress was suffocating, and the dreams of making it home were often fleeting. Any distraction from the horrors of war was cherished. The men treasured mementos of home. Letters from loved ones were rare prizes. Card games, puzzles, music, and the occasional sports game helped pass the hours waiting for action or sleep to come. Yet mail could be frustratingly irregular — sometimes taking as long as four or five months to arrive — and games and the energy to play them could not always be mustered after a long day of training or fighting. To keep morale from sinking, there needed to be readily available entertainment to provide some relief from war.

The story of the Armed Services Editions — portable, accessible, and pervasive paperbacks like the edition of *A Tree Grows in Brooklyn* that so moved a young Marine to write Betty Smith — is a remarkable one. They were everywhere: servicemen read them while waiting in line for chow or a haircut, when pinned down in a foxhole, and when stuck on a plane for a milk run. They were so ubiquitous, one sailor remarked that a man was "out of uniform if one isn't sticking out [of] the hip pocket!" They were the most dependable distraction available on all fronts. Whenever a soldier needed an escape, the antidote to anxiety, relief from boredom, a bit of laughter, inspiration, or hope, he cracked open a book and drank in the words that would transport him elsewhere. Every soldier and sailor abided by a strict policy of swapping and exchanging books, no matter how worn. The print could be smudged, the pages ripped or falling out, and still a book would continue to make the rounds. As one sailor said, "To heave one in the garbage can is tantamount to striking your grandmother."

They weren't just for entertainment and diversion. Books also served as the premier weapon in fighting Adolf Hitler's "war of ideas." Nazi Germany sought control over people's beliefs, not just their bodies and territory. From the 1933 state-sanctioned book burnings in Germany to the purging of libraries across Europe as nations were conquered by the Nazis, "un-German" reading material was threatened with extinction. The scale of destruction was impressive. By V-E Day, it is estimated that Germany had destroyed over 100 million books in Europe.

And yet the story of the Armed Services Editions is largely untold. It was an astonishing effort. The government supplied more than 120 million free books to ensure that America's fighting men were equipped with spirit and resolve to carry them through their battles.

With books in their pockets, American GIs stormed the beaches of Normandy, trekked to the Rhine, and liberated Europe; they hopped from one deadly Pacific island to the next, from the shores of Australia to the backyard of Japan. Some read to remember the home they had left behind, others to forget the hell that surrounded them. Books uplifted their weary souls and energized their minds. As the letter to Betty Smith reveals, books had the power to soothe an aching heart, renew hope for the future, and provide a respite when there was no other escape. For many of America's servicemen, books were their most important equipment.

After the war, the accessibility of mass-market paperbacks — together with the GI Bill — helped build a new literate middle class, spreading reading to a wide and democratic public. The wartime book programs had made *The Great Gatsby* into a classic, engaged dozens of authors in pen pal relationships with thousands of soldiers, and touched the minds and hearts of millions of men and women.

This is the story of pens that were as mighty as swords.

WHEN BOOKS
WENT TO WAR

ONE

A Phoenix Will Rise

What is to give light must endure burning.

— VIKTOR E. FRANKL

E VEN THE MISTY drizzle that blanketed Berlin did not dampen the merriment surrounding the grand parade held on May 10, 1933. Thousands of students, proudly wearing their university colors, walked through the foggy streets by glittering torchlight as they made their way toward the Bebelplatz, the main plaza between the Friedrich Wilhelm University and the Opera House. Forty thousand spectators gathered in the plaza to behold the spectacle that was about to unfold; another forty thousand assembled along the parade route. In the center of the Bebelplatz, a massive pyre of crossed logs, twelve feet long and five feet high, awaited. As the first revelers arrived, they threw their torches onto this peculiar structure. Blue flames shot skyward. It was a breathtaking sight. Soon the skeleton of logs erupted into a glowing mass of fire.

Meanwhile, a procession of automobiles snaked along the periphery of the Bebelplatz. Some of the students formed an orderly line between the cars and the crackling flames. The crowd watched as one student reached into the first vehicle, taking a book from a pile stacked inside. The book was then passed down the line, from one hand to the next, until it reached the student standing closest to the fire, who hurled it into the flames. The crowd burst into applause. In this manner, one book after another quickly made its way to the blaze. Some students grabbed armfuls of them, pacing between the automobiles and the inferno, fueling the fire each time they passed.

The initial destruction was interrupted only briefly, so that one of the student organizers could deliver a speech about the purpose for the gathering. To ensure the purity of German literature, he said, it was necessary to burn all "un-German" books and documents that threatened the national movement of Nazi unity. This included all works by Jewish authors, for "the Jew, who is powerful in intellect, but weak in blood ... remains without understanding in the presence of German thought, fails to dignify it and, therefore, is bound to injure the German spirit." The extermination of these offensive volumes would make the nation stronger by ridding it of ideas antagonistic to Germany's progress. When the book burning resumed, another student announced the names of authors whose books were being destroyed, and explained why their ideas were harmful to Germany. Sigmund Freud was denounced for falsifying German history and degrading its great figures. Emil Ludwig was criticized for his "literary rascality and high treason against Germany." Erich Maria Remarque was condemned for denigrating the German language and the nation's ideals. Author after author was named. Book after book was burned, and the crowd cheered as if they were watching a sporting event. And so it continued for hours into the night.

Although it had been rumored that the book burning was solely orchestrated by an overzealous student organization, it became clear that it was done with the blessing of the Nazi Party when Dr. Paul Joseph Goebbels, the "Minister of Public Enlightenment," arrived to make a speech. Goebbels oversaw the Reich Chamber of Culture, which regulated Germany's literature, press, radio, theater, music, art, and film. He used his influence to mold German society to suit Hitler's ideology. Goebbels was wary of politically progressive authors who championed such causes as pacifism, socialism, reform, and sexual freedom. Books that so much as hinted at such themes were condemned to the flames.

When Goebbels ascended the swastika-draped rostrum, he declared that "Jewish intellectualism is dead" and that "national socialism has hewn the way." Gesturing toward the scene before him, he continued:

> The German folk soul can again express itself. These flames do not only illuminate the final end of the old era, they also light up the new. Never before have the young men had so good a right to clean up the debris of the past. If the old men do not understand what is going on, let them grasp that we young . . . men have gone and done it.
>
> The old goes up in flames, the new shall be fashioned from the flame of our hearts.

After Goebbels's speech, the song "The Nation to Arms" punctuated the night air and the students again took to throwing books into the mountain of fire.

To ensure that Berlin's book burning would have a wide audience, it was broadcast live over the radio and filmed. Movie theaters across Germany soon showed footage of Berlin's bonfire with commentary explaining that harmful books eroded German values and must be destroyed. As this message spread,

ninety-three additional book burnings were held, each attract-
ing a large audience and intense media coverage. The students
of Kiel University assembled two thousand examples of literature considered harmful to the German spirit, built a giant bonfire, and invited the public to watch as they burned the offensive
books. In Munich, students led a picturesque torchlight parade
before collecting one hundred massive volumes from the university library to be publicly burned. At another event in Munich, five thousand schoolchildren gathered to burn Marxist literature, and were urged that "as you watch the fire burn these
un-German books, let it also burn into your hearts love of the
Fatherland." In Breslau, five thousand pounds of heretical works
were destroyed in a single day.

As book burnings spread across Germany, the Nazis also
targeted any individuals who harbored anti-Nazi sympathies.
Those suspected of entertaining views harmful to Germany
were subjected to house searches; if anything objectionable
was found, the offenders were punished. Some were never seen
again. Quiet hysteria spread; many people preemptively destroyed documents and books that might be problematic. According to one report, when a local woman was given a tip that
she should make sure her home was "really clean," she "immediately burned [her] books and papers and the next day endured
a search." Nazis published lists of books fit for burning; among
the authors named were Karl Marx, Upton Sinclair, Jack London, Heinrich Mann, Helen Keller, Albert Einstein, Thomas
Mann, and Arthur Schnitzler.

Helen Keller wrote an impassioned letter to the student
body of Germany, expressing her shock and disbelief that the
birthplace of the printing press had become a crematory for
this invention's posterity. "History has taught you nothing, if
you think you can kill ideas," she scolded. "Tyrants have tried to

do that often before, and the ideas have risen up in their might and destroyed them." "You can burn my books and the books of the best minds in Europe, but the ideas in them have seeped through a million channels and will continue to quicken other minds," she said.

Others joined Keller in censuring the youth of Germany. Nobel Prize winner Sinclair Lewis denounced the book burnings, stating the works being destroyed were some of the "noblest books produced by Germany in the last twenty years." He added that the authors whose writings were thrown into the flames "should feel nothing save satisfaction at receiving this unintentional tribute from an organized mob." In London, H. G. Wells gave a defiant speech on intolerance, echoing some of the same sentiments as Keller. Book burnings "had never yet destroyed a book," Wells said, as "books once printed have a vitality exceeding any human being, and they go on speaking as though nothing had happened." "It seems to me," he went on, "that what is happening in Germany is a clumsy lout's revolution against thought, sanity and books." Although he admitted that he did not feel safe in England, and believed that authors could one day be lynched or sent to concentration camps because of the perceived danger their books presented, he found comfort in a single idea. "In the long run," he said, "books will win, and the louts will be brought to heel, and sane judgment will settle with all the braying and bawling heroics of these insurgents." In the meantime, Wells protested Germany's actions by providing a refuge for endangered titles. With the cooperation of other authors, Wells established the Library of Burned Books, which opened in Paris in the spring of 1934. The library housed copies of all books banned or burned by the Nazis, and held in safekeeping writings and books donated by German refugees and anyone who felt their books might be at risk.

American editorialists also voiced their disapproval. It seemed incongruous that universities, which had long been a chief glory of Germany, had become one of her shames, one newspaper said. The *New York Times* dubbed Germany's actions a "literary holocaust," commenting that "such an exhibition of the new national spirit, silly and shameful as it seems, bespeaks a mass-movement plainly touched with insanity." *Time* magazine referred to the incident as a "bibliocaust" and reported the ghastly details, including how a band played Chopin's "Funeral March" as books were cast into a bonfire in the Romerberg, Frankfurt's medieval marketplace. Many Americans gathered in public protests — eighty thousand in New York, fifty thousand in Chicago, and twenty thousand in Philadelphia.

How could Germany, an educated nation renowned for its philosophers and thinkers, tolerate the purging of its libraries and the destruction of its books? These acts were not isolated events, but rather one piece of a carefully orchestrated plan devised by Adolf Hitler to manipulate German culture in accordance with his policies and dogmas. Once he gained power, Hitler passed laws to ensure obedience to the new order he was establishing. For example, in 1935 *Mein Kampf* became state-sanctioned reading; a copy was gifted to every couple who married, and it was used as a textbook in every German school.

The führer's involvement in transforming Germany's cultural institutions to bolster his policies extended far beyond books. Hitler worked to create the impression that only pure-blooded Germans had made culturally and artistically significant contributions worthy of display in museums. He founded a new holiday, the Day of German Art. As the presider over the day's festivities, he selected which artworks would be exhibited, and awarded top honors to pieces he deemed ideologically appropriate. Thereafter, he dictated where each work would be displayed within galleries, and set the value of each creation. The pieces that reinforced his vision of Germany were displayed prominently, and their price tags were correspondingly high. Museums were similarly "purified" by Hitler and Goebbels, as they forbade the display of pieces created by Jews or others considered to be inferior to full-blooded Germans. By exhibiting only those works that would herald the accomplishments of the Aryan race, Hitler aimed to give the impression that only they were capable of bringing glory to Germany.

Education was reorganized to reflect Hitler's ideology. On the same day as the Berlin book burning, Dr. Wilhelm Frick, Germany's minister of the interior, lectured German school administrators on changes to the educational system. He mandated that students be instructed on "everything concerning the fatherland and German history — with special emphasis on the last twenty years" and on "race science, heredity and genealogy." As to the latter, Frick explained that schools must "consistently emphasize that the infiltration of the German people with alien blood, especially Jewish and Negro, must be absolutely prevented," and that lessons on "race biology must also bring out mental and spiritual differences between the different races and must bring home to pupils the dangers of race deterioration." Under Frick's guidelines, children were instructed that pure-blooded Germans were a superior race. Concomitantly, Jewish and left-leaning lecturers were dismissed from their employment; at some schools, vacancies ran as high as 33 percent.

Hitler also exploited radio and film to disperse his ideas to even the remotest places. Radio broadcasting was considered an efficient means of publicizing, and ensuring obedience to, the führer's dictates. Goebbels endeavored to make inexpensive radios available to the masses so that families across Germany could listen to Hitler's messages. German movie studios were pressured to produce entertaining films containing propaganda, and Hitler and Goebbels personally worked with producers to see that their vision for Germany was adequately reflected on the big screen. Goebbels wielded enormous power; he approved scripts, prevented "un-German" films from being made, and determined whether completed films were worthy of being shown. When the public criticized the dull, propaganda-laden films offered in German cinemas, Goebbels blamed movie critics for planting such ideas in their reviews. In 1936, film criticism was outlawed.

By 1938, the Nazis had banned eighteen categories of books, 4,175 titles, and the complete works of 565 authors, many of whom were Jewish. Yet some Jewish authors remained on bookshelves, to the utter frustration of the Nazis. German newspapers published furious missives censuring institutions that allowed the continued influence of Jewish writers. German librarians were forced to carefully comb through their collections and ensure that every book inimical to Hitler's policies was eliminated.

In that year, Nazi policies moved from books to people. On October 18, 1938, Hitler deported over twelve thousand Polish Jews from Germany. Yet only four thousand were allowed to enter Poland, leaving thousands stranded on the German-Polish border. When Herschel Grynszpan, a young Jew living in France, learned that his family was among those languishing on the border without food or shelter, he stormed into the German embassy in Paris and, in a fit of rage, fatally shot German diplomat Ernst vom Rath on November 7, 1938.

The incident spawned an anti-Semitic wave of terrorism across Germany. By November 9, news of the assassination had spread, and violent anti-Jewish demonstrations erupted in Berlin. Squads of young men roamed the city, breaking store windows with metal batons and weapons. Shops were emptied, merchandise was thrown into the streets, and looters descended like vultures. The *New York Times* reported that gangs of young Germans, who appeared to be officials or members of the Nazi Party, vandalized Jewish-owned businesses as onlookers joked and laughed. By the following day at least ninety-one Jews had been killed. Almost all Jewish businesses in Berlin were gutted. Eleven synagogues were burned, countless temple books and Torah scrolls were destroyed, and thousands of Jews were imprisoned, sent to concentration camps, or driven to suicide. November 9, 1938, became known as the Night of the Broken Glass — Kristallnacht.

As the foreign press demanded answers and details, Goebbels stepped forward to set the record straight. The *New York Times* reported that he "openly sanctioned the wave of terrorism, destruction and incendiarism that swept over Germany," and even promised that "there would be further anti-Jewish laws for a comprehensive solution of the Jewish problem in a manner that will equalize the status of the Jews in Germany in conformity with popular anti-Semitic sentiment." "The reaction of the German people to the cowardly murder in Paris" signified "the nation follow[ing] its healthy instincts," Goebbels said. He confessed that he sympathized with the rioters and vowed to silence all foreign criticism by threatening that Germany's Jews would pay the price for any lies and exaggerations published overseas. As for the victims of the attacks, Goebbels said: "If I were a Jew ... I would remain silent. There is only one thing the Jew can do — shut up and say nothing further about Germany."

Kristallnacht provoked little outrage within Germany. Hitler's policies beginning in the late 1920s had paved the way for acquiescence of such blatant persecution. After years of devaluing Jewish contributions to German society and culture, the Nazis had created a climate where violence against Jews was generally condoned.

Some Americans, however, found Germany's barefaced anti-Semitism shocking. Newspapers were flooded by letters voicing concern and incredulity. For example, from Saint Paul, Minnesota, a man wrote: "The extent and severity of this outbreak of terrorism [are] unbelievable," and the "assassination of a minor official cannot justify wholesale retaliation in this manner. Reprisal against a whole people for the crime of an overwrought youth is a throwback to barbarity." A San Franciscan wrote a letter to that city's *Chronicle,* marveling that "one madman could infect a whole nation of intelligent, sensible, essentially kindly people with his own fanatic madness." In Boston, a writer to the *Herald Tribune* remarked that "the noblest feature of modern civilization, respect for human life, has been abandoned for the time being in Germany." This Bostonian noted that while the "internal affairs of Germany are her own business . . . there are some practices which are so revolting to mankind, such a setback for civilization, such a debasement of the human spirit that absence anywhere of protest against them is almost equivalent to approval of them."

Germany declared war on Poland on September 1, 1939. Britain and France were compelled by treaty to declare war against Germany. Yet as the German military pushed into Poland, France and Britain were invaded initially not by tanks and bombs, but by words. Hitler's psychological warfare paved the way for a quick succession of German victories.

France and Britain each knew they would be attacked after Poland, but France was more vulnerable, with its long land border with Germany. Hitler prepared for battle by infiltrating

France's airwaves. Germany hired native-French broadcasters to lure unsuspecting listeners to tune in to amusing radio shows and popular music. Many listeners were oblivious to the propaganda that was subtly included. These radio commentators expressed worry over the German army's dominance and military strength, and predicted that France could not withstand an attack. The doubt Hitler's radio programs planted in French minds quickly spread. Edmond Taylor, a correspondent for the *Chicago Tribune* who lived in France during this period, witnessed Hitler's intricately choreographed propaganda campaign and how it crumbled France's resolve. Describing it as a "strategy of terror," Taylor reported that Germany spent enormous amounts on propaganda and even bribed French newspapers to publish stories that confirmed the rumors of Germany's superiority. According to Taylor, Germany's war of ideas planted a sense of dread "in the soul of France that spread like a monstrous cancer, devouring all other emotional faculties [with] an irrational fear [that was] . . . uncontrollable." So weakened was the confidence of the French that something as innocuous as a test of France's air-raid-siren system generated ripples of panic; the mere innuendo of invasion somehow reinforced the idea that France would undoubtedly be defeated. Although the French government made a late attempt at launching an ideological counteroffensive by publicizing the need to defend freedom, it was as effective as telling citizens to protect themselves from a hurricane by opening an umbrella. When the invasion finally did come, France capitulated in six weeks. By similarly destroying the resolve of his enemies before invading them, Hitler defeated Poland, Finland, Denmark, Norway, Belgium, the Netherlands, and Luxembourg in addition to France, all in under a year. Over 230 million Europeans, once free, fell under Nazi rule.

As France succumbed to its fate and surrendered to Germany, Hitler prepared to send a powerful message to the world, showing how seriously he took his role in avenging Germany's military humiliation in World War I. France's defeat was an opportunity to display the might of the German army and intimidate other nations that would be invaded in the future.

On June 17, 1940, Hitler met with what remained of the French government to sign a formal armistice. Employing every dramatic device to mark the event, Hitler insisted on re-creating the scene of Germany's defeat in World War I, aboard Marshal Ferdinand Foch's private railway car in France's forest of Compiègne. The rail carriage had long been stored in a French museum; on Hitler's orders it was moved to the exact location where it had stood on November 9, 1918. Clearly, it was France's turn to be humiliated. The führer personally delivered the terms of capitulation to the French officials. After the armistice was signed, Hitler decreed that Foch's railway car and a monument dedicated to France's World War I triumph be transferred to Berlin, where they would be displayed in a museum to mark Germany's victory over its longtime enemy across the Rhine.

Once a nation fell to Germany, great care was taken to re-fashion that country's concepts of culture, history, literature, art, media, and entertainment in an effort to solidify and re-inforce Hitler's power. Often, the first cultural pillar to be toppled was the library. Hitler created the Einsatzstab Reichsleiter Rosenberg (ERR) to confiscate desirable books and other artifacts in occupied territories. They were intended for a Nazi university to be built after the war. Undesirable books, by contrast, were destroyed. In Eastern Europe, the ERR burned a staggering 375 archives, 402 museums, 531 institutes, and 957 libraries. It is estimated that the Nazis destroyed half of all books in Czechoslovakia and Poland, and fifty-five million tomes in Russia. Libraries in occupied nations that remained open were reorganized to serve the Nazi agenda. Poland's libraries were restructured along National Socialist lines through a process of Germanizing records, supplementing collections with Nazi-approved literature, and removing all undesirable materials. After Holland was defeated, recent German books were displayed in order to impress the public with German achievements. When France fell, one of Germany's first actions was to issue the "Liste Bernhard," which identified 140 forbidden books. In September 1940, a more comprehensive list was published, naming nearly 1,400 titles. Many libraries in Paris were simply closed. H. G. Wells's Library of Burned Books, ironically, was carefully preserved by the Nazi occupiers. According to Dr. Alfred Kantorowicz, the library's general secretary, the Germans kept it "under lock and key," and although it was "practically impossible for foreigners to use the books," Germans consulted them for reference. Hitler's attention to libraries became so well known that, throughout Western Europe, librarians and curators took preemptive measures, moving their most valuable holdings to caves and castles, hoping to hide and preserve treasured collections.

As American newspapers reported Hitler's cultural attacks, the war began to be defined as having two fronts or dimensions. One journalist explained: "There are two series of conflicts going on at the same time: the vertical conflicts in which nations fight one another, and the horizontal conflicts which are ideological, political, social and economic." Other descriptions referred to the war as involving physical and mental components, and as being fought on the battlefield and in the library. Regardless of the terms used, a unanimous understanding emerged that the war was not waged on battlefields alone: the ideas a nation espoused were also under attack. Hitler sought to destroy not only armies, but also democracy and free thought. This new brand of combat was pegged "total war."

Although Americans took solace in their physical distance from Germany's army, it soon became apparent that Hitler's ideas had long reach. Just as it invaded France with radio broadcasts before sending in its military, Germany relied on the radio to engage American minds long before there was any suggestion of American involvement in the war. Radio sets of the 1930s and 1940s typically included shortwave bands for international listening. For eighteen hours each day, Germany (with Japan's help) broadcast programs that would reach North America; the war of ideas against the United States had begun. If America could be weakened as efficiently as France, Germany would be able to trounce the nation with very little struggle.

In order to make its propaganda more palatable to Americans, German officials searched for American expatriates to hire as announcers, as their accents would conceal their loyalties. In exchange for such benefits as ration coupons, which were only distributed to German citizens, and protection in an increasingly volatile Germany, several Americans joined Reichsradio. Iowa-born Frederick William Kaltenbach and Illinois-born Edward Leo Delaney were among the first American radio hosts. Later, Reichsradio would turn to the infamous Mildred Gillars, better known as Axis Sally, to deliver some of its greatest propaganda punches.

The campaign had little effect, however. The American media readily exposed Germany's radio shows for what they were. The *New York Times* reported that Germany's broadcasts were smartly arranged, copying the format of typical American radio shows: they read the news, played music, and presented skits. Yet while domestic radio stations included sales pitches for soap and breakfast cereal, the *Times* warned that Germany was out to sell a point of view.

Beyond calling out the propaganda campaign, some Americans discussed counterattacking. France's quick defeat demonstrated how effective Germany's radio campaign was. One of the loudest voices to address this issue belonged to the American Library Association (ALA). Librarians felt duty-bound to try to stop Hitler from succeeding in his war of ideas against the United States. They had no intention of purging their shelves or watching their books burn, and they were not going to wait until war was declared to take action. As an ALA publication observed in January 1941, Hitler's aim was "the destruction of ideas . . . even in those countries not engaged in military combat."

Throughout late 1940 and early 1941, librarians debated how to protect American minds against Germany's amorphous attacks on ideas. The "bibliocaust" in Europe had struck a nerve. America's librarians concluded that the best weapon and armor was the book itself. By encouraging Americans to read, Germany's radio propaganda would be diluted and its book burnings would stand in marked contrast. As Hitler attempted to strengthen fascism by destroying the written word, librarians would urge Americans to read more. In the words of one librarian: if Hitler's *Mein Kampf* was capable of "stir[ring] millions to fight for intolerance and oppression and hate, cannot other books be found to stir other millions to fight against them?"

When Goebbels spoke in Berlin on the night of May 10, 1933, he declared that from the ashes of the burned books smoldering before him there would "arise victoriously the phoenix of a new spirit." As he uttered these words, Goebbels envisioned German nationalism, fascism, and Nazism emanating from the books' remains.

Within ten years of Goebbels's speech, from the embers arose a renewed dedication to democracy and freedom. From the remains of those tomes blackened and licked by flames arose a spirit dedicated to spreading ideas, including those contained in the books that had been destroyed. Soon, thanks to America's librarians, towering piles of books would rise in libraries, department stores, schools, and movie theaters — not for burning, but for donation to American servicemen. Rival publishing companies would come together, pooling their resources and expertise to print tens of millions of books for American servicemen on all subject matters and professing all manner of viewpoints. From the ashes, books would arise and flourish.

TWO

$85 Worth of Clothes, but No Pajamas

In all phases of administration, training, and operation make every effort to keep your men informed.
Nothing irritates American soldiers so much as to
be left in the dark regarding the reason for things.

— ARMY BASIC FIELD MANUAL

A S WAR SPREAD across Europe in 1939 and 1940,
most Americans opposed getting involved. In June
1940, the recently invented Gallup poll revealed
that only 7 percent of Americans were in favor of an immediate declaration of war against Germany. Yet many understood
that America might not have a choice. That same month, the
New York Times, along with several other major newspapers, endorsed the unpopular position that the United States needed
to immediately adopt a national system of compulsory military
training. The *Times* explained:

The most powerful mechanized army that the world has ever seen
is now striking at Paris. We must consider realistically the consequences of that army's victory. If we are not to be caught without
warning, we must face in all frankness the worst that can possi-

bly happen. That worst is France defeated and knocked out of the war; England in no position to defend herself in 1940 owing to the loss of her supplies in Flanders; Hitler becoming the master of all Europe, either in possession of the British fleet or in possession of shipbuilding facilities which are many times our own, in Germany, Norway, Belgium, Britain, Holland.

Hitler had declared himself the enemy of democracy, and the United States was one of the largest, richest, and softest of them all, the article said. Plus, it was no secret that Hitler's "whole strategy has been to strike before his opponents were prepared."

Hitler did not conceal that he considered the United States an enemy, or that he expected his military to face America's. In a December 1940 speech given at a Berlin antiaircraft-gun factory, Hitler dubbed America, Britain, and France the "haves," while deeming Germany a bullied "have-not." Yet he was not simply motivated by revenge for Germany's defeat in World War I. He had a vision. "Two worlds are in conflict, two philosophies of life," and "one of these worlds must crack," he said. With an army of only 174,000 men (as of 1939), the United States was in fact vulnerable. Popular or not, conscription was necessary. As Congress worked on legislation during the summer of 1940, President Franklin D. Roosevelt reminded the nation time and again that conscription, no matter how despised, was essential to adequate defense.

In September 1940, Congress passed the Selective Training and Service Act. Under this legislation, approximately 16.5 million men between the ages of twenty-one and thirty-five were required to register for military service (later amendments extended this age group to eighteen to fifty). On October 16, 1940, brothers, husbands, sons, boyfriends, uncles, friends, and neighbors turned out in droves to registration centers that had sprouted across the United States. Although there was concern that a contingent of isolationists and pacifists might threaten the process, the day passed surprisingly smoothly. In New York City, where 991,000 men registered for military service, only two arrests were reported; one transpired when two men broke into a fight over who should register first, and the other involved a man who spent several hours preparing himself for registration in a saloon. Election Day was less than one week away, and some thought the timing of the draft would cost Roosevelt another term, but it did not. Not only did Roosevelt take the unprecedented step of conducting the first peacetime draft in American history, but within a week of doing so he won an unparalleled third term as president.

In order to accommodate the hundreds of thousands of civilians called into service, the U.S. Army planned to construct and furnish forty-six new training facilities. However, because federal funding was not approved until the fall of 1940, the Army was in the unique position of having to conscript men and train them while also acquiring basic supplies and building the very camps needed for the conscripts and the training. The scope of the job was monumental. As one historian noted, "Land had to be cleared, hills leveled, valleys filled, trees uprooted, roads surfaced, and drainage systems installed before the construction of barracks, laundries, officers' quarters, and rifle ranges could begin." It was estimated that construction of the camps would require 400,000 laborers, 908,000 gallons of paint, 3,500 carloads of nails, and 10 million square feet of wallboard.

The timing of conscription first and camp construction second was disastrous for morale. The first men assigned to the new camp areas could hardly believe the extent of the military's unpreparedness. They were greeted by great stretches of barren land. Although workers feverishly built heated barracks, in many camps there was inadequate shelter, which was especially distressing to those who were drafted into service during the coldest time of year. Winterized squad tents were provided before there were barracks, with six or more enlistees to a tent. Each night, surrounded by strangers, the men were blanketed by numbing cold and lulled to sleep by the howl of the wind. Homesickness ran rampant.

It was not just the new camps that were deficient. Even facilities created during World War I proved unready. One man assigned to Fort McClellan in Alabama (which had been used as an infantry training camp in 1917) described the place as a "hell hole," and elaborated that it was "dirty, stinking, [and] muddy." Every aspect of the camp was makeshift and unfinished. All men initially slept in sixteen-by-sixteen-foot tents with six to eight of their fellow soldiers. A single stove was used to heat each group, but sparks frequently burned holes in the tent material, and small fires constantly had to be extinguished. While roads around the camp were generously described as "cleared," in actuality they were riddled with tree stumps that the soldiers-in-training were ordered to remove. There were many other dirty jobs assigned. "You'll haul coal and ash and ashes. You'll unpack rifles that are buried in heavy grease and you'll clean that grease from them. You'll stoke fires, you'll mop floors, and you'll put a high polish on the windows," Sergeant Marion Hargrove explained in his famous account of military life. There would be times when "you'll wonder if you've been yanked out of civil life for *this*" and "you will be thoroughly disgusted with your new job," Hargrove added.

Beyond buildings and facilities, camps lacked even the most basic supplies. Once a man arrived at his training camp, a mountain of gear was supposed to be given to him for his new military life. The Army quartermaster (QM) planned to provide infantrymen with a "field uniform of steel helmet, shirt, trousers, leggings, shoes, underwear, and, depending on the weather, raincoat or coat and overcoat . . . ; a haversack, for his mess kit; cup and canteen; first-aid kit; pack holding blanket, shelter tents, poles, pins, toilet articles, gas mask; intrenching tool, reserve ration; weapon and ammunition." As one magazine quipped, the men were given "some $85 worth of clothes, but no pajamas." In reality, the first wave of recruits was missing a lot more than just pajamas. Because the QM had not yet procured their khaki regimentals, men were forced to wear hated wool uniforms from World War I.

Many camps also lacked ammunition, weapons, and equipment for training drills. The men felt foolish as they were forced to pretend a mop handle propped on a sawhorse was an antiaircraft gun. At Fort McClellan, trucks bore signs reading TANK, and logs were used as placeholders for artillery. Even General Dwight D. Eisenhower recalled in his memoir, *Crusade in Europe,* that "troops carried wooden models of mortars and machine guns and were able to study some of our new weapons only from blueprints." The use of these pretend weapons "added little to the new infantryman's *esprit,*" he admitted.

In addition to the demoralizing reality of the training camps' unpreparedness, draftees experienced growing pains in adjusting to the regimentation of military life. Up at 6:00 a.m., the men stumbled out of bed and into the dark to spend hours learning how to march and maneuver in freezing temperatures. When ammunition and weapons were available for drills, the Army strove to simulate battle conditions. The men would crawl under barbed wire while live ammunition whizzed a couple of feet above their heads. The sound of grenades, rifle fire, and TNT bursts penetrated the air as dummy enemy soldiers were dropped from trees. The men spent additional hours in classrooms watching films, reading charts, analyzing mockups, and studying how their equipment functioned and was best utilized. They were frequently tested and ranked, with failing students shifted to other courses or training. There was constant pressure to perform well. Top grades meant promotion, a pay raise, and an elevated social status. Most men would do anything to avoid the disgrace of being held back because of academic failure. Military training proved both physically and mentally draining.

The transition from civilian to soldier did not come easily to the great majority who found themselves wandering around training camps in the early 1940s. Although newspapers and magazines romanticized the experience, in reality, many men were completely miserable and struggled with loneliness, isolation, and melancholy.

At the end of each day, most men craved solitude and escape. But unless granted a furlough or leave, it was impossible to get away. The only place an enlistee could spend his off-duty hours in an unfinished training camp was his squad tent. There was no opportunity for the men to enjoy a little distance from their military service. They found themselves surrounded by it even in their free time. It was especially difficult for those who were drafted. Former civilians did not anticipate how disoriented they would feel as they lost access to their hobbies and interests while being drilled into patterns of uniformity and sameness. It felt foreign to them to be told when to wake up, how to dress, what to eat (and when to eat it), the beat at which to march, and when to go to sleep. Privacy and individuality were the luxuries of civilians — not soldiers. It was the same in the U.S. Navy. "You learned that your days of privacy were over while you were in the navy and they would not return until you were back in civilian life again," James J. Fahey recounted in his memoir of Navy life. "When you ate, slept, took a shower, etc., you were always part of the crowd, you were never alone."

Despite the limited resources available, music (primarily singing) and athletics provided some diversion. But these communal activities were among the least popular at more established camps. According to one study, when given a choice, most men preferred to spend their leisure time engaged in relatively independent activities — writing letters, reading magazines and books, watching a movie, or listening to the radio. Only 16 percent preferred to spend their off-duty hours playing sports, and 5 percent chose to spend their time singing. For the most part, men craved an escape — from the camps they trained in, the strangers they lived with, and the possibility that they might be shipped off to war.

Army leaders knew that effective training would be impossible if morale and the quality of camp life were not improved. Comparisons between established and new training camps revealed a staggering difference in attitude and zeal for training. This disparity was attributed, at least in part, to the availability of entertainment. At Georgia's Fort Benning, satisfaction with military life was generally high. When off duty, men had access to pool tables, cards and games, musical instruments, a library of books and magazines, and a movie theater that could seat two thousand. While the training regimen was the same, the men at Fort Benning adjusted to military life with greater ease; they could genuinely relax after each day's training session and experience a temporary escape from their service. The War Department concluded that amusements and entertainment were crucial.

Yet the Army was struggling to secure the most basic supplies. It could not immediately build and furnish movie theaters and sporting venues when men did not even have buildings to live in or guns to shoot. What the Army needed was some form of recreation that was small, popular, and affordable. It needed books.

World War II would not be the first time the Army and Navy welcomed books into their ranks. Yet no other war — before or since — has approached the rate at which books were distributed to American forces in World War II.

The first American war where books made an appearance on the frontlines was the Civil War. Volunteer organizations collected used books, and some religious institutions even printed their own, such as *The Soldier's Pocket-Book,* a miniature tome of psalms, hymns, and prayers that the Presbyterian Church hoped would be more satisfying than "light and sinful reading." Although distribution was hit or miss, and the selection of titles was limited, the books that reached the battlefields were cherished. As one veteran of the Civil War, Homer Sprague, insisted over fifty years after the war had ended, "soldiers in the field hunger and thirst for reading matter." Yet with no meaningful support from the War Department in disseminating books, the chief force dictating whether a man received any reading material was luck.

There was a huge improvement in book services for the American forces in World War I. A mélange of civilian organizations — the Red Cross, the YMCA and YWCA, the Knights of Columbus, the Jewish Welfare Board, the Salvation Army, and the ALA, among others — shouldered the task of providing donated books to soldiers in training camps. Millions of volumes were collected. The work performed by these organizations was universally lauded, particularly by those who received the benefits. Thomas Marshall Spaulding, a major in the Army, said that books "made life worth living for our own soldiers and the soldiers of other countries who fought alongside ours," and inspired "that amazing spirit of American troops." Even units weary from battle, dispirited and drained, emerged with renewed vitality after convalescing with books. Although they were trained to kill and subjected to indescribable brutalities on the frontlines, the presence of books seemed to verify that "the members of our army [are still] human beings," Major Spaulding said.

After World War I, the War Department decided to make books a staple in its training camps. In 1921 the department created an Army Library Service, responsible for the maintenance of the 228 libraries at Army posts in the United States then in existence. In the words of Colonel Edward Munson, the chief of the Army's Morale Branch at the time, books were considered not only "a valuable means of recreation and an essential agent in education and instruction," but also a "channel for the . . . betterment of character and behavior." War was a "clash of wills even more than one of arms," he said, and books enabled soldiers to strengthen their minds.

Although it began with the most noble of intentions, the Army Library Service soon fell into a state of neglect. As the nation was no longer at war, funding for the maintenance of each library's collection was cut year after year, and the acquisition of new titles became impossible. As the size of America's armed forces dwindled, state library agencies were permitted to pilfer the most popular titles from Army libraries for use by the broader public. As a result, when conscription for World War II began in 1940, existing Army libraries lacked almost any desirable titles. Outdated textbooks were practically useless, and modern bestsellers were nonexistent. And new training camps lacked books and libraries altogether. Faced with a morale crisis, a need to educate its charges on why they were in training, and a dearth of modern textbooks to enable the more ambitious to study and improve their rank, the Army prioritized the modernization of its library collections.

Starting in late 1940, the Army made plans to purchase tens of thousands of books and to build recreational facilities, including libraries, for all training camps. Initial proposals provided for a limited number of books and tiny libraries (with seating for as few as twenty-four men). But these paltry arrangements never made it past the drawing board, thanks to the vision of one man.

Raymond L. Trautman was a thirty-four-year-old reserve first lieutenant with a professional library degree when he was selected to become the chief of the Library Section of the United States Army. Before earning his degree at Columbia University in 1940, Trautman had managed several bookstores and learned the commercial side of the book business. He also spent five years working with the Civilian Conservation Corps, which was jointly operated by the Army and the Department of the Interior. This rare combination of Army know-how and book-industry expertise made Trautman an ideal candidate to head the Army's Library Section. Whenever obstacles arose that threatened the quantity and quality of books reaching the Army, Trautman fought for his men and took whatever measures necessary to ensure that they received the books they wanted. Thanks to Trautman's guidance and sheer determination, exponentially more books were provided to servicemen during World War II than the Morale Branch had envisioned in 1940.

An early goal established by the War Department was to purchase books to the tune of one for every enlisted man. In reality, the quantity of books each Army unit or training camp received fell short of this mark. In 1941 large units of five thousand or more men were supplied a generous budget for books, but small outfits of fewer than one thousand men were entirely unfunded. This shortcoming was unacceptable to Trautman. Early surveys on the use of books in those training camps that had well-stocked library facilities revealed circulation rates so staggering that it was a wonder the print had not been wiped clean from the pages. Trautman knew what he needed to do. He needed to purchase millions of books for dozens of camps. But he lacked funding.

As word circulated of the camps' slumping morale and empty bookshelves, Trautman's fellow librarians came to his rescue. Feeling a moral and professional obligation to do something, librarians volunteered to host local book drives to gather books for nearby training camps. In the words of the publicity director for the New York Library Association's 1941 book drive: "Books are available to amazingly few men in the service. The librarians of the state feel that when there is time and inclination for reading there should be books to read—and so they are setting out to get them." Grassroots campaigns mushroomed across the United States and were greeted with a hearty response. Librarians asked for pleasure reading—fiction, comics, books of humor, and short stories—as well as textbooks and technical treatises. Local newspapers publicized these book drives and helped spread the message of how important books were for the sustenance of morale in the training camps. Tens of. thousands of books were collected in short order.

The ALA took notice of these many successful local drives. If thousands of books could be collected by a single librarian, how many millions could be gathered if librarians across the country threw their effort behind a single campaign? At its 1941 annual meeting, the ALA announced that it was investigating the possibility of hosting a national book drive. A chorus of support greeted the idea, and advice poured in from experienced librarians who had undertaken book drives during World War I, or had hosted recent drives. Overcome by the incredible show of support, the ALA sent its executive secretary, Carl Milam, to Washington, where he met with Army and Navy officials as well as Charles Taft, assistant coordinator of the Office of Health, Welfare and Related Defense Activities (Taft was the son of former president William Howard Taft). Taft, who would prove to be both a chief proponent and nuisance, was amenable to the idea of a nationwide book drive, but it was Lieutenant Colonel Trautman who sealed the government's approval. Despite the Army's aspirations to purchase adequate quantities of books, Trautman admitted that Army posts with fewer than five thousand men had no funds for reading material, and that if some soldiers were to have any books at all, they would have to be supplied by a book campaign. By the end of this meeting, the ALA was granted federal approval to launch a national book-collection drive.

In a matter of months, a blueprint for the project was whipped together. With the United Service Organizations (USO) and American Red Cross each donating $50,000 to cover costs, the ALA's National Defense Book Campaign (NDBC) made plans to collect as many as ten million volumes in 1942. Office space in the Empire State Building was donated by the USO for the campaign's headquarters, and the ALA hired Althea Warren, who was considered "#1 in the field of Women Librarians," to run the campaign for a four-month term, the maximum amount of leave she could take from her position at the Los Angeles Public Library. Warren proved the perfect candidate for the job. In fact, she devoted so much time

and energy to nurturing the campaign, her closest friends referred to it as "Warren's child."

Warren's personality, work ethic, and library experience suited
her for the challenging work of heading the NDBC. After earning a library degree, Warren secured employment at Chicago's
Sears, Roebuck branch library. Physically connected to a Sears,
Roebuck store, and created for the education and pleasure of
the store's employees, this library proved to be as hectic and demanding an environment as one could imagine. "Before opening, at the lunch hours, and at closing time I stood in the midst
of a throng and learned to hand out as fast as a ticket agent the
book that best matched each person," Warren recalled. " 'Give
me a book like *The Shuttle!*' 'I want a new set of adjectives to
describe colors in the spring catalog.' 'The head chemist in the
testing laboratory would like a certain government pamphlet
by Dr. Wiley,' " people eagerly barked and yelled over the din of
commotion. Warren's advice and expertise were in constant demand, and she did not disappoint. In one memorable episode,
Warren received a trusting note from a woman in the book-
keeping department via the library's pneumatic-tube system,
which ran between the library and store. "It's very slow here
on this rainy day," the bookkeeper complained. "Please send
me one of those novels you have had to withdraw from circulation as unfit for a lady to read." Warren fulfilled the request and
was surprised the next day to receive the book back, discreetly
wrapped, with the message: "Blessings upon you! You're quite
right. This is not fit for anybody to read. Please send another
just like it."

Warren later moved to California and worked her way up
to the position of head librarian of the Los Angeles Public Library. Colleagues were impressed by the magic she brought to

her work. Warren's spirit and professionalism motivated her colleagues; it was said that her coworkers were inspired to work as hard as she did while trying to emulate her personable manner.

As Warren traveled cross-country to New York City in late November 1941 to take her seat as director of the book campaign, she already had ideas about running the drive. She had been involved in the provision of books to soldiers at Camp Kearny, outside San Diego, during World War I. Having witnessed the therapeutic and utilitarian uses of books then, Warren was determined to collect millions of volumes for the growing number of men in uniform.

Her task was simple to define and challenging to execute: to inspire a nation to give. Regardless of how people felt about the United States entering the war (with most Americans firmly opposed), Warren was confident all could agree that men in training camps deserved books for morale and entertainment. "Most of us believe, whatever our convictions concerning the war, that . . . it will be a great satisfaction to scramble to get the books for [the men in camps] which they will genuinely enjoy," Warren said in an editorial for *Library Journal*. She added: "Librarians know from their own experiences that some printed pages are medical plasters to extract pain, others are tourists' tickets out of boredom or loneliness to exhilarating adventures, still others are diplomas for getting promotion and drilling ideas into a quick-step." While she described the creation of libraries for servicemen during World War I as "probably the finest accomplishment in the annals of our national growth," she told her fellow librarians that they were now being asked "to gather more books than are contained in any existing library in the world." She concluded simply, "Let's do it!"

THREE

A Landslide of Books

The soldier at the front needs to have a cause in his
heart as well as a gun in his hand.

— EMILY MILLER DANTON, LIBRARIAN

VOLUNTEERS FOR THE NDBC worked feverishly
throughout November and December 1941 to organ-
ize and promote the largest book drive in American
history. Time was fleeting and the project was monumental. As
Althea Warren admitted to her colleagues: "It is going to take a
full month of radio spots, pictures, stories, editorials, and half a
million printed posters to get the mass mankind of our country
to give in quantity." The campaign needed a publicity director.
Marie Loizeaux, the former publicist for the New York Library
Association's 1941 book drive, was hired immediately.

Loizeaux aimed to blanket the nation with book-drive posters, and shower every village, town, and city with receptacles for
donations. There would not be a library, school, department
store, or train depot that did not advertise the campaign or inform the public of where books could be donated, so far as she
could help it. Loizeaux worked with major corporations, pub-

lic transportation, and chain stores so that her publicity efforts would have the largest impact. She yielded impressive returns. National Transitads promised to display twenty thousand posters advertising the campaign in the trains it serviced. Bus tickets were redesigned to include a reminder to donate books. Safeway supermarkets agreed to display donation boxes and a book-campaign poster in each of its twenty-four hundred stores. Hundreds of radio programs — from college-run to nationally syndicated shows — vowed to advertise the book drive on the air. Newspaper reporters offered to announce information on the campaign, such as directing townspeople to book drops and identifying the types of books that were in highest demand.

The efficacy of Loizeaux's publicity work was evident before the campaign even began. Donations from the public flowed in to the campaign's coffers, and one eager publishing company sent a gift of one hundred thousand paperbacks. The nation's willingness to give caused both delight and panic: if so many books were donated before the campaign even started, a landslide of books might overwhelm volunteers once it actually began. Turning to newspapers for help, Warren made a frantic appeal for additional helpers to apply at branch libraries.

Just as the campaign was taking shape, Japan waged its surprise attack on Pearl Harbor on December 7, 1941. Congress promptly declared war on Japan, and Germany followed by declaring war on the United States. Suddenly the nation faced one struggle in the Pacific and another in Europe and Africa. American troops began shipping out to fight Hitler's army, and yet some wondered why the United States was taking action against Germany when it was Japan that had attacked Pearl Harbor. Librarians understood that the conviction to go to war would not last long if fueled only by hatred and a desire for revenge. Now they vowed not only to collect books for the servicemen, but to illuminate why the nation was at war.

The NDBC was renamed the Victory Book Campaign (VBC) to reflect the nation's entry into the conflict. After being blessed with the support of President Roosevelt and the First Lady, who publicly donated books for the servicemen, the campaign officially began on January 12, 1942. The public turned out in droves to donate books and support their servicemen. "Carrying the books themselves, sending their chauffeurs with volumes stacked high on back seats, or calling up voluntary and library services to help move the larger contributions, New Yorkers began yesterday to fill the sorting table of the Victory Book Campaign," the *New York Times* reported. Many celebrities helped raise awareness of the importance of the VBC. One of the grandest displays of publicity and patriotism occurred on the steps of the legendary New York Public Library on Forty-Second Street in Manhattan during the last two weeks of January 1942. The American Women's Voluntary Services arranged for a series of programs featuring movie stars, popular bands, local personalities, Broadway performers, and military officials to build interest in the VBC and collect books. Several of the programs were recorded and broadcast on the radio to audiences across the United States. Each day, thousands of spectators besieged the library to catch a glimpse of their favorite Hollywood idols and donate to the drive. Benny Goodman, Kate Smith, Raymond Massey, Wendell Willkie, Katharine Hepburn, Chico Marx, and Kitty Carlisle were among the famous who threw their support behind the campaign.

Of the dozen or so performances given at the New York Public Library that month, the one that seemed to strike the deepest chord was actor Maurice Evans's reading of Christopher Morley's speech "The Gutenberg Address." In the 1940s, Morley was a household name; he was an author, contributing editor of the *Saturday Review of Literature,* and an organizer of the Sherlock Holmes enthusiast group the Baker Street Irregulars. A lover of literature and poetry, Morley began his writing career in 1912 and went on to publish countless novels, short stories, and poems. More than three thousand New Yorkers braved the cold to hear the dramatic reading of his address. Many thousands more listened on the radio.

Morley's speech begins with the description of a young man packing a duffle bag before leaving home to join the services. Although there is some debate over his need for certain items, there is no doubt when it comes to the seven books he tucks into his bag. These books are his ration on pleasure. They will fortify his mind and keep him in good spirits. Morley attests to the fact that books provide company, soothe homesickness, and are vital armor in the fight against Hitler. Germany had weaponized books, as evidenced by the publication of *Mein Kampf* and the shameful book burnings. But Americans could use books to their benefit by reading whatever they desired and spreading the ideas they found between two covers. "Wars are won in the mind before they can be won in the field," Morley observes.

In the address, Morley draws a parallel to America's bloodiest conflict, the Civil War, and Abraham Lincoln's most famous speech, the Gettysburg Address. Honoring the lives lost on that battlefield, Lincoln dedicated the nation to ending the war and proving that democracy and freedom could endure the test of time. Morley's Gutenberg Address would honor the printed word and freedom of thought:

> Twenty five score years ago a German workman brought forth a new idea, conceived in worship and dedicated to the proposition that men's words can travel, that their thoughts can freely com-

municate and multiply, and are worth preserving. Now we are engaged in a *world* Civil War, testing whether that freedom of mind
and word, or any other freedom, can long endure.

Through the efforts of librarians, politicians, authors, teach-
ers, and the media, Americans came to understand that the nation was going to war in the name of freedom, not only to vin-
dicate their losses in Pearl Harbor. Liberty itself was menaced.
Europeans who had fallen under Hitler's rule lost the freedom
to read and discuss many ideas, and Americans began to realize the same could happen to them. The war began to feel less
distant and more personal and immediate, especially as America's armed forces swelled in size, and seemingly everyone knew a
young man who was being sent off to war. By early 1942, one out
of every three men between the ages of eighteen and forty-four
left home to serve the nation. Those left behind on the home
front were stirred by the VBC's call for books. Not only would
they try to meet the campaign's goal of donating more books
than the number housed in the libraries of the five largest cities in the world, they hoped to exceed it. After all, if Morley was
correct, and wars were won first in the mind, American servicemen would need an awful lot of books.

Within two weeks of the campaign's start, 423,655 books were
collected. By the end of January, 100,000 books were sorted,
bundled, and loaded onto Army trucks and shipped to camps.
The VBC volunteers were impressed by the public's response
to the drive. "Although we realized that in setting our starting
date we were giving scant time for preparation we rejoice [that
though] we began half-cocked . . . we were ready to meet the requests . . . for books for troops in transit," read the minutes of a
January 1942 VBC board meeting.

Post librarians with empty bookshelves were overjoyed when shipments of victory books arrived. "It is hard for me to express my deep thanks for the very wonderful collection of books that the Book Campaign donated to our Post Library," one library officer wrote to VBC volunteers. "Our library here is starting out from scratch," and "I had spent days trying to figure out how I could get my shelves partly filled with the very limited funds that the Post Library had to spend," he said. But the VBC had changed everything. This librarian reported that his shelves were now filled, and "I have had any number of people comment on the very fine choice of books." Another librarian wrote, "You have started something here that I hope catches hold and spreads throughout the country, for these new and recent books are something that all the Army Camp Libraries are very much in need of." It would take time for all post libraries to receive books; alongside letters of earnest thanks came pleas from desperate librarians for help in filling their empty stacks.

Yet inevitably, the initial fanfare faded. Although one million books were collected in the campaign's first month, some felt this was nine million too few.

"Something's wrong somewhere," began a February 1942 editorial in the *Saturday Review of Literature,* a widely read periodical at the time. "It seems incredible that a nation of 130,000,000 people, who frequently buy one million or more copies of a single book, and where approximately 750,000 hold memberships in book clubs, should be so sluggish and indifferent about contributing books for men in the services ... The goal of ten million books should have been reached in the first week, instead of one-tenth that number in a month." It was not for lack of publicity that the campaign was off to such a start, for newspapers, radio programs, and magazines cooperated in giving the campaign prominence. Posters were hung on every surface that could accommodate them. They were in libraries, stapled onto telephone poles, and plastered on the walls of train stations and schools. What was the problem? The editorial concluded that perhaps the sacrifice being asked seemed too inconsequential compared to some of the more significant demands being made of the public. "Is it possible that the national psychology emphasizing bigness has caused us to think only in those terms — to the detriment of the small things that have to be done if we are to win the war?"

To be sure, an overwhelming list of demands was made on the public. Collection drives for all manner of goods were held, and Americans were expected to do their part and contribute. When the nation faced a crucial shortage of aluminum in the summer of 1941, it seemed airplane production would grind to a halt. Frantically, the Office of Production Management threw together a two-week nationwide aluminum-scrap drive in July, with hopes that fifteen million pounds of aluminum would be donated, enough to manufacture two thousand planes. Americans turned their homes upside down searching for every last bit of the metal they could spare. As one historian described: "Enthusiastic householders, delighted at the call for service, hauled an astonishing collection of aluminum wares to their village greens — Uncle Mike's coffeepot, Aunt Margaret's frying pan, the baby's milk dish, skillets, stew pots, cocktail shakers, ice-cube forms, artificial legs, cigar tubes, watch cases, and radio parts." Even when the unbelievable news was reported that no airplanes could be made from the donated aluminum (officials learned after the drive that only virgin aluminum could be used), the drive's success in uniting the nation remained a badge of glory.

Households were also asked to donate paper, rags, metal, and rubber. Families learned to think twice before throwing anything in the garbage. Paper was used to package everything from fuses to antiaircraft shells. Rags, such as old draperies and bedsheets, were needed to wipe clean the engines, power plants, and gun mechanisms in battleships to keep them smoothly operating. Rubber was so essential that when the United States faced a crippling shortage in the summer of 1942, the chairman of the Petroleum War Council announced that there was "not enough nonessential rubber outside the stock-pile to make an eraser for a lead pencil." President Roosevelt begged Americans to donate any item made of rubber to help the nation overcome this crisis. Once again, the home front did not disappoint. In two weeks, more than 218,000 tons of rubber were collected nationwide, and at the end of the drive, the average contribution was approximately seven pounds of rubber for each man, woman, and child.

In his January 1942 State of the Union address, the president optimistically said that America's "workers stand ready to work long hours," to "turn out more in a day's work" and "keep the wheels turning, the fires burning twenty-four hours a day and seven days a week" to supply much-needed war material. Ironically, just as millions of Americans took jobs in the defense industries and were paid handsome wages, consumers were asked to curb their spending so factories could focus their efforts on war production. "Life under a war economy will be like living at the depth of a great . . . depression," the *Wall Street Journal* reported, to many a worker's chagrin.

Rationing was another hardship on Americans. From cooking stoves and sugar cubes to rubber and gasoline, many items were in short supply. Instead of new automobiles rolling off assembly lines, there came vehicles for the war. General Motors manufactured planes, antiaircraft guns, aircraft engines, and diesel engines for submarines. Ford produced bombers, jeeps, armored cars, troop carriers, and gliders. Chrysler built tanks, army trucks, and mine exploders. Gone were the days when families would pile into their jalopies and go pleasure driving; the rationing of cars, gasoline, and rubber put an end to that. Pleasures grew simpler, as people spent more time at the movies, entertaining at home, playing board games — and reading.

Some adjustments were easier than others. As rationing was extended to even the most common goods, hysteria occasionally crept in. Within a couple of years, sugar, coffee, butter, cheese, canned goods, meat, paper, and clothing were all added to the list of restricted goods. By the end of the war, almost every food, with the exception of fruits and vegetables (which were often grown in backyard victory gardens), was rationed or unpredictably stocked. The appearance of even the most basic items on a store shelf could cause unbridled elation. Even years after the war, one man would never forget the spectacle his mild-mannered neighbor made, running down the street, screaming at the top of her lungs that, at long last, toilet paper was available at the local supermarket. While the director of the Office of Civilian Defense kept a chipper tone about these restrictions ("Whether or not we have more than one cup of coffee a day, or more than one spoonful of sugar in it, has little effect on us, though it may have a large bearing on the outcome of this war"), some found it difficult to take rationing in stride. A mere rumor of a new restriction could set off a stampede as people rushed to stores to stock up before an item was gone for good. When the Office of Price Administration announced civilian consumption of rubber products would be slashed by about 80 percent, one of the greatest buying rushes ever recorded in the sale of sporting goods occurred, as men flocked to stores to buy tens of thousands of golf balls. Women grabbed handfuls of corsets, girdles, and brassieres (the elastic threads used for undergarments were made, in part, from rubber). Panic trumped patriotism, and hoarding became such a problem that even retailers denounced it. "If it is news when a man bites a dog, it is certainly news when a merchant urges a customer not to buy," one newspaper quipped.

President Roosevelt occasionally reminded Americans that rationing, supply drives, volunteer activities, and defense work were necessities in fighting total war. In one April 1942 fireside chat, the president maintained that the price for victory was not too high. "If you don't believe it, ask those millions who live today under the tyranny of Hitlerism. Ask the workers of France and Norway and the Netherlands, whipped to labor by the lash," Roosevelt said. "Ask the women and children whom Hitler is starving whether the rationing of tires and gasoline and sugar is too great a 'sacrifice.'" The president gravely concluded, "We do not have to ask them. They have already given us their agonized answers."

Considering the myriad ways that the public was asked to contribute to the war effort, that the VBC did not collect ten million books overnight was understandable. Instead, a steady stream of books flowed into the campaign's donation bins as the drive inched toward its goal.

As late February gave way to March, Althea Warren's four-month term as director of the Victory Book Campaign neared an end, with the goal of ten million books far from reached. Warren turned to publishers for help, asking for large donations of newly printed titles. Tens of thousands of new books were shipped to the VBC as a result. The VBC also asked publishers to advertise the need for readers to donate books after they finished reading them. Pocket Books did its part by printing a full-page notice in its paperbacks, asking readers to support sailors

and soldiers by bringing their books to a local library for donation, or mailing them to one of the addresses provided (one was
for Army libraries, another for Navy libraries).

By early March 1942, 4 million books had been collected.
Yet VBC sorting centers rejected 1.5 million of them as unsuitable for the training camps. Many of the early pleas for books
did not mention the (seemingly obvious) need for the public to
provide books specifically suited for young men in the services.
In some instances, it seemed that the public may have confused
the book drive and the waste paper campaign. Newspapers had
a field day reporting some of the titles donated. *How to Knit, An
Undertaker's Review,* and *Theology in 1870* were among the million and a half books that would not be sent to the servicemen.

The VBC did what it could with these titles. It sold decrepit
books to the waste paper drive and used the proceeds to purchase textbooks or other highly desired books that were not frequently donated. Children in need benefited from 5,679 juvenile titles, via the VBC and the Save the Children Federation.
Books that were topically off-kilter for young men were sent to
overburdened libraries in war-industry areas. (Palatial war factories were built in many small towns, causing thousands of
people to migrate to them to secure employment; but there was
often a shortage of homes, food, and resources to support these
burgeoning populations. Libraries in these areas could not meet
demand, and the VBC's donations were greatly appreciated.)
Valuable books, such as first editions or extremely rare tomes,
were sold and their proceeds were used to purchase books requested by the camps.

While the VBC did not waste a single book, it could not
continue to act as a clearinghouse for all unwanted books in the
United States. Newspapers assisted the campaign by publicizing
the types of books that Americans in the armed forces would

want most. Books "musn't be dirty, worn or juvenile," and the "soldier's preferences are for fiction, biography, history and technical works in that order," one newspaper instructed. The Red Cross suggested: "Be sure they are of the kind your own son would want to read if he were in the service."

Meanwhile, hundreds of thousands of Americans were leaving training camps and going to war. By the early spring of 1942, American warships were deployed in the Atlantic, Arctic, Mediterranean, Indian, and Pacific Oceans, and American troops were stationed in South America, Greenland, Iceland, the British Isles, the Middle East, Africa, Asia, Australia, and the Pacific Islands. Americans were scattered around the world.

They faced a mix of hardship, exhaustion, boredom, and fear. The infantry who served in North Africa slept on the ground every night, and quickly developed the survival instincts of soldiers. Almost reflexively, the slightest hum of an airplane sent dirt flying. "Five years ago you couldn't have got me to dig a ditch for five dollars an hour," one man said. "Now look at me ... Any time I get fifty feet from my home ditch you'll find me digging a new ditch." Besides developing a penchant for foxholes, the infantry acclimated to months without bathing, weeks without clean socks or clothing, and long periods of eating unsavory rations out of tin cans and packets. They were always filthy, tired, and overburdened. There were times when the men marched all night, could not move a muscle during the day (or risk being detected), and "lived in a way that is inconceivable to anyone who hasn't experienced it," as war correspondent Ernie Pyle described. The infantry—or "the God-damned infantry, as they liked to call themselves"—"had no comforts, and they even learned to live without the necessities," he added.

The amount of time spent twiddling thumbs, waiting for

something to happen, was almost as miserable as when the fighting started. As Private First Class H. Moldauer complained: "Monotony, monotony, all is monotony. The heat, the insects, the work, the complete absence of towns, women, liquor ... The irregular mail, which has become regular in its irregularity." He even found himself resenting "the monotony of prefixing the name with those three little — awfully little — letters: pfc." While most accounts of war focus on battles, skirmishes, and combat, the everyday life of a soldier consisted of far more waiting than fighting. And there was perhaps nothing that weighed so heavily on the mind and body as waiting. In the words of war correspondent Sergeant Walter Bernstein, war "is nine-tenths ordinary grind with no excitement and a great deal of unpleasantness." But when excitement came, "it is mostly the loose-boweled kind that you would just as soon be without."

When a battle began, the fear of death overwhelmed almost all else. Artillery and mortar fire were terrifying. Their deafening noise was only a precursor to the appalling destruction they unleashed. At their worst, they could atomize a man's body, sometimes resulting in near-obliteration. A man might be talking to a friend one minute and be unable to recognize him the next. Shells and flak ripped through flesh, limbs were severed, and explosions threw mangled body parts into the air and covered the ground with human carnage. Besides the dangers from above, the earth underfoot was riddled with German mines. One wrong step could change a life. This lurking danger became so ingrained in men's minds that, even years after the war, veterans would think twice before walking across a patch of grass, preferring to instead traverse an asphalt or concrete pathway.

Being exposed to a stream of death changed the way the men understood the war and their own role in it. Just as they felt they had checked their individuality at the training-camp gates, in combat the men came to the depressing realization that they were mere cogs in the military's machine. Like broken equipment that was exchanged for new gear, the Army sent in fresh troops to take the place of those wounded or killed in battle. But the very concept that human beings were treated as replaceable — casting off one man after his life was lost or his body incapacitated and plugging in another who might also be replaced down the line — brought on the uncomfortable feeling that the military viewed men as expendable. According to E. B. Sledge, who served in the First Marine Division on Peleliu and Okinawa, this realization "was difficult to accept." "We come from a nation and a culture that values life and the individual. To find oneself in a situation where your life seems of little value is the ultimate in loneliness," Sledge said.

The discomforts, dangers, and stressors of war were a brutal yoke to bear. Lacking relief from the strain, some men inevitably reached a breaking point. As Lieutenant Paul Fussell explained, the soldier "suffers so deeply from contempt and damage to his selfhood, the absurdity and boredom and chickenshit" of military life, "that some anodyne is necessary." While rest periods provided a temporary relief from the fighting, they offered no escape from the servicemen's surroundings. Letters from home and books were favorite items because they could be carried anywhere and retrieved whenever one needed a moment of solace, even on the frontlines. Yet overseas mail service was notoriously irregular and painfully slow. Americans in North Africa reported going months without mail. Misunderstandings and frustrations abounded. War correspondent Ernie Pyle reported that one soldier in his unit, who had gone three months without a single letter from his wife, became so disgusted by her remissness that he wrote her of his plans to get a divorce. After mailing this letter, the same man received one huge batch of fifty letters covering the entire three-month period. He immediately sent a telegram to his wife to take back his divorce threats.

In the absence of mail delivery or diversions afforded by sports equipment and movies, books were often the only entertainment the men had. And they were treasured. According to one Army chaplain, books gave the men "something worthwhile to occupy their minds and make it possible for them to more easily keep their minds on something constructive rather than dwelling too much on the destructive aspects of the war itself." In addition to merely distracting the men, studies dating back to World War I concluded that books had a therapeutic quality, enabling humans to better process the difficulties and tragedies they endured. Army psychiatrists agreed that books helped divert the mind, providing relief from the anxieties and strains of war. Reading was credited not only with improving morale but easing adjustment and averting the onset of psychoneurotic breakdowns. According to one article: "When we read fiction or drama, we perceive in accordance with our needs, goals, defenses, and values," and a reader will "introject meaning that will satisfy his needs and reject meaning that is threatening to his ego." From books, soldiers extracted courage, hope, determination, a sense of selfhood, and other qualities to fill voids created by the war.

Many men who were injured in the war found hope and healing in the books they read as they recovered. Charles Bolte, who was wounded in Africa, hospitalized, and distressed over his future as he faced the amputation of his leg, remembered a momentous day. A friend (who was being treated for a bullet wound) walked up to Bolte's bed, triumphantly waving a copy of Ernest Hemingway's *The Fifth Column and the First Forty-Nine Stories,* which he had found in the hospital library. Bolte

found comfort in a story about a hero who discovered that cry-
ing relieved the pain in his broken leg. Until then, Bolte had
never dared cry. The story convinced him to cover his head with
his blankets and give it a try. "It helped me, too," Bolte said. Although he endured multiple amputation surgeries, Bolte turned
to reading throughout his hospitalization and credited books
with helping him mend and move forward. "What happens
during convalescence from a serious wound can sour or sweeten
a man for life," Bolte remarked. For him, the latter occurred.
"It was the first time since grammar school that I'd had enough
time to read as much as I wanted to," he said. While there were
many things that helped him heal, Bolte placed the dozens of
books he had read as among the most important. Tens of thousands of men would share Bolte's experience over the course of
the war, finding in books the strength they needed to endure
the physical wounds inflicted on the battlefield, and the power
to heal their emotional and psychological scars as well.

The therapeutic effect of reading was not a new concept to
the librarians running the VBC. In the editorial Warren published on the eve of commencing her tenure as director, she
discussed how books could soothe pain, diminish boredom or
loneliness, and take the mind on a vacation far from where the
body was stationed. Whatever a man's need—a temporary escape, a comforting memory of home, balm for a broken spirit, or
an infusion of courage—the librarians running the VBC were
dedicated to ensuring that each man found a book to meet it.

They needed more of them. Training camps' stores were being depleted as men were encouraged to take a victory book
with them when they left for overseas service. Thousands of donated books were loaded onto Navy ships embarking on a mission. It was not an uncommon sight for piers to be lined with
boxes of victory books; servicemen would grab a title before

they boarded ship. These journeys could last weeks, and were notorious for their tedium and emptiness. Books were an ideal way to pass the time. As millions of volumes accompanied men as they shipped out overseas, millions more were needed to replenish training camps and keep up with demand.

In March 1942 Warren left the campaign, replaced by her close friend John Connor, who had served by her side as assistant director. Connor had degrees in business administration and library science, and had worked as an assistant librarian at Columbia University before joining the VBC. He passionately opposed censorship during wartime and was a champion of civil rights. Despite his strong opinions (which were not always popular), his personable manner made him well-liked. As one colleague described Connor, "He was always there with a smile, a handshake, and a kind word."

Under Connor's direction, librarians went into overdrive during the early spring of 1942 and were rewarded with an upswing in book donations. They harped on the types of books soldiers wanted, advertised the books that were most popular, and reminded (and begged) the public to give. Sorting centers happily reported that these efforts impacted not only the quantity of contributions but the quality of books received as well. By April 1942, book donations had climbed to 6.6 million volumes.

If momentum continued to build, it seemed possible that the campaign's goal would soon be met. Turning to the White House for help, the VBC requested that Friday, April 17, 1942, be designated Victory Book Day. The president obliged. At a press conference, he "asked the cooperation of all citizens, newspapers and radio stations to make [it] a success." When reporters asked President Roosevelt what types of books should be donated, he responded jokingly: "Anything except algebra," before stating simply that the public should give the same books that they had read and enjoyed. The Army and Navy were composed of civilians, and their reading tastes were no different from the home front's.

The president, who described himself as a "reader and buyer and borrower and collector of books" for all his life, held the VBC and other book organizations in high esteem, for he sincerely believed that books were symbols of democracy and weapons in the war of ideas. Shortly after he declared April 17 as Victory Book Day, Roosevelt released a statement on how books played an essential role in the fight for freedom:

> We all know that books burn—yet we have the greater knowledge that books cannot be killed by fire. People die, but books never die. No man and no force can abolish memory. No man and no force can put thought in a concentration camp forever. No man and no force can take from the world the books that embody man's eternal fight against tyranny of every kind. In this war, we know, books are weapons.

With the president's Victory Book Day declaration, Connor worked volunteers into a frenzy to prepare for the final charge to meet the campaign's goal of ten million volumes. Librarians were impressed by the public's response. Stories of citizens and businesses going the extra mile proliferated. A man in New York City's Chinatown painstakingly went from one apartment to the next collecting books in a rickshaw. Milkmen collected books from their customers' doorsteps. Libraries prominently posted thermometer charts that tracked book donations. Even children got involved. Boy Scouts and Girl Scouts pounded the pavement, collecting books through door-to-door solicitations in their neighborhoods. One Boy Scout troop collected an astounding ten thousand books in a single day. Around the nation, heaps of books were piled into donation bins. Nearly nine million books had been collected by the end of April 1942.

One million to go. As most commencement ceremonies for colleges and universities were held in May, the VBC decided to ask American universities to protest Germany's book burnings—which had begun at its universities—by assembling books for donation. Letters were mailed to every college and university in the United States proposing this idea. The letter urged that books be exhibited in a conspicuous place, such as at the center of graduation festivities. It would be a powerful contrast: American colleges collecting piles of books for donation to the services to memorialize the piles of books collected by the Nazis for burning. In the event that universities wished to remark on the significance of the books collected, the VBC recommended a passage from Milton's *Areopagitica:* "Books are not absolutely dead things, but do contain a potency of life in them to be as active as that soul whose progeny they are; nay, they do preserve as in a vial the purest efficacy and extraction of that living intellect that bred them."

Although the VBC's letter was not sent until the beginning of May 1942, many schools organized last-minute collections to coincide with graduation festivities. Among them were the University of Arkansas, Tougaloo College, the University of Denver, the University of Kansas, the University of Scranton, and Bowdoin College. Several universities used the VBC's suggestions as a blueprint for their own book ceremonies, right down to reading the passage by Milton.

. . .

The VBC was not the only organization to think back to the 1933 book burnings that May. With the passage of nine years and a formal declaration of war, the book burnings were cast in a new light: a warning of the destruction that would follow. In nine years' time, cities were destroyed, millions of lives were lost, and devastation had spread across Europe like a plague. As one newspaper remarked, "Hunger, forced labor, imprisonment, concentration camps, unarmed crowds of fleeing citizens slaughtered from the skies, nations murdered without cause"—these "are the spectacles that have succeeded those bonfires of books."

One of the most acclaimed book-burning memorials of 1942 was the radio program *They Burned the Books*, by Stephen Vincent Benét, a Pulitzer Prize winner. Renowned for his epic poem *John Brown's Body*, and the short story "The Devil and Daniel Webster," Benét was known for his ability to intertwine history with fable in striking prose. Aired by the Columbia Broadcasting System, *They Burned the Books* was such a sensation that copies of the script were immediately printed and sold in book form. Over the next four years, this program would be retransmitted over the airwaves countless times.

They Burned the Books begins with a stark warning: "Justify the enemy. Appease him. Excuse him. Pardon, condone or accept him. And, by any intelligent process of thought, you will arrive at the diabolical, tortured, debased world of Germany and her Axis partners." A bell then tolls nine times, after which the Berlin book burnings are reenacted for listeners. The narrator introduces several of the authors whose works were destroyed, and recounts the reasons given by the Nazis for throwing their books into the flames. One was the Jewish poet Heinrich Heine, whose well-known poem "The Lorelei" had been famously set to music by Friedrich Silcher:

I know not if there is a reason
Why I am so sad at heart.
A legend of bygone ages
Haunts me and will not depart.

The air is cool under nightfall.
The calm Rhine courses its way.
The peak of the mountain is sparkling
With evening's final ray.

The lyrics of "The Lorelei" had been memorized by millions of Germans; burning copies of the song would not eliminate it. Instead, the Nazis, "with totalitarian courtesy . . . kept the song—and blotted out [Heine's] name." "Author well-known—since 1842. Author unknown—since 1933," the narrator scoffs. "That's what they do to soldiers of humanity, that's how they rob the soldier of his sword."

After discussing the works of Heine, Albert Einstein, Sigmund Freud, Thomas Mann, Ernest Hemingway, Theodore Dreiser, and many other authors whose books were burned, the narrator urges that they could live on in the minds of those who had read them, but only if Americans chose to fight for their preservation, and for intellectual freedom. "This battle is not just a battle of lands, a war of conquest, a balance-of-power war. It is a battle for the mind of man." Although America did not realize in 1933 that the book burnings were the beginning of Hitler's total war, "we know it now," the narrator intones. The war being fought was for all the books that had been burned, for all the voices the Nazis tried to silence, and for all the innocent people whose blood had been spilled. History featured many instances of people trying to squelch freedom of thought, but the most egregious offender of them all was Adolf Hitler.

"We are waiting, Adolf Hitler. The books are waiting, Adolf Hitler. The fire is waiting, Adolf Hitler. The Lord of Hosts is waiting, Adolf Hitler."

By 1942, the words that Goebbels spoke one dreary night in 1933 had begun to come to fruition, but not as he had hoped. The pile of ashes in Berlin's Bebelplatz was not forgotten. Those ashes were now a symbol of the freedoms at stake and the danger that the Axis powers presented. Now books would flourish in numbers greater than before. Authors would not be silenced. A new phoenix would arise: an army of words, thoughts, ideas, and books.

Within one month of the ninth anniversary of the Berlin book burning, another million books were collected by the VBC. The campaign's goal had been met. Librarians across the United States celebrated. Letters from appreciative servicemen emphasized what a difference a box of books could make. From Africa, a man wrote "to let you know that your efforts of boosting morale of the troops going overseas are not in vain. On our voyage over here," he said, "there were thousands of us on the ship, [and] we were all overjoyed beyond words to find that we had some books to read to pass the time during our leisure moments, and there were many." A lieutenant in the Army Air Corps stationed in Alaska thanked the VBC for not forgetting the men in his remote corner of the war. He noted that, even as he wrote his letter, men were reading the books the VBC had sent, "and I can assure you that they are very grateful." From the United States Naval Station in Rhode Island, a captain reported that books were being devoured. As the men were not permitted to leave the station, the reading room was one of the few places where they could relax and lose themselves in books.

As the armed forces swelled in size, however, the need for

books grew. Many felt that the VBC, having met its goal, could not simply stop its work. But even its continuing efforts would not be enough. There were two problems: the exhausted supply of donated books and the growing pool of millions of men in the services who needed to travel light. Hardcover books were fine for training libraries, and even onboard battleships. But they weighed down every soldier who had to carry them into the field.

The VBC struggled for renewal in 1943. It bore the brunt of scathing criticism from Isabel DuBois, the head of the Library Section of the Navy. DuBois oversaw nearly a thousand Navy libraries and eight hospitals, and took great pains in developing lists of quality books with which to stock them. The VBC trespassed on DuBois's duties, and she did not appreciate the intrusion. She had opposed the 1942 VBC and vehemently resisted the notion of a 1943 campaign. After receiving a shipment of victory books in the summer of 1942, DuBois wrote to Connor that if the books she received were a "sample of the books which have been sorted by librarians, it is the worst indictment of my profession I have ever seen. These were the same titles which I discarded in 1917 and 1918 and the 25 years in between has not made them any more valuable." She added: "When I think of the tremendous waste in transportation and handling, it leaves me simply appalled. In other words, are gift books worth it? As you know, I never thought they were, but I am more firmly of the opinion than ever."

The VBC also faced stiff political opposition from the government's Charles Taft, who only reluctantly approved funding the campaign again, despite his complaint that he was "positive it is not making an impression in the larger centers." He was "convinced that this is because the librarian has been made chairman." "I raised serious questions at the very first meeting as to the use of the librarians in this capacity," he said. "If this were just a brief drive I would not say anything about it but it is expected to be a continuing effort, and I am satisfied that it is going to bog down unless you establish as a general policy that a live wire layman be put in charge of the campaign effort in every large center." Between 1870 and 1900, librarianship had swung from 80 percent male to 80 percent female, though men held the majority of executive posts and women generally played second fiddle. The VBC's first director, after all, had been described as "#1 in the field of *Women* Librarians." Taft clearly was not a fan of the female-dominated group.

When John Connor and the VBC survived the funding scare, he wrote to Althea Warren, describing the ordeal. "Taft began once again his gospel of the inadequacy of librarians and his preference to have business men do the job. He was permitted to speak his piece," Connor said, but when others had "finished extolling the efforts of the librarians in the VBC effort, there was little that Charlie could do by way of rebuttal." Connor expected a sympathetic response, and Warren did not disappoint. "How glad I am to have missed Mr. Charles P. Taft! Didn't he make you want to haul off and slap him in the jaw? He is so full of criticism and with no suggestions to help," she said.

The 1943 campaign produced fewer books than 1942, and many of them were not useful to the troops. Connor made arrangements to route unwanted books to organizations and areas that would appreciate them. An outspoken proponent of racial equality, he sent volumes to Japanese internment camps and begged the Army to send more to its African American troops.

Connor also sent books to American POWs, though it wasn't easy and had to be done via the YMCA's War Prisoners' Aid division. The books donated to the YMCA had to be rigorously sorted, as the rules governing what books would be accepted were onerous. For example, nothing published after September 1, 1939, was allowed, nor were materials that had any relation to geography, politics, technology, war or the military, or "any subject which may be considered doubtful." Books had to be new or in mint condition; no signs of previous ownership or erasure were permitted. Anything written by or including material of Jewish authors or "émigrés from enemy or enemy-occupied countries" was rejected because such books would not be allowed in German-controlled POW camps.

The VBC turned to publishing companies for help. In the month of March 1943 alone, the campaign collected fifteen hundred books from Funk & Wagnalls, over fifteen hundred from Harper & Brothers, four thousand from Doubleday, Doran, two thousand from W. W. Norton & Company, one thousand from G. P. Putnam's Sons, and sixteen hundred from Alfred A. Knopf—to name just a few. Of them all, Pocket Books was consistently generous in donating its popular paperbacks. The five thousand books given to the campaign by Pocket Books in March 1943 supplemented the sixty thousand provided the month before. Beloved by the servicemen because they were lightweight and smaller than the traditional hardcovers, they easily made the rounds overseas as well as in camps and hospitals.

As donations from the public continued to slow, the question arose: why shouldn't the armed services provide millions of books as part of its budget? Between 1941 and 1943 the Army and Navy had experimented with distributing magazines to the troops. The success of this program doomed the VBC.

Despite early setbacks, delivery of popular periodicals was one of the greatest transformations in recreation for frontline soldiers to date. Originally, the Army and Navy ordered thousands of subscriptions to more than a dozen magazines, and planned to sort them into sets by bundling one copy of each into a single package for shipment around the world. In the Army, one set of magazines was supposed to reach each unit of 150 men. In reality, fifty- and seventy-pound packages, each containing two hundred copies of the same magazine, piled up at overseas postal-distribution centers, where they languished for months. More often than not, the magazines were never sorted, and instead hundreds of identical magazines would eventually be shipped to one unit. The next month, the same unit might not receive any periodicals. This haphazard distribution was incredibly frustrating for those in the services. As the Pulitzer Prize–winning cartoonist Bill Mauldin observed, magazines arrived "late and tattered, if they arrived at all," and "half of the magazines carry serial stories, which are a pain in the neck to the guys who start them and can't finish them" because they never receive the next issue. It would take almost two years to straighten out these problems.

The 1942 reorganization of the Army's Special Services Division, which was responsible for serving the morale needs of the servicemen, brought an end to slipshod magazine delivery. Special Services set up a giant assembly warehouse near the New York Port of Embarkation, where tens of millions of magazines were received, sorted, and bundled into sets. Initial offerings included: *American Magazine, Baseball Magazine, Collier's, Detective Story Magazine, Flying, Infantry Journal, Life, Look, Modern Screen, Newsweek, Omnibook, Popular Mechanics, Popular Photography, Radio News, Reader's Digest, Superman, Time,* and *Western Trails.* Each weekly set included one copy of most magazines; for titles such as *Life* and *Time,* three copies were provided to keep up with demand. (In 1945, a special "WAC

Magazine Kit" was developed, which was distributed to hospitals and Women's Army Corps units overseas and consisted of *Harper's Bazaar, Glamour, Good Housekeeping, Ladies' Home Journal, McCall's, Mademoiselle, Personal Romances, True Confessions, True Story,* and *Woman's Home Companion.*)

The first sorted sets were mailed in May 1943, and from that point forward, magazine deliveries became regular, and the popularity of periodicals continued to grow. Between July 1943 and January 1946, the number of magazine sets distributed to the servicemen increased sevenfold. Due to the overwhelming demand, additional titles were added to each set, including *Overseas Comics,* the *New Yorker, Pic,* and *Hit Kit.* To keep magazine service affordable for the Army and Navy, publishers sold their magazines at cost. The average price for the September 1944 monthly set of one hundred magazines (based on four weekly deliveries of twenty-five magazines in a set) was only $3.86.

To minimize costs and make concessions for paper rationing, some magazines experimented with printing armed forces editions. Generally, these publications contained no advertisements, used twenty- to twenty-five-pound paper instead of the traditional forty-five- or sixty-pound paper, and were a fraction of their usual size. *Newsweek* published a "Battle Baby" edition, *Time* printed a "Pony Edition," and the *New Yorker, Science News Letter,* and *McGraw-Hill Overseas Digest* all printed special overseas editions. All of these magazines were roughly six by eight inches and used paper that was akin to newsprint. The miniatures saved paper, but the smaller print was brutal on the eyes. *Newsweek's* Battle Baby was a reproduction of the regular magazine shrunk down to size, which resulted in text that approximated seven-point font. Sergeant Sanderson Vanderbilt, an avid reader, joked that "after a few more years of squinting my way through pony-size overseas editions of *Time,*" he would surely go blind. One historian seconded this sentiment: "Even in good light one could not read it very long at a time."

Another magazine to embrace the miniature wartime edition was the *Saturday Evening Post,* which printed the smallest of them all, measuring a mere three by four and a half inches: *Post Yarns.* These booklets were truly pocket-sized, and contained articles, stories, and cartoons. The *Post* sent ten million copies to servicemen around the world, with a proviso that the *Yarns* be passed from one reader to the next. Ben Hibbs, the *Saturday Evening Post*'s editor, said that the *Yarns* were designed because "war correspondents are always telling me of the hunger for reading material that exists whenever American soldiers and sailors pitch their tents or hang their hammocks." The *Yarns* were the *Post*'s "attempt to make the lives of our fighting men a little happier," and were distributed "without charge as a token of the admiration and gratitude of the *Saturday Evening Post* and the folks back home," he said. The Battle Baby, Pony Edition, and *Post Yarns* were the most striking magazines produced during the war — and in the history of magazines. Small, lightweight, and entertaining, they were appreciated beyond measure.

So why not books? The proliferation of practically weightless miniature magazines made the provision of hefty hardcovers, and the VBC itself, seem obsolete. If an arrangement could be made to produce and distribute smaller books using magazine-service models, the Army and Navy would be hard-pressed to ignore such an opportunity.

FOUR

New Weapons in the War of Ideas

The first couple of days at sea our ship seemed to
mill around without purpose. Then we stopped
completely, and lay at anchor for a day. But finally
we made our rendezvous with other ships and at
dusk — five days after leaving London — we steamed
slowly into a pre-arranged formation, like floating
pieces of a puzzle drifting together to form a picture. By dark we were rolling, and the first weak
ones were getting sick . . .

After a while the sea calmed . . . The soldiers were
routed out at 6:30 a.m., and at 10:00 a.m. every day
they had to stand muster and have boat drill for
an hour. Outside of that they had little to do, and
passed the time just standing around on deck, or ly-
ing down below reading.

— ERNIE PYLE, "CONVOY TO AFRICA," 1942

I N MAY 1943 the *New York Sun* broke the news that the
Army and Navy no longer needed the VBC's donated
books. For the first time, the armed forces planned to purchase millions of paperbacks each month, with the help of an
organization that called itself the Council on Books in War-

time. "Too many people looked upon the voluntary campaign as an opportunity to get rid of books that nobody would want," the *Sun* said. The next day, the *New York Herald Tribune* picked up the story: "Public Campaign Fails, Army Will Buy Books," the headline read. "American soldiers are going to have books if the Army itself has to buy them," the article said.

Believing that a 1944 campaign was likely, VBC volunteers were disappointed to learn that their work had been dubbed a failure. Days after publication of the *Sun* and *Tribune* articles, the USO informed the VBC that it would not provide any funding for a 1944 campaign. The VBC had no choice but to close its doors. With heavy hearts, and after lengthy discussion, the ALA officers voted to discontinue the campaign as of October 1, 1943. Volunteers across the United States received a letter from the VBC headquarters stating that the War Department planned to purchase books, and that the VBC would stop its book drive, as it was no longer needed. Outraged librarians made their opinions known. One librarian wrote to the VBC demanding an explanation for why the campaign was ending when the need for books was insatiable and "our warehouse is almost empty." "If libraries are going to abdicate their peculiar war responsibilities and opportunities, they can expect to be treated with increased indifference," said an incensed librarian from Cleveland. "Certainly the need for which the Campaign was brought into being has not been fully met — in fact, [it] has scarcely diminished," wrote an exasperated librarian from the American Merchant Marine Library Association.

Yet the decision was hard to argue. There was a limit to the quantity and usefulness of donated books, and it was time for a larger-scale effort: printing new books chosen and constructed expressly for Americans at war. The design was as important as the choice of titles. Cartoonist Bill Mauldin, who documented

Army life in France, Italy, and Burma, once tried to explain for the home front the daily rigors an infantryman faced. He suggested:

> Dig a hole in your back yard while it is raining. Sit in the hole until the water climbs up around your ankles. Pour cold mud down your shirt collar. Sit there for forty-eight hours, and, so there is no danger of your dozing off, imagine that a guy is sneaking around waiting for a chance to club you on the head or set your house on fire.
>
> Get out of the hole, fill a suitcase full of rocks, pick it up, put a shotgun in your other hand, and walk on the muddiest road you can find. Fall flat on your face every few minutes as you imagine big meteors streaking down to sock you.
>
> After ten or twelve miles (remember — you are still carrying the shotgun and suitcase) start sneaking through the wet brush. Imagine that somebody has booby-trapped your route with rattlesnakes which will bite you if you step on them. Give some friend a rifle and have him blast in your direction once in a while.
>
> Snoop around until you find a bull. Try to figure out a way to sneak around him without letting him see you. When he does see you, run like hell all the way back to your hole in the back yard, drop the suitcase and shotgun, and get in.
>
> If you repeat this performance every three days for several months you may begin to understand why an infantryman sometimes gets out of breath. But you still won't understand how he feels when things get tough.

The physical demands made on an infantryman, or anyone fighting near the frontlines, required that all unnecessary items be removed from one's pack. "You look everything over and try to find something else you can throw away to make the load on

[your] blister[ed] [feet] a little lighter," Mauldin said. Even gas masks were routinely chucked because the men were so desperate to lighten the weight they carried. It is not surprising that a hardcover book was unlikely to survive the final cut. As Sergeant Ralph Thompson sarcastically said, if "you could see what an infantryman's normal impedimenta consist of, you'd understand why he doesn't run out and buy a couple of 1,000 page historical novels to top off the load."

Yet they craved their reading. Army newspapers and magazines, such as *Stars and Stripes* and *Yank, the Army Weekly,* were in high demand. When each set of popular domestic magazines arrived, they were snatched up, pored over, and passed on to the next guy in line. Mauldin said that "soldiers at the front read K-ration labels when the contents are listed on the package, just to be reading something." Books *were* wanted—but not hardcovers. What the Army and Navy needed were conveniently sized, featherweight volumes.

While paperback books might seem like an obvious solution, the softcover book had not yet been embraced by all publishing companies. The war (and most notably, rationing) had sparked a new trend away from hardcover tomes and toward smaller softcover books, mostly provided by new paperback publishers and imprints. The shift was stark. In 1939, fewer than two hundred thousand paperback books were sold in the United States; by 1943, this number had climbed to over forty million. Before the 1940s, the publishing industry and bookstores had snubbed the paperback. Booksellers refused to place the inelegant and inferior softcovers in their shops, which were almost all devoted to stately, sturdy hardcovers. The profit margin on a hardcover book, priced at about ten times the cost of a softcover, was a significant obstacle to publishers in thinking beyond the format. However, the tides began to turn when publishers' access to paper was slashed by rationing, and restrictions were placed on their consumption of cotton cloth used for hardcover book bindings (the government needed this cloth to make camouflage netting). As each publishing company faced the conundrum of producing books with only a fraction of the paper and cotton cloth they typically used, they came to grips with the idea that they would not be able to manufacture their usual quantity and quality of hardcover books using their ordinary methods.

Pocket Books, the first American publishing company to mass-produce paperbacks, demonstrated that it could secure robust profits by selling paperbacks in drugstores and five-and-dime chains (such as Woolworth's) instead of traditional bookstores. As its name suggests, Pocket Books printed smaller volumes that used less paper. Even the most stubborn proponents of hardcover books had to admit that paperbacks were well suited to overcome wartime restrictions. What emerged was a revolution in the American book industry. *Time* magazine declared that, between the budding paperback trade and off-the-charts book sales, 1943 "was the most remarkable in the 150-year-old history of U.S. publishing."

The concept for the Council on Books in Wartime was realized one fateful day in February 1942, when Clarence Boutell, the publicity director for G. P. Putnam's Sons, had lunch with George Oakes, of the *New York Times*. Oakes mentioned that the *Times* had recently refurbished and renovated Times Hall, a theater on Manhattan's Forty-Fourth Street, and that it was being made available to host programs by public-minded organizations. Boutell, who believed that books were an essential weapon for building morale and fighting the war of ideas, suggested that publishers assemble at Times Hall to discuss how books could be used to win the war. "The men of words shared the responsibility with the makers of guns and the users of them" to ensure victory and a lasting peace, Boutell averred. The two men agreed to ask their colleagues if they had any interest in such a program.

Back at his office, Boutell presented the idea to Putnam's president, Melville Minton, who was interested enough to suggest they meet with Malcolm Johnson, of Doubleday, Doran & Co., to discuss it further. Publishing was a second career for Johnson, who had graduated from MIT with a chemical engineering degree and then spent seven years with the Standard Oil Company on a project in China. However, once he discovered publishing, Johnson knew he had found his true calling. He began as a managing editor of the *Atlantic Monthly* before landing a job at Doubleday. Johnson worked in publishing for the rest of his life. He became a prominent figure in the industry, and his opinion of Boutell's idea carried weight. Luckily, he loved it.

Representatives from several large publishing houses and key figures in the industry formed a working committee. Boutell was voted chairman of the group. With Johnson, other members included Donald S. Klopfer of Random House; Frederic G. Melcher, editor of *Publishers Weekly;* William Warder Norton, president of W. W. Norton; Robert M. Coles of the American Booksellers Association; George Oakes and Ivan Veit of the *New York Times;* and Stanley P. Hunnewell of the Book Publishers Bureau, the industry's leading trade organization. At a March 1942 meeting, this group voted to form the Council on Books in Wartime, with the objective of exploring how books could serve the nation during the war. One week later, another meeting was held at which Norton suggested that the council's slogan be: "Books are weapons in the war of ideas." It was adopted on the spot. Membership quickly swelled to over seventy representatives of the publishing world.

During the early months of its existence, the council seemed to be "a committee in search of a project." All believed books had a definite role in the war, but how could they be mobilized into action? In the spring of 1942, the council hosted a meeting of publishing professionals at Times Hall to discuss this question. To spur discussion, each invited guest received an essay in advance written by council members, entitled "Books and the War." The essay began by noting that total war was underway, with fighting not only "in the field and on the sea and in the air," but also in "the realm of ideas." It said: "The mightiest single weapon this war has yet employed" was "not a plane, or a bomb or a juggernaut of tanks"—it was *Mein Kampf.* This single book caused an educated nation to "burn the great books that keep liberty fresh in the hearts of men." If America's goal was victory and world peace, "all of us will have to know more and think better than our enemies think and know," the council asserted. "This war is a war of books ... Books are our weapons." This missive did exactly what the council had hoped it would. Conversation flowed as writers and publishers contemplated their special role in the war. Interest in attending the Times Hall meeting burgeoned. So many requests for tickets to the event were received that many people had to be turned away.

On May 12, 1942, Times Hall was filled to capacity with writers, journalists, editors, publishers, major government figures, and all others who had a stake in the freedom to print and publish the written word. For two nights, the book world converged to examine the themes in the council's essay. The keynote speaker, Assistant Secretary of State Adolf A. Berle Jr., commenced the program by asking that "everyone who has anything to do with books ... take good care that the books are worthy of the place which is vouchsafed them." Hitler had waged war on ideas, Berle said, and "if authors still may write, if publishers still may print, if universities still may teach, it is because, and only because, many and many men for faith alone are prepared to give their lives, their children's lives, and all they have, for the defense of that right." *New York Times* columnist Anne O'Hare McCormick took the podium next. She spoke of how there were three pressing wartime needs that only books could placate: Americans needed books that could clarify the issues wrapped up in the war, prove that the problems that seemed insoluble could be solved, and fortify resolve and help them endure the hardships they faced. "The book written to express and inspire big thoughts, big dreams, mature and steady purposes in America, a book written to the scale of America, will fire a million guns and launch a thousand ships," McCormick's voice boomed as a clatter of applause engulfed it.

After its Times Hall convention, the council considered a number of different projects, with the two most significant being radio broadcasting and recommending relevant books for the public to read. First it turned to radio. Focusing on the home front, the council produced programs highlighting books that clarified the values at stake in the war and provoked debate about what the nation was fighting for and how peace could be achieved. These programs — *Books Are Bullets; Fighting Words; Mightier than the Sword;* and *Words at War* — consisted of author interviews, book discussions, and dramatizations of books. Of the hundreds of episodes that were broadcast, the most sensational of them all was the *Words at War* adaptation of Selden Menefee's book *Assignment: USA.* Rather than focus on how the war had unified the nation behind a common goal, Menefee boldly exposed the hypocrisy of fighting a war for democracy and freedom when inequality and social strife ran rampant at home. The radio dramatization of *Assignment: USA* took its listeners on a train ride around the United States, as a narrator commented on the problems Menefee witnessed in several cities. Nothing was ignored — labor disputes, isolationism, prejudice, racism, anti-Semitism. It proved to be one of the most controversial radio programs of the decade.

The program was first broadcast on Tuesday, February 22, 1944, at 11:30 p.m. (an hour so late that producers complained no one would be listening). At the beginning of the show, a narrator explains that listeners will hear actors reenact Menefee's experiences and conversations with Americans across the nation. The first town visited is Brattleboro, Vermont, where a furious father is heard refusing to allow his daughter to marry an Irishman. "No daughter of mine will ever sink *that* low," he bellows. The narrator then remarks: "In New England you will find a well established social hierarchy — a caste system unparalleled in America except by the white-Negro relationship of the South." The train moves on to Boston, where Menefee encounters a mutilated patriotic poster — with the word "United" changed to "Jewnited." "Isolationism, anti-Semitism, [and] pro-appeasement are more rampant in Boston than in any city in the land," the narrator intones. Describing anti-Semitic leaflets distributed in the subways, and violence directed against Jews, the narrator says he would expect such scenes in Nazi Germany, not in the United States.

As the train moves through the South, it stops in Mobile, Alabama, where the narrator observes booming shipyards, young girls soliciting in the streets, and rambunctious boys robbing stores and drinking alcohol. With a housing shortage and a city overrun with destitute families seeking employment, one native of the area tells the narrator that the "sooner the war's over the sooner we'll get 'em out of the shipyards, out of town and back to their pea patches and swamps where they belong!" As the train passes through Mississippi and Louisiana, the narrator observes that "large segments of the population are more interested in keeping the Negro in his place than in keeping Hitler and Tojo in their places." "The resulting dissension must be very gratifying to Dr. Goebbels," he concludes. Asked about the "racial question," a local politician insists there is none. "There is white supremacy, and there always will be white supremacy. We have no patience with fellas in Washington, with their antilynching bills, their anti-poll-tax bills, and their anti-discrimination clauses in war contracts," he says.

The train chugs through the Midwest, where the narrator comments that Chicago's black market flourishes; Detroit's race riots are "worse than most of the South has ever seen"; and Minneapolis seethes with anti-Semitism. On the West Coast, residents of California, Oregon, and Washington State can be heard complaining about food and housing shortages, absenteeism, labor turnover, and strikes. The narrator speaks of low morale plaguing the war plants, as management blames workers for being shiftless and dissolute, while workers blame management for long hours and difficult work conditions. Everyone blames the government for the lack of housing, childcare, and community facilities.

Yet following this damning account of division across the United States, the narrator asks Menefee to give his overall impression of America. He ends the program with a dash of optimism. "People are doing a wonderful job fighting this war, despite the mistakes that some are making," Menefee states. Public opinion polls showed that Americans knew what they were fighting for and were determined to win the war and a lasting peace. Menefee concludes that Americans generally agreed on the course the nation was taking in the war and were willing to fight for peace and freedom.

"Assignment: USA" made people talk. Some Americans were offended by Menefee's characterizations and curt comments, while others felt that the episode discussed the nation's problems with a refreshing dose of honesty. Magazines and newspapers jumped at the opportunity to cover the controversial program. *Variety* reported that if "Assignment: USA" had been broadcast earlier in the evening, "the phone calls would have burned the insulation off the wires of NBC." The substance of the show "scorched the air [and] made your ears burn"; it was just the type of program the country needed. The *New York Times* deemed it "the boldest, hardest hitting program" of the year. As word spread, NBC was pressured to rebroadcast the show at an earlier hour when more people could tune in and listen. NBC acquiesced, and when the program was replayed, some cities — such as Boston; Springfield, Massachusetts; and Mobile, Alabama — refused to carry it. According to *Time* magazine, "Boston was not amused" at the rebroadcast and had "heard all it wanted to hear . . . when the program first went on the air." Did the broadcast help in the war effort? Certainly it showcased the rigor of a free press and the right to dissent and raise a critical voice. The council was gratified by the segment's popularity and felt a sense of accomplishment in producing a show that sparked discussion about the issues plaguing the home front. It achieved precisely what the council had hoped.

While the council's radio programs enjoyed wide popularity, council members were concerned that the quantity of books recommended each week might overwhelm the public. The council decided to start a new project to promote only those titles deemed extraordinary, that clarified why the country was at war, what values were at stake, and under what terms the war should be ended. A War Book Panel was created to nominate and choose titles that could be published bearing the council's stamp of approval. Panel members included Irita Van Doren, editor of the *New York Herald Tribune;* Amy Loveman, associate editor of the *Saturday Review of Literature;* Lieutenant Colonel Joseph L. Greene, editor of the *Infantry Journal;* Admiral Harry E. Yarnell, retired; and J. Donald Adams, editor of the *New York Times Book Review.* The panel met periodically to discuss titles and vote on which would receive official endorsement. Selected books were republished and labeled "Imperative," their front covers emblazoned with a large *I.* All council members were obligated to advertise these books as essential reading — even books published by rival companies. While they would certainly benefit monetarily by promoting the sale of books, never before had publishers collaborated so wholeheartedly as to advertise books published by their competitors. Posters were displayed in libraries and bookstores to help publicize the new Imperative book program and the selected titles.

The first book branded Imperative was *They Were Expendable,* by W. L. White, which was chosen in November 1942. The book told the story of the servicemen who manned torpedo boats in the Philippines as Americans came under Japanese attack. Told from the perspective of four survivors (out of sixty men), the book did not shy away from the idea stated in the title: these men were considered replaceable and they knew it. "Suppose you're a sergeant machine-gunner, and your army is retreating and the enemy is advancing," one of the survivors proposed. He continued:

The captain takes you to a machine gun covering the road. "You're to stay here and hold the position," he tells you. "For how long," you ask. "Never mind," he answers, "just hold it." Then you know you're expendable. In a war, anything can be expendable — money or gasoline or equipment or most usually men ... They expect you to stay there and spray that road with steel until you're killed or captured, holding up the enemy for a few minutes or even a precious quarter of an hour.

Reviews pegged the book as the most significant personal war experience yet published. It was well deserving of the "Distinguished Service Medal, the 'I' for Imperative," one newspaper said.

About four months later, the council announced that John Hersey's *Into the Valley* would be its next Imperative. Hersey told of his experience as a war correspondent on Guadalcanal, where he accompanied a company of Marines on a mission to take the Matanikau River from the Japanese in October 1942. According to Hersey, after a long march into the dense jungle, enemy snipers opened up, Japanese machine guns rattled off rounds, and mortars were lobbed — their shrill whistling gave a brief, terrifying warning that a shell was about to burst. Hersey watched as Americans were unable to set up their own machine guns quickly enough and were forced to retreat, carrying injured and dying men back to camp. *Into the Valley* provided a realistic account of what battle was like, describing acts of heroism on the part of the Marines without overly romanticizing their experience.

In May 1943 the third Imperative was selected — Wendell Willkie's *One World*. The book told of Willkie's tour of Allied nations during the fall of 1942 as an American ambassador at large, and recorded his impressions of the leaders and people he encountered. Willkie urged Americans to shed their isolationist tendencies and recognize that countries needed to cooperate with one another to achieve peace and maintain it after the war. The fourth Imperative, announced in July 1943, was Walter Lippmann's *U.S. Foreign Policy*. This book argued that America's failure to readjust its foreign policy to account for its acquisition of the Philippines in 1898 and Germany's aggression during World War I rendered it completely unprepared for war in 1941 and threatened its ability to make peace. Lippmann provided a brief history of America's diplomatic relations and wars, challenged America's fondness for isolationism, and urged Americans to recognize their commitments to the world. The book was lauded for making foreign policy accessible to the masses, and widening the area of discussion from small groups of intellectuals to hundreds of thousands of people.

The fifth Imperative was another of John Hersey's, *A Bell For Adano,* which was the only work of fiction endorsed under the program. This book challenged Hitler's propaganda about America's heterogeneity being its weakness. (In September 1941, Goebbels had declared that the "America of today will never be a danger to us. Nothing will be easier than to produce a bloody revolution in the United States. No other country has so many racial and social tensions. We shall be able to play many strings there.") The hero of Hersey's story is an Italian American GI who takes part in the invasion of Sicily and wins the trust of the Italian locals because of their shared heritage. Hersey advanced the notion that America's armed forces had an advantage in the world war precisely because they represented a melting pot of cultures and ethnicities.

The sixth and, as it turned out, final Imperative book was named in September 1944, Edgar Snow's *People on Our Side*.

Snow, a war correspondent for the *Saturday Evening Post,* took a seventeen-country tour from April 1942 through the summer of 1943. Primarily focusing on his experiences in Russia, China, and India, Snow described the political, economic, and social problems that plagued these nations.

It is not entirely clear why the Imperative program came to an end. Selection of a seventh book began, but the War Book Panel voted in equal number for two books, and it seems this tie resulted in a stalemate. In the spring of 1945, the panel selected Ralph Ingersoll's *The Battle Is the Payoff,* but this title had already become a bestseller; it seemed unnecessary to crown as an Imperative a book millions of people were already reading. And at that point, the end of the war was in sight.

Despite its modest number of titles, the Imperative program was a success. Indeed, as with Hollywood and the film industry, the war was good for reading and the book industry. Americans purchased about 25 percent more books in 1943 than they did in 1942. The new paperback format was a hit, as Americans craved simple pleasures in times of peril. This increase in book buying was indicative of an expanded market of book buyers. As *Time* magazine observed, by 1943, "book-reading and book-buying reached outside the narrow quarters of the intellectuals and became the business of the whole vast literate population of the U.S." No longer were books linked to wealth and status: they had become a universal pastime and a fitting symbol of democracy.

The council's greatest achievement was neither its radio programs nor its Imperative series. In 1943 it turned its attention to the book needs of U.S. servicemen. Publishers knew that soldiers, sailors, and Marines craved books, but hated the VBC's bulky hardcovers. Although the council had reached out to the VBC to offer assistance in supplying the servicemen with books, the relationship between these two organizations never warmed. In fact, when council members Richard Simon (of Simon & Schuster) and John Farrar (of Farrar & Rinehart) met with VBC members in December 1942, Farrar cryptically described the meeting as a "fairly complicated one and inconclusive," and then added: "I had best report on it orally." The two organizations never meaningfully worked together.

As of early 1943, no book existed that met the specific needs of servicemen stationed on the frontlines. It would have to be invented. As publishers puzzled over how to affordably produce small-sized paperbacks, a few men worked on a blueprint that would revolutionize the industry. After consulting with Lieutenant Colonel Trautman and graphic artist H. Stahley Thompson, Malcolm Johnson presented a proposal to the council to reconstruct the book — inside and out. Although they would leave the meeting with more questions than answers, the plan met a chorus of approval. The "Armed Services Edition" was born.

Over the next several years, the production of these books would be beset with challenges. But with the cooperation of every major United States publishing company and the Navy and War Departments, the council championed the most significant project in publishing history. The organization in search of a project had finally found a lasting one.

FIVE

Grab a Book, Joe, and Keep Goin'

Dear Sirs:

I want to say thanks a million for one of the best deals in the Army — your Armed Services Editions. Whenever we get them they are as welcome as a letter from home. They are as popular as pin-up girls — especially over here where we just couldn't get books so easily, if it weren't for your editions.

— PRIVATE W. R. W. AND THE GANG

THE PUBLISHERS FACED a forbidding task: fashioning a new style of book suitable for mass production while operating under wartime restrictions. For starters, there was paper rationing. In 1943, publishers were allocated only 37.5 percent of the paper they used in 1939. Many found this constraint infuriating when the country was in the midst of a war of ideas. As a columnist for the *Chicago Daily News* said: "We don't burn books in America, we merely slash the paper allotment. The motives are vastly different, but some of the results are the same." But the government considered books a necessary piece of equipment; just as aluminum and rubber were funneled to factories to produce airplanes, the government agreed to provide nine hundred tons of paper per quarter year for the production of Armed Services Editions (ASEs).

To maximize the number of books that could be printed with this supply, and to ensure that the ASEs best fit the servicemen's circumstances, the council resorted to unprecedented formatting and manufacturing techniques. Of course, the council had to rely on paperbacks. This saved space and weight, and the books gained pliability so they could be tucked more easily into a pocket or full pack. Next, the size of each book had to be reduced. In the 1940s, a standard small hardcover book was five by eight inches and could be up to two inches thick. The ASEs would be produced in two sizes: the larger would measure six and a half by four and a half inches — similar to the mass-market paperbacks in drugstores — and the smaller, five and a half by three and three-eighths inches. The largest ASE was only three-quarters of an inch thick, and the smallest was less than an eighth of an inch thick. These measurements were not arbitrary. The council researched the pocket dimensions of standard military uniforms to ensure that the larger ASE could fit in the pocket of a soldier's pants, while the smaller could be tucked away in a breast pocket. Even the longest ASE, which was 512 pages, could slip into a hip pocket. The smaller books were essentially the size of a wallet. Even soldiers on the frontlines could stow away or summon such a book in an instant.

No book press existed that was capable of printing such tiny books. The council solved this problem by turning to magazine presses. Many benefits flowed from this decision. Perhaps the most important was that these presses used thinner paper than what was normally used for hardcover books. This helped keep ASEs incredibly light and slim. Thanks to their paperback cover, small size, and featherweight pages, the ASEs weighed one-fifth or less than their hardcover counterparts.

Since magazine presses were not designed to produce pocket-sized publications, the council printed the books "two up": two books were printed on each page, one above the other, and were then sliced into two by a horizontal cut. The magazine presses for *Reader's Digest* were used to produce smaller books, and the larger were printed on pulp-magazine presses. One disadvantage to the two-up method is that it forced the council to yoke one book to another, requiring staff members to count pages, words, and characters in order to match similarly sized books. This was a chore that was both time-consuming and tedious. If different-sized books were coupled together, the shorter book would have blank pages — blasphemy in the age of paper rationing. Indeed, when the Army noticed blank pages in some early ASEs, it insisted that the council fill up these pages with biographies, puzzles, or the like. The council obliged by including an author's biography when space allowed. Over the course of pairing books, the council took great pains to ensure that they were not edited to achieve a desired word count or size. If a book was condensed, the front cover always included a disclaimer.

Knowing that battle conditions were stressful and lighting conditions were unlikely to be optimal for reading, the council aimed to create books that would be easy on readers' eyes. Traditional hardcovers had four to five inches of text per line, and were taller than they were wide. For its ASEs, the council bound the books on their short side, making them wider than they were tall, so that each page could accommodate two columns of two and a half to three inches of text. It was believed that battle-weary soldiers would find the shorter lines of text easier to read.

Another benefit of this double-column format was that 12 per-cent more words could be squeezed onto a page. The finished prototype was "small, light and attractive ... and completely readable even under trying conditions of light and motion," the council said in a memorandum on the project.

The council aimed to make the exterior of the ASEs as at-tractive and functional as possible. Rather than shrink the im-age of the hardcover edition's dust jacket to fit the smaller size, book covers were redesigned. A thumbnail image of the original dust jacket appeared on the front cover, and the book's title and author were prominently displayed. The covers were printed on sturdy, heavyweight paper in vibrant colors. To alert read-ers of the other titles that were available in that month's batch of books, the inside back cover listed the council's latest offerings. The back cover of each ASE provided a brief description of its contents.

Book covers were printed by one firm, the Commanday-Roth Company, and were distributed to the several printing houses that reproduced the interior pages. The ASEs were then assembled and bound, and the conjoined books sliced into two. Although hardcover books were typically glued and sewn to-gether, the early ASEs were bound by staples instead. (Accord-ing to one newspaper, staples were favored because many ser-vicemen were stationed in locales where insects would feast on glue, or the dampness of jungles and other wet climes would cause the glue to loosen or dissolve.) Once production was com-plete, the ASEs were shipped to distribution points selected by the Army and Navy.

In addition to being made a convenient size and weight, the books needed to be as affordable as possible, to meet the budget constraints of the Army and Navy. The council agreed to sell the ASEs to the government at cost, plus a one-cent royalty that was split between the author and the original publishing company. According to the council, "the prices at which [the ASEs] are being manufactured are probably the lowest at which comparable books have ever been produced in the United States." Initially, the average cost of each book was only slightly more than seven cents per copy. They were such a sensation that demand necessitated the production of additional millions per year, dropping the average cost of production to 5.9 cents per book.

At the project's inception, the Army and Navy requested that the council provide 50,000 copies of each of fifty titles—or 2.5 million books—per month. Eighty percent would be distributed to the Army, and the rest to the Navy (which was in rough proportion to the number of men in each service). By the time the council signed its contract with the armed forces in July 1943, its initial goal was reduced from fifty to thirty titles each month, since the manufacturing and editorial challenges were daunting.

A three-part process was used in selecting titles. First, the publishers gleaned from their stock lists books that would be appealing to servicemen. Next, the council's staff of readers, a group of people outside the publishing industry who provided their opinions about each book's merit, narrowed the selections. The third step was to seek government approval from Lieutenant Colonel Trautman on behalf of the Army, and Isabel DuBois, the head of the Library Section of the Navy. At any time, however, the Army and Navy could request that the council print certain titles, and feedback from the servicemen was always welcome. The main consideration in book selection was variety. The goal was for each series to consist of a range of titles so there would be a book to fit the tastes of every man. The most popular genre was contemporary fiction (almost 20 percent of the ASEs fell under this category), followed by historical novels, mysteries, books of humor, and westerns. Other categories included adventure stories, biographies, cartoons, classics, current events, fantasy, histories, music, nature, poetry, science, sea and naval stories, self-help and inspirational books, short story collections, and travel books.

One of the most remarkable aspects of the council's ASE endeavor was that it set broad benchmarks and worked to avoid censorship of the soldiers' reading. This is not to say that the council was permitted to print any book regardless of content. Once publishers and the council narrowed their list of potential ASEs, the council's readers flagged any passages that might be offensive to America's allies, give aid and comfort to the enemy, conflict with the spirit of American democracy, or be offensive to any religious or racial groups, trades, or professions. These guidelines were liberally interpreted, but they did prevent the issuance of certain books. For example, although it passed the Army and Navy's review, the council recommended dropping George Santayana's *Persons and Places* (an autobiography) because the book expressed a view deemed "dubious as to democracy." When Zane Grey's *Riders of the Purple Sage* (a western whose heroine befriends gunslinging cowboys who urge her to break away from the evils of the Mormon Church) was on the verge of being printed, a reader objected to it because of its "bitter attack on the Mormons."

Both books were rejected. The council generally believed it was better to not print a book than to perform surgery on it to eliminate offensive words or passages. The latter reeked too heavily of censorship, and the council did not want to skew an author's intent or story. As the government was funding the project in the name of boosting morale, it is understandable why the council avoided books that were objectionable to or discriminatory toward certain groups.

Still, all told, the titles produced as ASEs cut a very wide swath. John Jamieson, an expert on publishing during World War II, said that the ASEs consisted of "just about everything... except text and technical books and the juvenile and feminine fields." There were classics (*David Copperfield,* Shakespeare's poetry), modern classics (*A Tree Grows in Brooklyn, The Great Gatsby*), westerns (*Sunset Pass, Six Gun Showdown*), mysteries (*Harvard Has a Homicide, The Murder That Had Everything*), biographies (*The Story of George Gershwin, Benjamin Franklin*), comics and art (*Soldier Art, Cartoons for Fighters,* and *The Sad Sack*), and sports (*The Brooklyn Dodgers, The Best Sports Stories of 1944*). Plus, there were books about math (*Mathematics and the Imagination*), the sciences (*Your Servant, the Molecule*), history (*The Republic*), and current affairs (*U.S. Foreign Policy*). There were titles to cheer the men up (*Laugh It Off, Happy Stories Just to Laugh At*) and others whose titles, alone, provided comfort by posing questions that the men asked themselves (*Is Sex Necessary?, Where Do People Take Their Troubles?*). By the time its mission was complete, the council had printed approximately twelve hundred titles.

Authors whose books were selected as ASEs were rewarded with a loyal readership of millions of men. Word spread quickly about the titles that were perennial favorites, even reaching the home front. F. Scott Fitzgerald's *The Great Gatsby,* which was written in 1925, was considered a failure during Fitzgerald's lifetime. But when this book was printed as an ASE in October 1945, it won the hearts of an army of men. Their praise reverberated back home, and *The Great Gatsby* was rescued from obscurity and has since become an American literary classic.

For authors, learning that their book had made the cut for

ASE publication was a great honor. Emily Kimbrough, who cowrote *Our Hearts Were Young and Gay,* said that she and Cornelia Otis Skinner were "more proud of . . . that edition than of being selected Book of the Month." David Ewen, author of *The Story of George Gershwin* and *Men of Popular Music,* once explained that the publication of both of his books as ASEs had a "particularly significant meaning." At the time, he "was in the armed forces and knew only too well what a solace books could be to the tired, lonely men stationed in far-off places." When David Lavender learned his first adult novel, *One Man's West,* had been chosen as an ASE, he was incredibly grateful to receive such recognition. "Fifty-three thousand copies! I could scarcely believe such figures . . . And I am inclined to believe that having those fifty-three thousand copies spread far and wide gave the book a running start toward three hardcover editions, followed by its paperback reprint." To this day, the book remains in print.

The books chosen for publication each month were collectively dubbed a series. Each early series was assigned a letter, and each book was assigned a number. For example, the first month of titles consisted of the A-series, numbered one through thirty: A-1, A-2, and so on. Beginning with the J-series, thirty-two titles were printed each month. The Q-series marked the beginning of forty titles per series. The T-series was the last to designate a letter-number combination on the books themselves (although the council's records continued the letter-number assignment; the Z-series was followed by the AA-series, BB-series, and so on); thereafter, beginning with the number 665, each book was assigned a number only. Over time, the print run for each series steadily rose; 125,000 copies of each title were printed beginning with the Q-series, and a staggering 155,000 copies of each title were printed from the W-series to the Z-.

Managing the production of the ASEs was Philip Van Doren Stern. Formerly the executive editor of Pocket Books, Stern had a background in paperbacks and was familiar with both the editorial and production aspects of the paperback industry. The task before Stern was herculean. As manager of the Armed Services Editions branch of the council, Stern had to maintain constant relations with five different Army and Navy offices, a paper firm (Bulkley Dunton) and its mills, five printers, a dozen or more composition (typesetting) houses, the entire membership of the Council on Books in Wartime (both individually as publishers and collectively through the council's management committee), and an advisory committee on book selection. Even with the help of a paid staff of ten people, the magnitude of the project and the number of moving pieces that Stern supervised was mind-boggling. That it all came together, and month after month the books were chosen, printed, and distributed, is a testament to the dedication of all parties involved. The project certainly was not without its headaches.

For example, after meeting with a dozen leading commercial printers to price the cost of printing, the council decided to work with five firms that promised a deep discount: the Cuneo Press, Street & Smith, the W. S. Hall Company, the Rumford Press, and the Western Printing and Lithographing Company. However, by November 1943, Western Printing began grumbling about this deal and even threatened to quit. Representatives from the Army spoke directly with Western's representatives and tried to convince the company to continue printing the ASEs. One frustrated colonel advised the council that it avoid such episodes by having the ASEs declared essential by the government. In the end, Stern was forced to negotiate a 10 percent increase in the prices paid to Western Printing in order to secure this company's uninterrupted service. Throughout the project, Stern would face similar obstacles that threatened the timely production of the ASEs. He became quite adept at hurdling them.

By September 1943, the A-series was delivered to the Army and Navy, totaling 1.5 million of the smallest paperback books ever mass-produced in the United States. In just seven months, the idea was hatched, "planned, organized, and put into effective operation"; contracts were drafted, signed, and executed and the books were manufactured and delivered. It would go down in history as one of the best-coordinated production programs of the entire war.

As the American media closely followed the 1942 and 1943 VBCs, a curiosity surrounded the council's ASE plan. After all, millions of Americans had contributed to the VBC, and they wanted to know more about the organization that had replaced it. One of the first publications to reconcile the change of the guard was the *New Republic*. It began by explaining that the servicemen's appetite for reading proved to be greater than what the VBC could accommodate, thus the council was printing special paperbacks exclusively for men in uniform. The article reported that, each month, the council would publish fifty thousand miniature reprints of twenty-five or more titles. As many as thirty-five million ASEs would be printed in a single year. Despite this impressive feat, the *New Republic* was disparaging of the council's work. "The books themselves are designed for cheapness, convenience and wear-outability," the article said. By printing the books on "flimsy newsprint," the books would weigh less than hardcovers, but the author of the article, Malcolm Cowley, doubted they would hold up for long. "My impression from handling one of the advance copies, is that it would fall to pieces after two or three readings," Cowley wrote.

The council had hustled for months, created a book unlike any other, and pushed these literary novelties through production lines in record time. Understandably, it was disappointed by this uncomplimentary description. Archibald Ogden, the council's executive director, wrote a letter to the editor of the *New Republic* in defense of the ASEs. Describing the article as "a little unfair," Ogden went on to set the record straight. First of all, the ASEs were *not* printed on flimsy newsprint. "The paper selected for the Armed Services Editions is two grades higher than newsprint and more expensive; it is also more durable," Ogden countered. With respect to the article's statement about the books falling to pieces after a couple of readings, Ogden estimated that each book would survive six readings (and possibly more if it was not roughly handled). Ogden explained that these "editions are by all odds the strongest of any paper book in comparable size on the market." Finally, as to the "expendability" of the books, Ogden said that the ASEs were inexpensively produced so that millions of good books could be provided to men stationed around the world in a format that suited their circumstances. A serviceman would be able to choose whatever book interested him, take it wherever his missions sent him, and pass it along to someone else when finished. Reinforcements would arrive each month to supplement the books that remained in good condition and replace the ones that were not.

In the end, the *New Republic* was alone in expressing misgivings about the ASEs. By all other accounts, the project was a resounding success. Months after the Malcolm Cowley piece, the *New York Times Book Review* ran a story on the ASEs, reporting that "mountains of books — good books, including classics, current best sellers, history, biography, science and poetry — are being distributed among our fighting men overseas by a novel publishing arrangement between American book publishers and the Army and Navy ... Bundles of these books have been flown into the Anzio beachhead by plane. Others were passed out to the marines on Tarawa within a few days after the last remnant of Japanese opposition had been extinguished on that atoll. They have been dropped by parachute to outpost forces on lonely Pacific islands, issued in huge lots to the hospitals behind combat areas in all points of the world; [and] passed out to soldiers as they embarked on transports for overseas duty."

The account in the *New York Times* was confirmed by many letters, mailed from exotic locales, to ASE authors. For example, Leo Rosten, whose *The Education of H*Y*M*A*N K*A*P*L*A*N* (published under the pseudonym Leonard Q. Ross) was the first ASE to be printed (A-1), received countless "moving, even heart-breaking" letters from men in the armed forces. One that stood out in his mind, even forty years after his ASE was printed, said:

> I want to thank you profoundly, for myself, and more importantly, [for] the men here in this godforsaken part of the globe. We fry by day and freeze by night. What we are doing near the Persian Gulf ... no one knows. All we have ... for recreation is a ping-pong set — with one paddle only.
>
> Last week we received your book on Mr. K*A*P*L*A*N. I read it and simply roared with laughter. As an experiment I read it one night at campfire. The men *howled*. I have not heard such laughs in months. Now they demand I only read one K*A*P*L*A*N story a night: a ration on pleasure. I read the stories with an accent; I hope you would approve.

. . .

When the Army and Navy received their first shipment of ASEs in September 1943, the response from top brass was overwhelmingly enthusiastic. The Army immediately asked the council to increase the number of books published each month. As the project was in its infancy, and the production of thirty titles proved to be a significant undertaking, the council could not promise an instant reply. Yet when the B-series of thirty books was made ready for shipment in mid-October, Lieutenant Colonel Trautman requested that the council increase the print run for each title from fifty thousand to sixty thousand copies. Still no commitment was made by the council. In January 1944, Trautman attended a council meeting and reported that ASEs had made it even to the most remote locations: Guadalcanal, Bora Bora, and many other small islands in the South Pacific. Trautman trumpeted the success of the program and begged for more books. Or rather, commanded it. The council was ordered to increase the quantity of ASEs produced from fifty thousand copies of each title per month to seventy-seven thousand copies; each book run thereafter was to be increased by three thousand copies each month.

The council was eager to learn how the men in the armed forces felt about the new editions. Although ASE authors began to receive mail from servicemen, the council itself had received little feedback. Considering the enormity of the project, the amount of resources required to produce the books in such numbers, and the unprecedented cooperation among rival companies to bring about this common goal, many hoped that the council's work was not done in vain. Questions abounded. What if there were too many westerns? Were biographies and history books even wanted? Was there some genre of books that the council had overlooked? Were the ASEs standing up to the rigors of war and multiple readings? Council members could only hope that the gifts of literature, humor, biography, poems, nonfiction, and short stories were being received with the same enthusiasm with which they were manufactured.

Not all council members patiently waited for word from overseas. Stanley Rinehart, of Farrar & Rinehart, sent a note to his friend Charles Rawlings, a war correspondent for the *Saturday Evening Post,* asking if Rawlings could give him some idea of how the program was faring. Rawlings replied from an outpost in Australia in June 1944 — almost nine months after the ASEs were first sent to the Army and Navy — surprised that the council remained in the dark about its efforts. "What the hell, Stanley," Rawlings exclaimed in the opening of his letter. "Do you mean to say you publishers haven't been told what those limp, elongated, little reprints are doing? Told! You should be given DSM's [Distinguished Service Medals]."

> Dog-eared and moldy and limp from the humidity those books go up the line. Because they are what they are, because they can be packed in a hip pocket or snuck into a shoulder pack, men are reading where men have never read before — in this SWPAC [Southwest Pacific] theatre anyway. I've seen GI's with them ... three days after the beach head at Hollandia. The kids were hungry on ... iron rations and they were up to their buttocks in that terribly disappointing Hollandia marsh mud, but there they were, guarding a captured Jap plane against souvenir hunters or in their sack in the beach camp or mooning out after ... chow, reading a book.

Rawlings told a story of how, one day, as he was driving along in a jeep, he noticed a big crowd outside a PX (post exchange) and was curious to learn the source of this ruckus. "Even the ice cream hand-out counter was deserted," he said. As there had been a rumor that long-awaited cigarette lighters were due any day, Rawlings concluded that "nothing less could have caused the furor and I needed one of those things myself." So he stomped on the brakes and joined the melee. It wasn't lighters that were the main attraction—"it was your books." "They had come in ... those taut-corded brown paper bundles that seem to protect them very well and the PX help was cutting the bundles open and dumping the things into a big bin," Rawlings said. A line quickly formed, and the men urged one another along. "No time to shop and look for titles. Grab a book, Joe, and keep goin'. You can swap around afterwards," the men called out. As for the lucky soldier who grabbed *A Tree Grows in Brooklyn*—"the guy that got that one howled with joy," Rawlings said. With such a popular book came a great responsibility to read it quickly and pass it on to the next in line. "He'd have to sleep on it to ever get to finish it," Rawlings said. The books were not only enjoyed on land. The ship that carried him to Australia had two bundles of ASEs, Rawlings continued, and "we read out twenty-five blessed days on them." There was nothing else to do, and everyone was thankful to have them. With complete confidence, he assured the council that any worries or concerns about the books were unfounded. Rawlings concluded his letter by goading the publishers never to quit, since twenty million books were not nearly enough. He also asked that the publishers not "feel sore—as I do—that no one has ever mentioned the good job."

Other war correspondents penned unsolicited reports about the superb work of the council—noting the popularity of books in their published articles and also in letters written directly to council members. Lewis Gannett, whose column "Books and Things" was published in the *Herald Tribune* from 1930 through 1956, felt compelled to write the council once he saw the ASEs in action. A hardcore book lover and well-respected journalist, Gannett had critiqued some eight thousand books over the course of his career. His opinion of the council's book program carried weight.

The council was gratified to learn that it had earned Gannett's compliments and respect. "From hospitals in England, from Negro service units in Normandy, and ... the Army besieging Brest"—"your books [are] everywhere—in the front lines and at the rear, in jeeps, in pillboxes, in planes, [and] at bases," Gannett said. They were exceedingly popular with the troops. Men were reading wherever and whenever they had spare time. Gannett reported that he had "even seen a Piper Cub pilot, bored with a milk run from Rennes to Charbourg, pull one out from beside him while letting his plane do a bit of piloting on its own." He also recalled "a division where the noncoms and privates at the back of the general's war tent were all reading and discussing constantly—they had a lot of time when they were just on duty, with nothing to do except be on duty, and they wanted good books." Gannett said that there were "lots of boys in the army with a hunger for good reading" and many "lonely boys over here with a lot of time on their hands." In expressing his general impression on how the ASEs were received, Gannett said: "it would do all your hearts good to see how the boys gobble your books. It's a grand job."

Another journalist who gave an early appraisal of the council was Gretta Palmer. Palmer began her journalistic career with the *New Yorker,* and also wrote for the *Sunday World* and the *World-Telegram.* Known for expressing her thoughts on controversial topics, Palmer was not one to temper her strong opinions no matter how contentious or unpopular. As a war correspondent, she spent several months in the Mediterranean theater writing handfuls of disparaging reports criticizing what she had observed. In her own words, she had published "bad-tempered articles, telling various military and civilian organizations what I thought was wrong." When the council received a letter from Palmer, publishers likely assumed they were in for a blistering evaluation.

They found the opposite. In light of her critical essays about other war organizations, she wrote that it was "only fair that I should lay a wreath of orchids on your council which is, I truly believe, doing the best job of any group which has made an effort to make the soldiers' lives bearable," she said. Palmer marveled that a soldier was "allowed to pick [an ASE] up in a hotel in Casablanca and take it off with [him] on [a] plane, leaving it for someone else to read in a hospital in Marseilles." She observed that the format of the books was "superb for hospital patients: they are the only books I've seen that a patient can read with comfort, while he's flat on his back." Having been hospitalized twice while on assignment, she personally appreciated the distraction the ASEs provided as she convalesced. Palmer said that the titles could not be bettered. "If it weren't so ridiculously impertinent of me, I'd thank you on behalf of the soldiers, but I can at least thank you for the hours of pleasure you gave me," she wrote.

Over the course of the war, the ASEs' ability to shore up exhausted, disgusted, weary soldiers would be tested time and again — and the men who were counting on them were rarely disappointed. As the summer of 1944 approached, the council's mission to provide morale-boosting books would be tried like never before. The Allies were poised to wage one of the most elaborate and long-awaited offensive attacks of the war.

Guts, Valor, and Extreme Bravery

I've just been told that over 3,000 of our American boys died in the first eleven days of the invasion of France.

Who died? I'll tell you who died.

Not so many years ago, there was a little boy sleeping in his crib. In the night, it thundered and lightninged. He woke and cried out in fear. His mother came and fixed his blankets better and said, "Don't cry. Nothing will ever hurt you."

He died...

There was another kid with a new bicycle. When he came past your house he rode no-hands while he folded the evening paper in a block and threw it against your door. You used to jump when you heard the bang. You said, "Some day, I'm going to give that kid a good talking-to." He died.

Then there were two kids. One said to the other, "I'll do all the talking. I just want you to come along to give me nerve." They came to your door. The one who had promised to do all the talking said, "Would you like your lawn mowed, Mister?"

They died together. They gave each other nerve...

They all died.

> And I don't know how any one of us here at home
> can sleep peacefully tonight unless we are sure in
> our hearts that we have done our part all the way
> along the line.
>
> — BETTY SMITH, "WHO DIED?" JULY 9, 1944

B Y THE END of 1943, the question was not if, but where
and when, the Allies would launch an attack on Western Europe. Germany faced a three-front war and a
huge territory to defend. The Eastern Front, which ran through
Russia, spanned two thousand kilometers. The Mediterranean Front, which spread across Africa and Europe, was nearly
three thousand kilometers long. And in Western Europe, German troops faced a six-thousand-kilometer front to protect. As
thousands of Americans prepared for this deadly venture, they
tucked ASEs into breast and hip pockets.

In the meantime, Hitler prepared for the invasion by directing his propaganda machine at the American servicemen. One
of Germany's greatest weapons came in the form of an American voice. Mildred Gillars, whom servicemen affectionately referred to as Axis Sally or the Berlin Bitch, was a Maine-born ex-
pat living in Berlin. When the war broke out, she became an
on-air host for Reichsradio and immediately gained popularity
among the men; they liked her American accent, her seductive
tone, and the popular music she played. But behind her voice
and music was a program designed to discourage those who listened. "Hello, Gang. This is Midge, calling the American Ex-
peditionary Forces in the four corners of the world tonight,"
one program began. Playing off the name of a popular song, she
said: "Well, kids, you know I'd like to say to you 'Pack Up Your

Troubles In Your Old Kit Bag,' but I know that that little old
kit bag is much too small to hold all the trouble you kids have
got ... There's no getting the Germans down." Although the
program was laced with propaganda, it was usually transparent
enough for the men to laugh it off. Yet Axis Sally, from time to
time, disclosed uncanny intelligence information that disturbed
even the most steadfast listeners. One night she said, "Hello to
the men of Company E, 506th PIR, 101st A/B in Aldbourne.
Hope you boys enjoyed your passes to London last weekend.
Oh, by the way, please tell the town officials that the clock on
the church is three minutes slow." Her information was spot-on.
As much as Americans enjoyed Sally's music, they were eager to
put an end to her gibes.

The details for the invasion of France were settled by the
spring of 1944. The battle would begin at night with an Allied all-out aerial and naval assault to batter the German em-
placements along the French coast while creating craters in the
beaches that the infantry would later use for protection. American and British paratroopers would land behind the zone of
bombardment, and would secure various bridges and land-
marks to facilitate the massive land invasion that would occur
later that morning. Naval gunfire aimed at the beaches and fortifications would stop five minutes before an armada of LCTs
(Landing Craft Tanks) made their way ashore, carrying tanks,
all manner of weapons, and infantrymen. Army engineers and
light artillery would accompany the first wave of infantry, and
would be followed by additional waves of men and supplies.
Each segment of the attack was choreographed and timed down
to the minute. The elaborate plan required complete cooperation among the Allied nations participating, as well as between
the naval, air, and ground forces so that each element was executed in time for the next component to commence.

The likelihood of survival seemed to lessen as the men learned more information about the dangers they would face. One private recalled that when his company was briefed on the invasion, they were told the first wave could expect 30 percent casualties and "we were them!" Considering the dangers that awaited, many believed casualties would run even higher. As one historian explained: "The GI hitting the beach in the first wave at Omaha Beach would have to get through the minefields in the Channel without his LST [Landing Ship Tank] blowing up, then get from ship to shore ... [while] taking fire from inland batteries, then work his way through an obstacle-studded tidal flat of some 150 meters crisscrossed by machine-gun and rifle fire, with big shells whistling by and mortars all around." Next, the GI would be "caught in a triple crossfire — machine guns and heavy artillery from the sides, small arms from the front, mortars coming down from above." Barbed wire and mines (the Germans laid 6.5 million mines in the beaches and bluffs) awaited the GIs who survived the landing and headed across the beach. The men would need nerves of steel and unfathomable courage.

Under the leadership of General Dwight D. Eisenhower, the plans for D-day were formally set into motion beginning on May 31, 1944, with the expectation that the invasion would occur on June 5. In the final days leading to the boarding of the landing craft, the men readied themselves. They crammed into their packs dozens of pounds of ammunition, provisions, extra weapons, and other necessities. Although the recommendation was that the men not bring more than forty-four pounds of equipment, it was estimated that some men weighed at least three hundred pounds as they waddled under the weight of their packs.

Because the invasion could only occur in clear weather, an exact date was not set until the eve of battle. Knowing some men would have a long wait between arriving in England and the start of the invasion, the Army Special Services Division grew concerned about keeping morale elevated as servicemen bided their time. At least initially, many men remained in good spirits as they waited for action. Even when they learned they would have to rub foul-smelling impregnating grease on their uniforms to be impervious to a possible mustard gas attack, the men took it in stride. A war correspondent for the *New Yorker* reported that when one sailor noticed he was being watched as he greased his shoes, he jokingly called out, "This is the first time I ever tried to get a pair of shoes pregnant, sir."

"No doubt you tried it on about everything else," another sailor retorted as he, too, worked on his shoes. As the invasion neared, moments of levity were fleeting.

General Eisenhower took an especial interest in the morale of his troops. As he noted in his own memoirs, "morale, given rough equality to other things, is supreme on the battlefield." Eisenhower was known to read western novels to relax and relieve stress, and the men who would be doing the fighting deserved no less. Anticipating the time it would take to assemble all of the men needed for the mission, and the boredom and anxiety associated with the chore of waiting, General Eisenhower's staff had approved a recommendation from the Special Services Division to distribute ASEs in the marshaling areas — one book per person. When the C- and D-series were shipped to the Army and Navy, approximately eight thousand sets of each were reserved specifically for those who would participate in the D-day invasion. Among the books included in these series were: *The Selected Short Stories of Stephen Vincent Benét,* Charles Courtney's *Unlocking Adventure,* Lloyd C. Douglas's bestseller

The Robe, Esther Forbes's *Paul Revere and the World He Lived In,* John P. Marquand's *So Little Time,* Joseph Mitchell's *McSorley's Wonderful Saloon,* Marjorie Kinnan Rawlings's *Cross Creek,* Betty Smith's *A Tree Grows in Brooklyn,* Charles Spalding and Otis Carney's *Love at First Flight,* Booth Tarkington's *Penrod,* and Mark Twain's *The Adventures of Tom Sawyer* and *The Adventures of Huckleberry Finn.* Dozens of other titles joined the men on the shore of the English Channel.

Since all details of the D-day assault phase were kept secret, the council had no knowledge of the Special Services' plan to saturate the marshaling areas with ASEs. In fact, in late May 1944, the council was concerned that ASEs were "pil[ing] up in the warehouses and shipment to the Army and Navy was delayed." Some council members worried that this buildup of books indicated a lack of interest in the ASEs. It was a great relief when the council later learned that the imminent invasion of Normandy was the explanation, and that the Army had actually considered books so important to morale that they had earmarked almost a million for the men boarding transports.

Prior to the invasion, the Special Services blanketed the shores of Great Britain with some of the soldiers' favorite items. Packs of cigarettes were shoved into pockets, candy bars were grabbed by the handful, but of all things, the most sought-after item was the ASEs. As one Special Services officer recalled, palpable tension mounted in the staging areas, and books were the only thing available that "provided sorely needed distraction to a great many men." When the loading process finally began, many men, realizing how much weight they were carrying, stopped to unburden themselves of unnecessary items near the docking area. The ground was littered with a variety of objects, but among the heaps of discarded inessentials, "very few Armed Services Editions were found by the clean-up squads that later went through the areas." Weighing as little as a couple of ounces each, ASEs were the lightest weapon that the men could bring along.

After all were aboard, the ships had nowhere to go — the troops would await orders from General Eisenhower, who wanted to be certain that the weather, moon, tide, and time of sunrise were aligned in the Allies' favor before announcing the attack. In the meantime, there was little for the men to do but worry, pray, or read. Silence pervaded. A rosary could be seen in many a hand. According to one man, "Priests were in their heyday. I even saw Jews go and take communion. Everybody [was] scared to death." It did not help matters when the men caught another Axis Sally broadcast and she assured them, "We are waiting for you." Almost everyone was anxious to get going.

On the morning of June 4, the first vessels began to move out into the English Channel. Yet the weather soon deteriorated, with drizzle turning into a cold, hard rain. The LCIs (Landing Craft Infantry) and LCTs offered no shelter; the men aboard were thrown this way and that as their uniforms became soaked, and the waters more turbulent. The conditions were perfectly miserable. Things only grew worse for the troops when General Eisenhower was forced to postpone the invasion for a day because of the poor weather. An impenetrable cloud cover made a bombing campaign impossible for the air forces. Holding their positions, the flat-bottomed transports quaked in the churning waters; many men turned greener with seasickness by the minute as they waited. (When they finally made it to France and beheld the dead bodies of those who arrived before them, one man could not help but remark, "Them lucky bastards — they ain't seasick no more.") Others were anchored in harbors or up rivers; no one was allowed to leave their crowded transport. They just cursed, vomited, and waited.

Conditions grew grim aboard the landing craft. Even years later, many men would recall the nauseating combination of the smell of diesel oil, backed-up toilets, and vomit that wafted across the decks. Some men listened to the radio to try to pass the time, but when they caught another Axis Sally broadcast, they soon preferred silence. She had taken the liberty of refashioning the lyrics to the popular song "I Double Dare You" into a chilling threat about the invasion: "I double dare you to come over here. I double dare you to venture too near. Take off your high hat and quit that bragging. Cut out that claptrap and keep your hair on. Can't you take a dare on?"

Thank God for the ASEs. According to one second lieutenant, "so many [were] insensible to discomfort because of their interest" in what they were reading. A. J. Liebling, a war correspondent for the *New Yorker,* observed how the ASEs eased boredom and anxiety as the men waited for action. He saw members of the First Division "spread all over the LCIL ... most of them reading paper-cover, armed-services editions of books." So calm were the men of the First Division that Liebling commented that they appeared to be going on just another practice run, and not a deadly invasion. As one infantryman told Liebling: "These little books are a great thing. They take you away."

When word finally came that the invasion would begin during the early-morning hours of June 6, the news was a great relief. As members of the airborne forces suited up for their night mission, Axis Sally issued a final blow before they paid the German army a visit. "Good evening, Eighty-Second Airborne Division," she personally greeted them. "Tomorrow morning the blood from your guts will grease the bogey wheels of our tanks." Although some were bothered by Sally's comments, others just shrugged them off. After all, she had made similar taunts for days. As the Navy and Army Air Forces prepared to bomb to smithereens Germany's pillboxes and coastal fortifications, they took comfort in knowing they were taking a momentous step toward ending Axis Sally's threats.

Meanwhile, back at home, President Roosevelt spent the evening of June 5 delivering an important radio broadcast. He announced that Rome was the first major Axis capital to fall, and branded the event a great achievement toward total conquest of the enemy. Roosevelt was quick to acknowledge that there was "much greater fighting [that] lies ahead before the Axis is defeated." "We shall have to push through a long period of greater effort and fiercer fighting before we get into Germany itself," he said. "The victory still lies some distance ahead," but the president assured Americans that the "distance will be covered in due time — have no fear of that." After congratulating and thanking all those involved in the Italian operation, President Roosevelt concluded his address, "May God bless them and watch over them and over all of our gallant fighting men." Although his listeners had no inkling of it, the president knew that as he uttered these words the invasion of France had already begun.

Roosevelt spent the early-morning hours of June 6 drafting and reciting a prayer for an Allied victory in France. With his blackout curtains drawn, the president kept vigil. Detailed invasion reports trickled in to the White House, informing the president of when the first vessels began their trips and, later, when the Allied forces first landed. The next morning, President Roosevelt dispatched a copy of his prayer to Congress, where it was read on the House floor and in the Senate; the prayer was also printed in newspapers across the country so the entire nation could recite the words along with the president during his radio address that night:

Almighty God: Our sons, pride of our nation, this day have set upon a mighty endeavor, a struggle to preserve our Republic, our religion and our civilization, and to set free a suffering humanity.

Lead them straight and true; give strength to their arms, stoutness to their hearts, and steadfastness in their faith.

They will need Thy blessing. Their road will be long and hard. For the enemy is strong. He may hurl back our forces. Success may not come with rushing speed, but we shall return again and again; and we know that by Thy grace, and by the righteousness of our cause, our sons will triumph . . .

Some will never return. Embrace these, Father, and receive them, Thy heroic servants, into Thy kingdom.

And for us at home — fathers, mothers, children, wives, sisters, and brothers of brave men overseas, whose thoughts and prayers are ever with them — help us, Almighty God, to rededicate in renewed faith in Thee in this hour of great sacrifice . . .

Give us strength, too — strength in our daily tasks, to redouble the contributions we make in the physical and the material support of our armed forces.

And let our hearts be stout, to wait out the long travail, to bear sorrows that may come, to impart our courage unto our sons wheresoever they may be . . .

. . . Lead us to the saving of our country, and with our sister nations into a world unity that will spell a sure peace . . . a peace that will let all men live in freedom, reaping the just rewards of their honest toil.

Thy will be done, Almighty God.

Amen.

The Americans who landed at Utah and Omaha Beaches had vastly different experiences. The American Fourth Division poured ashore at Utah Beach, meeting very little opposition. In fact, some men were a little let down at how anticlimactic the landing was; they described it as seeming like just another practice invasion. The early waves of troops landing at Omaha Beach, by contrast, faced near-certain death. As soon as the transports lowered their ramps, the exiting men were thrust into the line of fire. German machine-gun spray ripped across the boats, instantly killing the hapless Americans on them. For the first wave of LCIs that reached Omaha Beach, the death rate was nearly 100 percent; no one got off the beach. Later waves of troops faced grievous losses on the shore. Shell-shocked, many men simply froze, unable to move toward safety. Others who forded through the barrage of gunfire and mortar blasts and moved to the shelter of the cliffs at the top of the beach suffered injuries along the way. Unable to go farther, their shattered bodies dropped to the sand and stayed there until medics arrived. Many men who climbed the beach later that day would never forget the sight of gravely wounded soldiers propped up against the base of the cliffs, reading.

In the first twenty-four hours of the invasion, 1,465 Americans were killed, 3,184 wounded, 1,928 were missing, and 26 captured. These numbers billowed as the battle moved inland. Eleven days into the invasion, 3,283 Americans had died, and 12,600 were wounded.

Throughout the war, media reports of the growing number of GI casualties troubled those who were still fighting to no end. Many men objected to the anonymity the term "GI" conveyed. "When we think of GI we think of items of issue, but we are not issued," Sergeant Frank Turman explained. "When we walk over our dead buddies we wouldn't refer to them as dead GIs. And when we get home again, and see our buddies' loved ones, we just couldn't say: 'Your son died a GI's death.'" "Anybody can be a GI," Sergeant Turman said, "but it takes a man to be a soldier, sailor or marine." For those who were fighting on the frontlines, the dead were not nameless or faceless. The war claimed men they knew and loved, and it was torture. The pilot who negotiated his plane through storms of flak knew the crew member who was fatally struck; when the Marines charged a beach in an amphibious landing and enemy snipers opened up on them, they knew which of their friends had fallen; and when Japanese pilots swung their planes into Allied ships, damaging and destroying them, the sailors who survived knew who had perished. For the men at war, death was agonizingly personal. Yet they rarely talked about it.

Over the course of fighting, many things went unspoken. Soldiers knew the savagery of their war experience — it did not need to be discussed. Every man who went through battle felt the terror of it. Mental and emotional baggage accumulated over time, but there were few outlets that enabled the men to deal with the burdens they carried. Men rarely bared their hearts to family. Every letter mailed home was read by a censor to ensure that no sensitive information was divulged, in case the letter fell into enemy hands. Because each letter was read by another soldier, many men resisted the opportunity to tell loved ones how miserable they were; besides, servicemen did not want to concern family members with the truth of their unhappiness and stress. Unable to describe the battles they fought, or share the feelings they felt, most letters were reduced to weather reports and vague pleasantries.

Books, however, did provide a catharsis for many men. This intangible response becomes evident by the reactions of servicemen to certain books. One unlikely author to earn wide appeal was Katherine Anne Porter. Her short stories delicately exposed private, deeply personal experiences and emotions that tended to give readers the impression that she understood their innermost thoughts and feelings. Hundreds of men wrote to her after reading her ASE: some described how they had connected to a certain character; others felt as though a layer of loneliness and isolation had been stripped away as her prose washed over them. By writing to the person who had touched their hearts, servicemen brought to life the relationship they felt through the pages they read. These letters frequently delved into incredibly personal experiences and feelings; in fact, details that often went unexpressed to loved ones were divulged to authors.

One man had treasured Porter's *Selected Short Stories* to such a degree that he carried his copy with him throughout the war and kept it for his trip home. "Inching back eastward across the long wastes of the Pacific toward discharge and home, I've had an opportunity once more to read some of your stories — in the paperbound Armed Services Edition. We can read better, with leisure and the perspective of long absence, under the conditions; thus I've appreciated your writing more than ever before," he said. What attracted him to Porter's stories all along was her ability to "put bewildered little things who were you and I back in the world," and capture "frightening emotions where we all ... once lived — lost when rejected, content when loved, made into small witch-ridden animals when abused."

Another man had also found great comfort in Porter's words and wrote to tell her so. He was delighted to receive a letter back from Porter, who asked if he was hospitalized and disclosed concern for her nephew in the Ninth Field Artillery Regiment. This man immediately wrote back, admitting he was "almost glad that I can say I am a patient" if it might induce Porter to keep a correspondence with him. He had spent the last four months hospitalized with jaundice, and was thankful to have books, such as Porter's, to read. Porter's reference to her nephew opened a wellspring of pent-up anxiety this man felt for a friend, who also belonged to the Ninth Field Artillery. "I worry about him more than I do myself; he is a good man, and since the landings in Africa so long ago he has been going through all hell. His buddies have been killed before his eyes again and again; in January the five men of his group — his best friends — were killed and he himself was hit. I think to myself: 'Dear God! A man can only take so much! And yet he goes on and on.'" This man admitted that he had felt "ashamed to write to [his friend] before I came to the hospital" because as his friend faced death, he himself had toured Italy, taking in concerts, operas, and palaces, and then was stationed thirty miles behind the frontlines — always outside the zone of danger. Compared to his friend, he did not feel like a real soldier. Having cleared his conscience to Porter, he felt much better.

After the war ended, Porter reflected on the role she played in helping some men get through the war. "I had three [servicemen] in my own family, and more than six hundred letters from [soldiers]," she said, "and I hope I may be forgiven if I rather feel, on the evidence of these letters, that that was a very superior army indeed. Not all of them wrote to praise, either. I mention this out of pride and pleasure that at least a few GI's felt that I understood them very well."

Betty Smith's *A Tree Grows in Brooklyn* was perhaps the most popular ASE of them all. It provided such a vivid account of childhood that many men felt as though Smith were writing about theirs. When word spread that Smith had published an essay, "Who Died?," that personalized the thousands of Normandy casualties, servicemen wrote to her begging for a copy. Smith received a steady stream of letters from men around the world, thanking her for the effect her writing had on them.

"When I first picked up your book, I was down in the dumps, a sad sack, as the boys say," a sergeant said to Smith. But as he read, "my spirits rose until at the end I found myself chuckling over many of the amusing characters." He needed the lift that *A Tree Grows in Brooklyn* had given him. He had felt depressed and lonely for months, and nothing had given him any relief from these feelings, until Smith's book. "I haven't laughed so heartily since my arrival over here eight months ago," he said. A man in the Army Air Forces said that Smith's book "made [him] feel homesick," and that it was "the first time I've ever been homesick in my life." He was amazed at how capably her words transported him to what life was like back home — a life that he sorely missed and hoped to return to. Yet he did not write to complain. "After being in the Army only a short time and reading all types of novels and classics, I can sincerely say after reading *A Tree Grows in Brooklyn,* my cup runneth over." Many of the letters written to Smith echoed these sentiments. One man in the 716th Bombardment Squadron felt such a strong connection to Smith's characters that he compared *A Tree Grows in Brooklyn* to "a *good* letter from home."

From a hospital, one man wrote that *A Tree Grows in Brooklyn* was a "source of never-ending enjoyment" to him, as it reminded him of his own childhood in Brooklyn. "To me," he said, the book was like "living my life over again." Another man wrote in the hopes that Smith might be "nursing another literary seedling into full treehood." Smith's publisher received a note from a serviceman who previously did not care for books: "but for the first time, I found a book I really enjoyed reading, and that's Betty Smith's novel named *A Tree Grows in Brooklyn.*" He wanted to know what other titles she had written. Thanks to Smith, "books are one of our rare pleasures," he said.

As with other books, *A Tree Grows in Brooklyn* also helped

eclipse some of the everyday irritations that could get on a soldier's nerves. In one spirited letter from R.H., Betty Smith got an earful about an annoying bunkmate. R.H. lived with happy-go-lucky Gus, who one day waved a copy of *A Tree Grows in Brooklyn* before him and declared: "'*This* is a *fine* book.'" "Gus calls everything fine," complained R.H. "He doesn't seem to know any other adjective, and he uses the word indiscriminately. His girl is a fine girl. 'Dragon Seed' is a fine movie, his buddy is a fine boy, a B-29 is a fine plane, it's a fine day — almost every time he opens his damned mouth fine pops out," R.H. said. "And I grit my teeth and pray." R.H. joked that one day he might be driven to the point of punching poor Gus, but it would not do any good. "I can see him now, picking himself up from the floor and laughing (not able to believe I'm really angry) and saying, 'Gee, that was a fine blow you floored me with, friend.'" Getting to the point, R.H. said that he began reading *A Tree Grows in Brooklyn,* and it made his exasperation with Gus melt away. "I haven't the power to tell you, as I'd like, how it has affected me," R.H. disclosed. "But I know this: from now on I won't be annoyed the least bit when Gus speaks of it and calls it fine."

Smith once estimated that she received approximately four letters a day from servicemen, or about fifteen hundred a year. She responded to almost all of them. Servicemen were shocked when they received a note from her, sometimes accompanied by an autographed photograph (a common request). Without fail, these mementos became treasured possessions. From a hospital, one man wrote to Smith: "Thanks — *thanks* — [for] your letter." It had come at the perfect time, for he had "a tough week coming up. Every doctor in the place wants his cut. I don't know what they'll do with what remains of me after the carvings done. Pour gravy on me and put an ap-

ple in my mouth, I guess." Smith's letter would give him courage
through the surgeries he faced.

"When I received [your] letter," one man wrote to Smith,
"I thought, well, Betty has sent a Christmas card like the usual
celebrities thinking they were doing something for the boys,
but lo and behold, there is Betty Smith herself! I'm still bragging about it. I told the fellows it was my first wife, because
they are not as familiar with your picture as I." After carrying
Smith's photograph with him from Germany to Belgium, the
same man, who kept a regular correspondence with Smith, was
forced to ask for a new one. "I am going to need another because
I've carried this one around in snow, rain, mud, and combat, until it looks like it's been through a war," he said. Another regular writer to Smith also found great comfort in her photograph.
"You helped inspire me during some of my most trying days of
battle, and battle fatigue [and] depression. The picture I carried
of you — that helped me remember the one I love [referring to
his wife] and inspired me to carry on for the better things in
life that I was fighting for." He added: "Your tiny picture helped
give me the sincere happiness and joy I needed while I was on
what might have been the last limb of life." Months later, after
this man was wounded in battle, he wrote to Smith as he convalesced in a medical unit, again insisting what a difference she
had made in his life. He and his wife planned to have a child
when he returned home, and if it was a girl, they would name
her Betty Smith.

Smith and the council were so inundated with letters about
A Tree Grows in Brooklyn that the council decided to reprint the
book. "I think it's wonderful that the armed services edition is
going into a second edition," Smith told a friend. "Most of my
mail is from servicemen overseas and without exception, they
say that everything in [*A Tree Grows in Brooklyn*] seems so true

that it's not like reading a book — it's like being home in Brooklyn again." "Some letters bring tears to one's eyes," she admitted. "I am very much touched by the service men away from home thinking so much of the book. I feel that I have done some good in this world."

Rosemary Taylor's *Chicken Every Sunday* was another surprise favorite among the men. The narrator of *Chicken Every Sunday* is an adolescent girl who gives an amusing account of her mother's experience running a busy boarding house, appeasing a long list of zany characters and serving mouthwatering dinners each night. Its wholesomeness and wit captured everyday happenings with such feeling that many servicemen could not help but grow sentimental.

A first lieutenant wrote to Taylor to express his "thanks for the joy you have given me and to many other officers and enlisted men out here in New Guinea." He said that *Chicken Every Sunday* gave them "the refreshing sense that the way of life which we have temporarily left behind is a rich and delightful heritage that awaits our return." Another man wrote to Taylor from China, as *Chicken Every Sunday* was his favorite book and Taylor's description of her mother's cooking reminded him of his own mother, "cooking without measuring, the seasoning, the timing." It brought back such rich memories of his own home that he compared reading the book to taking a leave. "It took me home for a couple of hours. It alleviated my homesickness. I really forgot about the war, and laughed and lived for a little while back in that marvelous house with all those wonderful people." His only complaint was that Taylor's "graphic, tantalizing descriptions of [her] mother's baked potatoes, the slivered green beans, salads, desserts — were almost more than this human flesh can bear. Even the mention of ice water is enough to set us all aquiver over here," he quipped. He closed by asking

Taylor to write more books like *Chicken Every Sunday* because "we need 'em."

From the Aleutian Islands, a soldier wrote Taylor that he could not "resist the temptation to write you how thoroughly your book 'Chicken Every Sunday' is being read and enjoyed by an audience for whom in all probability it was not intended." In fact, he said, he was "not speaking for *one* or *two* when I said it is a book for soldiers, for I have watched it travel from bunk to bunk in my own particular hut and have listened to bursts of abdominal laughter from the owners of the abdomens, followed by quote-unquote passages for the whole crowd to share." And there were "reverberations from neighboring huts on at least two sides." This soldier recalled that, when one man "took 'Chicken' to work with him," he "could barely contain his enthusiasm when he returned that night." The book was the hottest commodity on the post. Because reading was one of the only forms of recreation available to those stationed in the Aleutians, this soldier said that he and his friends had become pretty discriminating in their reading tastes. He explained that the reason *Chicken Every Sunday* resonated with him and the men around him was because the characters in that book were "home folks and every GI Joe who reads about them ... nostalgically recalls their counterparts back home." "On behalf of the lot of us," he said, "let me thank you for many hours of swell fun." "We all hope there'll be more books by Rosemary Taylor." And there were. The council printed Taylor's *Ridin' the Rainbow*.

As these early testaments demonstrate, books played a special role at war. They soothed troubled minds and hearts, and they achieved these feats where other pastimes failed. Books were the saving grace for many men facing combat, as accounts from all fronts confirm. As one scholar on the role of books in war-time observed, men gratefully turned to books because they "remind[ed] them of home or express[ed] their own moods and thoughts, which had to stay dammed up, for the most part, in the noisy commonplaces and promiscuity of barracks life." The therapeutic role that books played in allowing men to process their own circumstances by reading stories about others kept them wanting to read more and more. Books of humor made them laugh when there was nothing funny about their circumstances. Tales of life back home transported them to the places they missed and hoped to see again. By reading, the men received the closest thing to a respite from war. As one private wrote from France, "Books are often the sole means of escape for GI's" and "I have seen many a man who never before had the patience or inclination to read a book, pick up one of the Council's and become absorbed and ask for more."

Lieutenant Colonel Trautman tried to explain why books were so popular among servicemen. He observed that the average soldier in World War II was a civilian who had an eleventh-grade education, and whose previous use of books was largely confined to required schoolwork. Most of the soldiers did not go to the library in their home communities, and their reading habits focused on "printed matter equivalent to a three-hundred-page book each week"—ranging anywhere from comics to newspaper and magazine articles. With the war underway, these men were sent to all parts of the world, including many places where there was nothing to read in English; where there were no newspapers, and every magazine and book had to be transported thousands of miles. Next to letters from home, these books and magazines were treasured because they allowed the men to tap into the life they had left behind in America.

Some men received such comfort from seeing a book in English or a familiar magazine that they were transformed into readers for life.

If there was any doubt about the value of the ASEs, the summer of 1944 would put them to rest. As Americans trekked across France to Paris and leapfrogged from one Pacific island to the next, they would be surrounded by nothing but the war, and comforted by little apart from their books.

SEVEN

Like Rain in the Desert

For days I've been hunting through our service club, bothering the Red Cross, scanning our library shelves and hunting unrelentlessly through the barracks — for what???? G-183! G-183! G-183!

— SERGEANT B. S.

A S THE ALLIES marched toward Paris, a very different war was being fought in the Pacific. Beginning just north of Australia and moving toward the shores of Japan, the Allies slowly made progress capturing one island after another from the Japanese. Assigned to perhaps the deadliest theater in the war, the Americans stationed in the Pacific faced a succession of suicidal assaults. Morale continually dipped as these men, lucky to have survived one amphibious invasion, were shipped out to another island to do it again, knowing full well what was in store. Over time, the Pacific developed notoriety for the savagery of the fighting and the horrendous conditions of island life. Men admitted feeling an incredible sense of loneliness and isolation as they fought for islands that seemed insignificant and uninhabitable. It was difficult for them to fathom why any country had an interest in territory as undesirable as some of the islands they invaded.

If ever there was a place where the troops needed an emotional lift, it was on the islands they compared to hell. To offset the barbarity of the conditions and warfare, recreational items and amusements were essential. In the early days of an invasion, books were one of the few diversions that were small enough to be carried by the men without being a burden. And escaping into a book, even for only a few minutes, could do wonders for their well-being. Come hell or high water (and there were both), Special Services officers did their damnedest to get books onto these islands as quickly as possible.

One of the early battles that initiated Americans to island warfare was for Guadalcanal, which came on the heels of the Allied victory at Midway. Guadalcanal — described by a war correspondent as "a steaming, malarial 'green hell'" with "no value in itself" apart from a strategically important airstrip — was fiercely defended by the Japanese. Conditions on the island were extreme. After a long day of rigorous fighting, sleep was nearly impossible. Incessant bombings and night raids kept Marines tumbling from their bedrolls to foxholes and back again, as if they were subject to the ebb and flow of a warped tide. A weepy tropical rain ensured their bedding was soggy, and mosquitos pursued the Americans with almost as much vigor as the Japanese. Snipers swarmed after sundown, keeping the Marines on alert at all hours. When a man tried to catch a few winks while a friend kept watch, he was lulled to sleep by the incessant buzzing of pestilential insects, punctuated by shooting and shrieking mortars. "The nights are passed in wet chill and discomfort and the days in mud and filth," one man said. In the words of a war correspondent: "Guadalcanal's greatest pleasure is . . . still being alive."

As the Marines suffered on the island, sailors in the United

States Navy fared no better offshore. In what has been described as the "worst defeat in a fair fight ever inflicted," the Imperial Japanese Navy sank four cruisers and chased a fifth away in a mere thirty-two minutes on August 9, 1942, in the Battle of Savo Island, sustaining only minor damage in return. Over the next several months, the Navy would continue to endure grievous losses. By the time the battle for Guadalcanal ended in February 1943, so many ships had been torpedoed, damaged, and sunk that the body of water between Guadalcanal, Savo, and the Florida Islands earned the nickname Ironbottom Sound.

Each battle that followed Guadalcanal proved more deadly than the last. Those who survived some of the Pacific's most extreme fighting found themselves poised to invade Saipan in June 1944. The first waves of troops to arrive faced a stream of death. The Japanese created a false sense that the invasion would be easy, patiently holding their fire until Marine amphibious tractors were within a thousand yards and then unleashing an avalanche of fire on the Americans. Dead and wounded men covered the beach. Those who survived the violent landing experienced unfathomable brutality. Two days into the invasion, Japanese tanks ripped through American lines and drove back and forth over the Marines' foxholes. "It was a case of keeping your head down while Jap tanks crunched over the slit trenches and foxholes ... hoping they would straddle your position instead of running the tread in your hole," one Marine said. "A tank ran over my hole," a dazed platoon sergeant reported. After the tank passed, he "lit a fuse and tossed a whole pack of demolition charges on top of the damn thing." Casualties mounted with ferocious speed. Over fifteen thousand Marines were wounded, killed, or missing by the end of the one-month battle, making Saipan the bloodiest battle of the Pacific — up to that point.

To temper the stress of battle and provide an escape from

the death that surrounded the men, recreation and rest periods were crucial. The Special Services Division worked miracles to try to get morale-boosting equipment onto each island in record time. Within four days of the first American landing on Saipan, the Marines were greeted with a boatload of books. Three days later, a library was established. Even if they could only steal a sliver of time to themselves — to read a passage from a book of humor or an excerpt from a western — a brief distraction could go a long way. When shipments of ASEs arrived, they were eagerly grabbed, stowed away, and taken into battle. Some never made it out. As one Marine on Saipan shared with the Council on Books in Wartime:

> The morning after a particularly trying night of heavy enemy mortar fire ... I was walking along the road when I saw some of the dead being loaded gently into the backs of several trucks which had been drawn up to take their bodies to the division cemetery. I looked to see if I recognized any of the dead marines. There were half a dozen stretched out, some on their backs, and several face down. One of the latter was a young, fair-haired private who had only recently arrived as a replacement, full of exuberance at finally being a full-fledged marine on the battle front. As I looked down at him I saw something which I don't think I shall ever forget. Sticking from his back trouser pocket was a yellow pocket edition of a book he had evidently been reading in his spare moments. Only the title was visible — *Our Hearts Were Young and Gay*.

More than a year into the program, and having distributed nine monthly shipments of books among the armed forces, the council was eager to hear from more servicemen about how the ASEs were being received. Turning to *Stars and Stripes,* a newspaper by and for soldiers, it arranged for the publication of a small blurb under the headline "Mail Call," asking for feedback and suggestions from the men themselves. Was the council sending the right selection of titles? What books would the troops like to see in future editions? Were the ASEs holding up?

The servicemen were delighted to be asked for their opinion. Their regimented military lifestyle rarely involved being asked what they thought; they were usually told what to do and followed orders. The opportunity to have their voices heard made them feel a bit like civilians again. Bags of mail were delivered to the council with letters that lauded its efforts, requested specific titles, told daring tales of reading under fire, or bitterly complained about a certain book. Every letter was read, and most were answered.

Enthusiastic letters announced the ubiquitousness and popularity of ASEs among the troops. A Red Cross field director said that it was "not an uncommon sight to see men in long chow lines reading from one of the editions. They carry them to the movie theater to await the start of the picture; to read between duty paroles; to kill a few minutes before 'lights out'; while waiting in the sick bay for treatment; or sweating it out in the barber shop." A major in the South Pacific reported that an ASE was stuffed into every pocket. "Soldiers carry your books with them and read them in jeeps, on ducks, in alligators and weasels, as well as on LST's, on landing barges, and while waiting for coffee to boil between lulls at command posts," he said. From the USS *Independence,* one man wrote that the ASEs were "so popular that one is . . . out of uniform if one isn't sticking out of the hip pocket!" Another serviceman weighed in from a hospital bed in England: "From the Airborne Infantry of the front lines to the chair-borne Finance Corps of the rear, you can find the boys reading as they never have before."

Many letters hailed the ASEs as the best feature of military life. "Proof at last," a second lieutenant declared, that "there are, come training and shipment overseas, despite the wife and girl you leave behind and the stridency of regimentation, advantages in the serviceman's life. I don't mean cigarettes [or] chocolate bars," he said, "I mean the stirring edition of your pocket-books—the Armed Services Editions, which, through someone's high-mindedness, sense of humor, and also appreciation of *many* tastes, is simply (but imaginatively) superb." Another serviceman wrote, "I do not know who you are or how your organization was ever started . . . however, I want to thank you for providing so many books in such a handy form for all of us in the service." A lieutenant in India extended "damned sincere thanks" for the publication of "everything from Zane Grey to Plato." From Italy, an American soldier remarked that sending books to the services was akin to making it "rain in the desert." "There are many times when the only entertainment, relaxation, and mental stimulation is reading, so you can see how welcome the 'Armed Services' books are," he said.

Anyone who had made a long trip by sea knew what a difference a box of ASEs could make. One sailor who left California for Pearl Harbor wrote that the eight hundred men aboard his ship had "six long tiresome days at sea to look forward to," but when the library produced a box of ASEs, the sailors "grabbed them up like children with a box of chocolates." "They have made a lot of sailors happy and entertained during the many days of travel at sea," he said. Another sailor wrote, "Since I have been in the service I have not seen any single thing more worthwhile (or comparable in any other respect) than the Armed Services Editions."

Many appreciated the council's eclectic selection of titles, for there was always a range of subject matters and genres in each month's delivery. A dubious infantryman, who had feared that the ASEs would be confined to rudimentary offerings such as Zane Grey westerns and Tarzan stories, wrote to the council that he was "gratifyingly pleased . . . that you have eschewed such monstrosities." (The council ultimately published several of Grey's westerns and two Tarzan books). Another man said that the council's book selectors were "worthy of a medal" based on the conviction they exhibited in "the intellectual curiosity of the average soldier."

When servicemen learned that the work of a favorite author had been printed in ASE format, they would do nearly anything to track down a copy. As the inside back cover of each ASE listed all of the titles published that month, the men could check for books they wanted to read and scavenge their unit to find them. "For days I've been hunting through our service club, bothering the Red Cross, scanning our library shelves and hunting unrelentingly through the barracks—for what???? G-183! G-183! G-183!" one man exclaimed. "Yes G-183," he said, *Low Man on a Totem Pole* by H. Allen Smith. Smith was a favorite author of this sergeant's, and he begged the council to send him a copy; he even offered to pay for one. A man stationed in England asked for copies of *The Robe* and *A Tree Grows in Brooklyn;* he had already searched high and low for them and harassed the Special Services Division, but no copies could be found. He added: "You have no idea how many hours of pleasure your books give us."

When the council asked for book suggestions, it unleashed a storm of ideas from men anxious to find favorite authors and popular titles. People from all walks of life and with completely opposing tastes wrote to ask for more books. A sampling of these letters reveals that the council could do no wrong so long as it continued to include as many different types of books in each series as possible.

One man wrote that many soldiers "would like to get hold of *Anna Karenina* (literally)," in addition to Dumas novels, and Balzac. Yet he advised to "ease up on the historical novels," and "it might not hurt to try a single classic a month." A petition-like letter signed by an entire unit asked for two books: a dictionary, and *Tad Potter* by Asa Wilgus. *Tad Potter* told the story of a young man forced to choose between living on his family's New England farm or moving to a big city with the woman he loved. A librarian at a station hospital in the Ryukyu Islands seconded the request for *Tad Potter*. That book "requires little 'sales talk,'" the librarian said. "To interest a GI reader you have only to turn to the first page about a boy coming home in the Spring." From another hospital, a request came in for more plays — Shakespeare, George Bernard Shaw, and Broadway comedies. One man's fondness for classics could be another man's nightmare. "There is just one bit of criticism that I have to offer," one sergeant said after complimenting the bulk of the council's work. "I believe that the majority of the fellows prefer fiction, especially of the modern type," he said. Another man wrote that his only complaint was that there were not enough sports books. "My personal preference is for history and biography, but I know from observation that no one of your selections goes neglected or unappreciated," an engineer wrote.

Many servicemen were interested in reading about the nations involved in the war. One corporal wrote from the Pacific, where he had been stationed for some time, to say he was appalled by how little Americans knew about the history of that part of the world. He asked the council to help them out and print books on the culture and history of the Far East. From New Caledonia, a private first class wrote that, although the council had printed histories of Britain and North Africa, he was disappointed that it did not publish works on France, Russia, China, and India. In addition to requesting histories of these nations, he urged the council to print books on the "recent history and people of the Axis" to build "soldier and sailor understanding of our foreign policy and what it should be."

Enthusiasm for the council's books and special requests for certain titles spilled into letters the men wrote to their loved ones. Many praised the council's work to such a degree that anxious mothers, wives, sisters, and girlfriends wrote to the council to see if they could purchase ASEs for a special occasion or to supplement their next care package. The wife of an American POW in Germany asked the council to send her a book that complied with all of the restrictions Germany placed on books. A Navy nurse wrote the council, telling of how enthusiastically the ASEs were received by her patients. However, her brother, who was in the Army, had complained in a letter that he did not have enough reading material, and she wanted the council to send books to him. A caring sister wrote to the council about her brother, who had told her all about the miniature books that were making the rounds where he was stationed. There were three titles that he was eager to read, but could not find, and he begged his sister to help. "He says that I couldn't send him a nicer gift than those three little books," she said.

In response to most letters requesting ASEs, the council offered to inform the Special Services Division that books were needed in a particular theater or unit. Although council employees wanted to fulfill requests for certain ASEs, they were contractually obligated to give the Army and Navy *all* the ASEs that were manufactured. The council even refused a request from the United States Treasury Department for five hundred sets of ASEs to send to Australia under a lend-lease arrangement.

Yet the council did break the rules on occasion. A Dutchman who was quartering American soldiers in his home in Holland wrote to the council about an American officer who had been living with him for several weeks. This officer's love of reading was undeniable — he carried a huge collection of ASEs, but he lacked his favorite book, *Tarzan of the Apes*. "Next month he will have his birthday and I should like to give it to him for that occasion," the officer's Dutch host wrote. The only problem was that he could not buy an English edition of the book in Holland. Although he knew it was not the council's "habit to send books to civilians," he asked that it make this one exception.

Another overseas request came from a soldier in the Australian Forces, who happened upon the ASE of *Lou Gehrig* when on a joint mission with an American unit. "Being an ardent baseballer myself," he said, the discovery of this "marvelous book thrilled me beyond expression." Although he managed to glance through the book before American troops moved out, he was desperate to read the entire thing. "I realize your own servicemen have all claims," he said, but he pleaded with the council to "spare a copy for me, for which I would be extremely grateful."

Although appeals like these were routinely rejected by the council, some exceptions were made: a copy of *Tarzan* was mailed to Holland, and the Australian soldier received a package containing several baseball books.

When word spread that a certain book was exceptionally good, waiting lists were created to keep track of which soldier was the next to have the privilege of reading it. Those who could not wait their turn bribed their way to the front of the line (with packs of cigarettes, money, or candy bars). The council received a slew of letters asking for more copies of titles that the men were desperate to read.

While requests for classics, sports tales, modern fiction, and history books did not cause a ripple of concern, some suggestions sparked dissension within the council. One such request came from a serviceman serving off the Gold Coast in West Africa. This soldier said that books such as *Forever Amber, Strange Fruit,* and *The Three Musketeers* (Tiffany Thayer's version) were what the men really wanted. "The books that are most read are the books that have at least an essence of — to put it bluntly — sex and a lot of it," he said. While his unit was lucky enough to have secured copies of *Forever Amber* and *Strange Fruit* (most likely because someone asked a relative to send them), both books were overused, with *Forever Amber* commanding a waiting list of at least thirty men, and *Strange Fruit* having one almost as long. Clearly, they needed more copies, preferably in the council's conveniently sized ASE format. Many men echoed these title requests. From the Aleutian Islands it was reported that the "fellas have a fever to read the novel *Forever Amber* by Kathleen Winsor." "If you've ever seen books that were completely worn out by reading," another man said, "it was the copies of *Forever Amber.*"

Requests for titles such as these created some agitation among the council's readers. First of all, *Strange Fruit* and *Forever Amber* were considered so indecent that the city of Boston had banned them. (For one captain, this was a selling point. "We're all looking forward to . . . *Forever Amber,* since it seems to have stirred up some excitement back home," he said. "We get curious about all books that are banned in Boston — and who wouldn't?") But, by the same token, Lillian Smith's *Strange Fruit* was a bestseller on the home front; even Eleanor Roosevelt had praised it for its moving treatment of sensitive social issues. It told the story of an interracial couple whose affair resulted in pregnancy. The couple could not marry because it was prohibited by law, the father of the child is murdered, and an innocent man is lynched for the murder. Far from being pure smut, *Strange Fruit* presented issues about inequality and the hypocrisy of living under a democratic form of government that did not extend the same rights to each of its citizens. It also happened to include racy descriptions of seduction, including exposed body parts and the tearing off of clothing. While *Forever Amber* was also a best-selling book, it told the bawdy story of how a young woman, Amber, climbed the social ladder of English society by sleeping with rich and powerful men and/or marrying them. Amber became the favorite mistress of Charles II, but all the while she lusted for another man. Eleanor Roosevelt never praised that one.

Servicemen were sexually frustrated, but the idea of providing books that catered to such prurient interests flustered some of the council's staff. The controversy grew so heated that Philip Van Doren Stern was forced to raise the issue at a council executive board meeting, where he disclosed that certain members of the editorial committee "objected to having to give their approval on a number of . . . books that they consider of a trashy nature." The executive board did not care what the editorial committee thought: "These books are supposed to serve a purpose regardless of what type they are." The executive board meeting minutes continued: "If these books . . . give the boys overseas the kind of release from tension that they want, then the committee should be delighted to give their approval of the books." As the council would do time and again, it erred on the side of providing a variety of reading material rather than limiting the types of books sent to servicemen. As America's army fought to preserve freedom, the council stressed the need to provide unfettered access to a diverse set of titles — even trashy ones.

In due time, the council assured the servicemen who had asked that "*Forever Amber* and *Strange Fruit* will be published in Armed Services Editions." Men around the world were grateful for the council's decision. The council's independence in selecting books, and willingness to print controversial titles, earned the respect of many servicemen. Some even wrote letters prodding the council to resist any pressures from religious organizations or other groups that might try to sway members against printing certain books. "Pay no attention, absolutely no attention, to whatever organization tries to influence your selection of books," one infantryman urged. "If the legion of decency approaches you, please leer at them in your most offensive manner and tell them to stuff it," he said. The servicemen did not have to worry. That even banned books would be printed as ASEs seemed to especially delight the council's director, Archibald Ogden, who managed to gloat as much to a Boston newspaper. Under the headline "Boston's Sons in Service Reading Those Awful Books," he was quoted as saying, "It's beginning to look as if all an author has to do to get into the armed forces library is to be banned in Boston."

Some of the most colorful letters received by the council described the extent to which reading was intertwined with battle. A man wrote from Luxembourg to report that he had just "literally crawled out of my wet and muddy slit-trench, that we refer to as a foxhole, for a breath of fresh un-American air, knowing that in a few minutes I will definitely have to dive back via a one and a half back flip to safeguard myself from that rain of death that [the Germans] quite frequently arch over." He had been playing this cat-and-mouse game for days. Just earlier, as fresh rounds of artillery were being lobbed in his direction, he retired into his "heavily roofed, deeply carved-out fortress, and after praying feverishly, I started to read the Armed Services Edition of *C/O Postmaster* by Cpl. Thomas R. St. George, with the aid of a GI flashlight." The "experience of the corporal held me in good spirits," he said, despite the sounds of death that filled the air.

One commanding colonel felt a duty to share how *A Tree Grows in Brooklyn* helped him and a group of his men keep their mental bearings while under attack. This colonel commanded a "light ack ack battalion," which he defined as "anti-aircraft, anti-tank, anti-personnel." He explained that:

> not long ago I was down inspecting one of my batteries in a pretty tough position and was in a gun pit when some [Germans] started in on us with 88's. It wasn't very pleasant, waiting for them to come on in after their whistle first sounded and waiting for them to burst (elsewhere — you hope). Anyway, I noticed one GI reading in between bursts. I asked him what he was reading and he told us "A Tree Grows in Brooklyn." He started to read us a portion about "giving the baby the gussie" — a part of the book — and we laughed like hell between bursts. It sure was funny.

They all survived the German attack, and this commanding colonel decided to read the book for himself. He rummaged around to find a copy, and when he finally succeeded and began reading it, his unit again came under attack. "Our column got hit by a boche battalion holed up in some woods above a road and we hit the ditches and had a fierce fight." The commanding colonel admitted that he could not help but feel a temptation "to read some more while they had us pinned down pretty tight, but I had to get up front and give a few orders and start them over the hill." The fighting continued through the day, and although he was ultimately wounded, thoughts of the book's protagonist, Francie Nolan, and Brooklyn, New York, kept intruding. "I was thinking about that book even under pretty intense fire," he said; "it was that interesting." Although he was never much of a reader before the war (by way of background, he said that he had attended the United States Military Academy, and "never was in the West Point library except by order"), he liked *A Tree Grows in Brooklyn*. "I sit here in a dug in blacked out command post tent at the front somewhere and write this in sheer gratitude," he said.

Another description of reading on the frontlines came from a private who explained that, just before he had gone to battle, essential supplies had reached him and his unit: cigarettes and books. He grabbed a copy of Lytton Strachey's *Queen Victoria,* read a few chapters, and then his unit was suddenly called into action. They slowly advanced through heavy artillery fire, and became "pinned down in a field by mortar and machine gun fire." As bullets whizzed past him, this private began to panic because he saw no place to take cover. In an act of desperation, he dove into "what appeared to be a solid growth of brambles and bushes," which gave way under his weight and sent him crashing into a deep ditch. He was injured in the fall and could hardly move in his cramped hole. As he wiggled his limbs, he felt "a lump in [his] pocket [that] turned out to be *Queen Victoria*." Knowing it was "pretty 'hot' above"—for "every once in a while a shell would burst" nearby—he could do nothing except wait for the shelling to end and help to come.

He began to read. "It was no use to stew and fret; events were completely beyond my control," the private said. When he heard a shell explode a mere twenty-five feet from him, he felt as though the shell "might as well have been on top of me, but no action of mine could alter the result." Instead, he "merely resigned to being completely at the mercy of chance" and escaped his surroundings by turning page after page of *Queen Victo-*

ria. The book calmed and occupied his mind until the shelling lifted and he could be taken to a hospital. Days later, bedridden, he finished the book.

Although the bulk of the letters from servicemen sang the council's praises, there were also criticisms. Perhaps even more than notes of compliment, letters of complaint revealed how crucial books were to the quality of life of the men fighting overseas. One issue that plagued several ASEs stemmed from the two-up printing process. In the course of assembling the books, pagination problems sometimes occurred. One dilemma involved missing pages; sometimes upwards of twenty pages could be inexplicably absent from an ASE. A corporal griped that he had started reading John T. Whitaker's *We Cannot Escape History* "only to discover that pages 26 to 59 inclusive are missing whereas pages 59 to 90 inclusive are included twice."

Another man, who had invested a great deal of time in the book he had been reading, wrote to the council: "If it is your mission in the war to cheer the lives of members of the Armed Forces by your Armed Services Editions, you may consider yourselves a failure as far as I am concerned. In short, I am greatly upset," he said, and "that's putting it mildly." This frustrated sergeant explained that the cause of his "great wrath" was that he had just gotten to the "most exciting part of the fine novel *The Gaunt Woman* when "at least twenty-five pages were missing." He clarified: "Not torn out, mind you, but never put in the book during printing." The book told a suspenseful tale of a Gloucester skipper whose ship, the *Gaunt Woman,* had to navigate around Nazi submarines in order to haul its catch to shore as a romance brews. When this sergeant discovered the missing pages, he became so livid that he "threw the book" away, not knowing whether the "hero 'got the girl' or 'got the works.'"

To put things in perspective, he said that he was never one to write a letter of complaint, but "at a time such as [this] when good books are so hard to get, I feel you should have the opinion of one disgusted soldier." He implored the council's printers to take better care in the future to ensure that such mishaps did not occur because, at least for him, it was the cause of great "mental anguish."

In less than a month, the same man wrote a letter to Philip Van Doren Stern, expressing gratitude for the complete copy of *The Gaunt Woman* that the council had sent him. The sergeant admitted to feeling ashamed of his prior hot-tempered missive. He explained that "out here time hangs heavy on the hands and minds of we men who are 'sweating out' this side of the war." The ASEs were doing a world of good for him and those around him. This man felt that, due to the ASEs, he and his friends were "better informed [and would be] more intelligent . . . after the war."

Another problem stemming from the two-up printings was that pages from one title could be haphazardly shuffled into another. A private first class wrote the council about one example. His unit had recently received a package of ASEs in the mail, which was often the source of "many happy and contented hours of reading." After taking his time in selecting a book, as there were many tempting titles from which to choose, he began to read Ben Ames Williams's *The Strange Woman*. The book told a riveting story of a manipulative young woman who plotted against friends and lovers, reaping benefits at their expense until she became tangled in her own web of deceit. Once this soldier picked up the book, he could "hardly lay it aside"; "I became engrossed," he said. However, "to my utter dismay, 16 complete pages were missing," and in their place were "16 pages of the book *The Education of Henry Adams*." As he was hanging

on every word, he desperately searched for a copy of *The Education of Henry Adams* to see if the missing pages of *The Strange
Woman* might have been misplaced within it. They were not.
"I'm writing," he said, "in complete hope of your organization
rectifying this seemingly trifling matter." The book, "in such
condition as it is now, is worthless."

When printing errors were reported, the council worked to
mollify frustrated servicemen as swiftly as possible. Despite its
policy of not sending books to individuals, the council always
made an exception when it came to defective ASEs, and a perfect copy was promptly mailed along with a letter of apology.

While rectifying a book with missing pages was relatively
easy, more subjective complaints proved difficult to remedy.
This was especially true of criticism about the subject matter of
certain books. Despite the precautions the council took to ensure that the titles being printed were befitting of the fact that
there was a war going on, a few soldiers expressed their disbelief
that some ASEs were allowed to be sent to the frontlines. One
incensed private explained that he had finished reading *North
Africa* and was trying "to discover the names of the fifth colum-
nists on the Council." He "violently" objected to its inclusion as
an ASE, and was so shaken by the book that he asked the council to clarify: "What are we fighting for?" "What excuse can the
Council offer for using precious paper to print, for the guidance of an American soldier, such a book as this?" he asked. "If
no better could have been found, then the Council would have
been better advised to have printed nothing," he said. The bulk
of *North Africa* describes the geography, economy, and history
of North Africa; the excerpt that this private found so offensive
cast France's expansion into North Africa in the 1880s in a positive light (perhaps he found it too similar to Germany's quest
for expansion in Europe).

William Sloane responded to this letter on the council's behalf, assuring the private that "there is no question of any fifth column in our ranks and yours is the only complaint which we have received about the book on these grounds, so far as I know." Sloane promised that the council's staff would "be more meticulous in the future," and expressed his hope that the private believed that the rest of the books the council had printed were acceptable. Although the bulk of the private's letter chastised the council, Sloane admitted to feeling some gratification that the ASEs had "done one thing which we hoped for, which is to keep the intellectual interests of the American soldier alive and growing."

A milder letter of rebuke was received by the council regarding *The Iron Trail,* a western by Max Brand. In this book, an outlaw decides to lead an honest life when a local criminal completes a jewel heist, leaving clues that point to the former outlaw as the perpetrator. Although the book had no apparent pro-German message, the council received a letter asking, "Don't you think that might well be a German Book-of-the-Month selection?" Although the ASEs were "one of the greatest educational contributions — probably the greatest — of this war," this soldier wondered whether there was "any responsible member of your Council" who had read *The Iron Trail* before producing it.

One notable omission in the responses to the council's *Stars and Stripes* request for feedback was any word from those serving in the Women's Army Corps (WACs) and the Navy's Women Accepted for Volunteer Emergency Service (WAVEs). While special magazine sets were distributed to the WACs and WAVEs, consisting of female-oriented periodicals such as *Good Housekeeping* and *Ladies' Home Journal,* the absence of letters from servicewomen to the council confirms that ASEs were only provided to men. Since books were meant to serve the morale needs of those facing the horrors of battle, the Army and Navy perceived no need to provide portable paperbacks to the women who served in noncombatant positions. Plus, these women could be served by stationary libraries containing hard-cover books. One wonders what titles would have been added to the twelve hundred ASEs if large numbers of women served in combat in World War II.

On the whole, the council did not need to worry about how the servicemen felt about the ASEs. As one Army medical officer wrote: "Next to penicillin the Armed Services Editions are the greatest improvement in Army technique since the Battle of the Marne." The letters received from around the world proved that the books did exactly what they were supposed to: they relieved boredom, elevated spirits, incited laughter, renewed hope, and provided an escape. There was a book for every taste, whether a man preferred *Sad Sack* comics or Plato. And everyone read. As one man said, "[I'd] bet dollars to GI Spam that half the men . . . never cracked a book before." Yet he observed men read until the pages of each book were "so dirty that you can't see the print." Even as their condition deteriorated, the men held on to their precious books. "To heave one in the garbage can is tanta-mount to striking your grandmother," he said.

EIGHT

Censorship and FDR's F - - - th T - - m

> If it is to be left to the Adjutant General to decide
> what the Army is to be permitted to read then we
> might as well join the Nazis and stop fighting them.
>
> — *LYNCHBURG (VA) DAILY ADVANCE*, 1944

A s ACCOLADES FOR the Armed Services Editions
poured in during the summer of 1944, the Council on
Books in Wartime waged a battle of its own — against
censorship. While the council used certain criteria to guide its
selection (avoiding books that might give comfort to the enemy, for example, or that professed discriminatory attitudes), it
aimed to publish a range of titles from a variety of perspectives.
This open-mindedness ran afoul of the government on occasion. In 1943, the council had come under fire for publishing an
ASE of Louis Adamic's *The Native's Return*. The problem was
that the first edition of this book, published years earlier, contained passages deemed sympathetic to Communism. When
Michigan congressman George A. Dondero, a Republican,
heard that the council was supplying this book to servicemen,
he denounced the choice and questioned the council's motives
in sending a book critical of democracy to American soldiers

at war. As it turned out, the problematic passages had been removed in a later edition of *The Native's Return,* and it was this edition that had been reprinted as an ASE. Opposition to the title ceased when the record was set straight.

The censorship fight waged in 1944 was spurred by congressional revision of the Soldier Voting Act. After the original law largely failed in making absentee ballots available to servicemen in the 1942 election (only twenty-eight thousand servicemen — out of millions — voted in 1942), Congress committed itself to drafting a new bill to facilitate wartime voting by those serving in the armed forces, as well as all others whose war work required their absence from home (for example, Red Cross volunteers). Instead of having each state set individual and possibly conflicting rules for casting a ballot, the federal law sought to provide a single method by which to cast a vote. As a joint letter to Congress from Navy Secretary Frank Knox and War Secretary Henry Stimson said, "the Services are unable to effectively administer the diverse procedures of 48 States as to 11,000,000 servicemen all over the world in primary, special and general elections."

Throughout late 1943, Congress debated the language for the new voting bill. As this legislation began to take shape, Ohio senator Robert A. Taft, the brother of Charles P. Taft and a political powerhouse, asserted that some safeguard was needed to prevent the Democratic-led government from rigging the election by distributing pro-Democratic literature to the millions of people in the services. Taft adamantly opposed a fourth term for Roosevelt, and he distrusted the Democratic Party, believing it would disseminate political propaganda to the servicemen unless expressly prohibited from doing so. Taft proposed an amendment to the 1944 Soldier Voting Bill, known as Title V. This provision placed restrictions on amusements distributed to the servicemen, including books, so long as they were provided by the government and made some reference to politics. Just as Charles Taft nearly derailed the 1943 VBC with his threats to discontinue funding, his brother's amendment to the Soldier Voting Bill would stymie the council's selection of ASEs and challenge the very freedoms at stake in the war. It is a remarkable coincidence that the greatest menace to the book programs of World War II happened to be a pair of brothers.

The Soldier Voting Bill underwent revisions that winter and returned to the Senate and House of Representatives in March 1944 for a vote. Without any discussion of Taft's amendment, the Senate approved the bill. Acknowledging that it was not the most effective legislation, senators agreed that it generally improved the likelihood that those who were in the services would have an opportunity to vote. On March 15, the House took up the bill, and a heated partisan debate followed.

It was common knowledge that the vast majority of Americans in the services planned to vote for Roosevelt in the upcoming election. A February 1944 poll of servicepeople in the South Pacific revealed that 69 percent of American soldiers, sailors, and Marines would vote for a fourth term for Roosevelt, and 77 percent preferred to return to the United States under "the present form of government." Thus, there was a political incentive for Republicans to complicate the procedures for overseas voting, while Democrats strove to simplify it. By the time the bill entered the House for debate in March 1944, it no longer seemed to be about voting, but about both parties manipulating the ballot.

Discussion of the bill in the House deteriorated into a mudslinging contest. Democrats accused Republicans of intentionally making voting difficult. Republicans attacked Democrats for insisting that absentee voters use a "bobtailed ballot" (instead of listing the names of each candidate running for office as ballots on the home front did, the bobtailed ballot required voters to write in the names of each candidate for whom they were voting next to each office at stake in the election: President, Vice President, Senate, etc.). Republicans reasoned that, after twelve years in office, anyone could name the Democratic candidate for president, and the bobtailed ballot would thus favor Roosevelt. Representatives on both sides of the aisle criticized the bill for how complicated it had become. Democratic representative Daniel Hoch said: "In order to get a ballot a soldier must take three distinct oaths. He must literally swear his life away. Then, after all this swearing, if the ballot reaches home in time and is satisfactory to the Governor of his State it will be counted." "If I were a soldier," Hoch said, "I think that in disgust I would give it up and would not vote." Republican representative Leland Ford spoke next: "Of all the hodgepodge, mixed-up measures that have ever come before this body for final determination, this so-called soldier-vote bill is the ultimate." The bill, he said, was "clear as mud."

Despite the spirited debate, the House voted the bill into law. Although he did not veto the act, President Roosevelt criticized it, calling it "wholly inadequate" and "confusing." In the end, if those in the services wanted to vote, they would have to use a bobtailed ballot, and each state was required to provide a list of candidates to the secretaries of war and the Navy for distribution abroad.

Lost in all the bickering, largely ignored, was Senator Taft's amendment to the bill—Title V. This provision prohibited the government from delivering any "magazine . . . newspaper, motion-picture, film, or other literature or material . . . paid in whole or in part with Government funds . . . containing political argument or political propaganda of any kind designed or calculated to affect the result of any [federal] election." It sounded simple, but what counted as propaganda? Any work of nonfiction with a political sway? If the act was violated, a person could be criminally charged and convicted. Punishment included a fine of up to $1,000, one year of imprisonment, or both.

The War Department immediately notified the council that the ASEs would be affected by the law. Title V "uses the broadest terms ('literature or material') which include every medium of information and entertainment," the department warned. And the clause "'political argument or political propaganda of any kind designed or calculated to affect the result' of a Federal election, is similarly broad in sweep," it added. In light of the penalty for violating the law, the War Department advised that "reasonable doubt as to whether material . . . is 'designed or calculated to affect the result of any election' should be resolved in favor of prohibition." If a book so much as touched on a political theme, the council was urged not to print it. Naturally, members of the council wished to avoid serving jail time, but they also refused to be bullied into complying with legislation that restricted servicemen's freedom to read.

Philip Van Doren Stern tried to get around the restriction by asking publishers to grant the council blanket permission to delete any sentences or paragraphs that referenced politics from proposed ASEs to avoid violating Title V. He drafted a letter stating that the "law is quite clear," and the council would have to adapt to Title V. "This is not a matter of choice, but of necessity," Stern said. This letter was circulated to a handful of publishers and the War and Navy Departments before being mailed to the council's entire membership. Stern's proposal was immediately quashed. "I hope you didn't send the letter out as it is," Richard Simon, of Simon & Schuster, replied. Not only was the tone "much too apologetic and frightened," but "that law is not clear." The "words 'political propaganda of any kind designed or calculated to affect the result of any election for the Federal offices mentioned above' make just about as unclear and loose a phrase as I can think of," Simon said. Echoing Simon's disapproval were the Army and Navy, both of which opposed editing books in order to make them acceptable under the law. The Navy noted that any deletions would "almost certainly result in coloring the intent of the author," and, perhaps more importantly, "such procedure will undoubtedly result in the charge that the War and Navy Departments ... are presenting 'half truths' to the armed forces," which would be "a most undesirable, if not dangerous, moral effect since there is involved one of the principles for which we are fighting." Better to omit a book than to edit it.

That same spring, a troubling series of incidents caused council members to wonder whether the government was as solicitous about preserving freedom as it professed. The first surrounded the publication of Lillian Smith's book, *Strange Fruit*. While many critics and reviewers praised the book's bold and poignant handling of a story that touched on important social and cultural issues, it was soon banned in both Boston and Detroit for its obscenity. Boston did not take this ban lightly. Abraham Isenstadt, a Massachusetts bookseller who ignored the ban and sold *Strange Fruit* at his store, was arrested, charged, and convicted of violating state law by "selling literature containing 'indecent, impure language, manifestly tending to corrupt morals of youth.'" On appeal, his conviction was affirmed. The Supreme Judicial Court of Massachusetts explained that the book's "four scenes of sexual intercourse," two of which featured "strongly erotic connotations," tended to "promote lascivious thoughts and to arouse lustful desire in the minds of" those who read it.

Boston's book ban became a topic of national discussion because it seemed incompatible with the ongoing war being fought to preserve freedom. In fighting the war of ideas, Americans were told that they should read any book they desired in order to exercise their freedom and protest Hitler's destruction of books. But not this book, in this city. Yet restrictions on books did not start and end in Boston. Shortly after Boston's ban of the book, the federal government became involved in policing, and even expanding, the restrictions on *Strange Fruit*. Beginning in May 1944, the U.S. Post Office Department barred shipment of *Strange Fruit* and notified the publisher, Reynal & Hitchcock, that if it continued to distribute the book by mail, those responsible could risk prosecution under a federal statute prohibiting the mailing of lewd books. Reynal & Hitchcock defied the Post Office's restrictions, and said it was willing to accept that risk. The postmaster, however, next broadened his position, announcing that any publication that contained an advertisement for *Strange Fruit* could not be mailed. Leading newspapers and magazines, such as the *New York Herald Tribune* and the *Saturday Review of Literature,* were individually warned by the postmaster to stop running advertisements. Norman Cousins, the editor of the *Saturday Review of Literature,* publicly rebuked the postmaster's actions, stating that he had every intention of continuing to sell advertising space to promote *Strange Fruit*. "Censorship is no trivial matter . . . So far as Americans are concerned it involves their very traditions. Who in the post-office is charged with the responsibility for seeing that these traditions are not easily and ignorantly brushed aside?" "We not only protest your order; we refuse to follow it without due process of law," Cousins defiantly added.

As the debacle over the ban on *Strange Fruit* unfolded, the council's executive committee held an emergency meeting at the

Morgan Library in Manhattan to draft a resolution emphasizing the importance of free literature in wartime, and renounc-
ing the "increasing tendency on the part of the government to
encroach that freedom." Between Title V's ban on ASEs containing even a passing reference to national politics or United
States political history, and the Post Office's stance on mailing
Strange Fruit, the council recorded "its anxiety over these man-
ifestations of intolerance on the part of its government." The
council accused the Post Office Department of resorting to "star
chamber action in denying the use of the mails to works which
deal honestly and courageously with basic problems of our democracy."

"Censorship of matters other than those affecting security
in wartime cannot be left to the arbitrary will of individuals,
even if legally authorized, without grave jeopardy to democratic
freedom of the press," the council said. Once passed, this resolution was mailed to President Roosevelt, the postmaster general,
the secretaries of war and the Navy, the Speaker of the House of
Representatives, and the president of the Senate.

Next, the council drafted a press release listing books it was
forced to reject for publication as ASEs due to Title V: Catherine Drinker Bowen's best-selling biography of Chief Justice
Holmes, *Yankee from Olympus;* Charles Beard's acclaimed history of American politics, *The Republic;* Senator James Mead's
anecdotal account of servicemen's lives overseas, *Tell the Folks
Back Home;* Mari Sandoz's novel about a family in Nebraska,
Slogum House; and E. B. White's compilation of articles previously published in magazines, *One Man's Meat.* The press release explained that, under normal circumstances, eighty-five
thousand copies of these books would have been published as
ASEs; however, because of the recent legislation, the council

could no longer provide the servicemen with these or any other titles that might offend the law.

Many authors expressed their appreciation for the council's decision to challenge the law. Banned author Mari Sandoz thanked the council for its "vigorous efforts on behalf of the [banned] books." Sandoz said that she believed the entire act was an alarming piece of political handiwork, for it did not provide an effective mechanism to streamline absentee voting, and the book provision seemed only to clarify the true nature of the act. "Even temporary infringement of liberty establishes dangerous precedents," she said. Title V reminded Sandoz of a conference she had attended in 1938, where she met Dr. Friedrich Schönemann, of the University of Berlin. At the time, she did not believe Dr. Schönemann when he said that "the Nazis would not need to establish a government ban on books subversive to their ideals in America. We [Americans] would do it for them." Now, to her horror, he seemed to be right.

The council decided it was duty bound to wage a fight for the repeal of Title V. From a monetary perspective, it did not matter to the council if one book was disqualified for ASE publication, since another would take its place. Yet the council could not tolerate the censorship of the servicemen's reading materials, or the precedent set by the legislation. As Archibald Ogden, executive director of the council, grumbled: "It looks as though from now until November, we can publish nothing but 'Elsie Dinsmore' and 'The Bobbsey Twins.'"

In late May 1944, the council began a campaign to pressure Congress to repeal the law. A letter was sent to editors of every major newspaper and magazine in the United States, which explained the council's ASE program and the effects of the Soldier

Voting Act. The council asked that newspapers and magazines, which surely valued the freedom of the press, publish articles that would alert the public to the government's infringement of the servicemen's basic freedoms.

The degree of cooperation from the media was extraordinary. Throughout June and July 1944, critical articles were published lamenting the plight of the council as it strove to print a variety of books while the government worked to censor its selections. "Censorship for political reasons is a Fascist device which has no place in the United States," avowed the *Syracuse Post-Standard*. It is "ridiculous to set the armed forces as a class apart from civilians in control of reading material." An article published in Columbia, South Carolina, explained that, "since every voter except those who blindly follow a party line makes his decision on the basis of political, economic, and social thinking, this can only be interpreted by the Army and Navy authorities to mean a ban from service men's libraries, reading rooms, and moving picture shows, of everything that inspires, however indirectly, social, economic, and political thought." It was difficult to believe that American libraries and reading rooms were being subjected to a "Goebbels's purge" because of a federal law, the article concluded. Virginia's *Lynchburg Daily Advance* lamented that, under the act, "almost any book except cook books, fairy tales, or text books on such subjects as astronomy and mathematics would be banned." "If it is to be left to the Adjutant General to decide what the Army is to be permitted to read then we might as well join the Nazis and stop fighting them." An article in the *San Antonio News* said: "One would think that the men who fight the Nation's battles would be quite able to decide for themselves what they would like to read," and that "maybe they would rather skip voting this year than to have their reading-material censored."

In May 1933, tens of thousands of books were burned in Berlin and in towns across Germany. By the end of World War II, more than one hundred million volumes were destroyed in Europe by the Nazis.

America's librarians responded to Germany's "bibliocaust" by urging Americans to donate millions of books to the armed services. Here, on the steps of the New York Public Library, thousands gather to catch a glimpse of their favorite celebrities and donate books.

The Victory Book Campaign's first director, Althea Warren, inspired librarians across the United States to gather millions of books for homesick and weary servicemen. "Librarians know," she said, "that some printed pages are . . . tourists' tickets out of boredom or loneliness to exhilarating adventures."

Celebrities including Kate Smith, a popular singer remembered to this day for her rendition of "God Bless America," raised awareness of the need to donate books to the VBC.

Eleanor Roosevelt urged Americans to give good books to the armed services and proudly gave on behalf of herself and the president.

VBC posters were hung everywhere: in train stations, department stores, movie theaters, and schools. In 1943, the public was asked to give more books than they did the year before.

In St. Louis, streetcar tickets were redesigned to include a book drive reminder. All libraries and schools served as donation centers.

In New York's Pennsylvania Station, a three-year-old girl donates hardcovers by depositing them into a novel drop box posing as the "world's largest book."

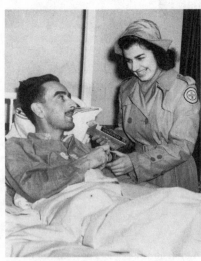

In hospitals, patients eagerly read books to pass the time. Here, a Red Cross volunteer gives a volume of Shakespeare to an American wounded in Tunisia.

Knowing hardcover books were unsuitable for men on the frontlines, Malcolm Johnson, of Doubleday, Doran & Co., helped develop troop-friendly paperbacks and revolutionized American publishing in the process.

During the war, Armed Services Editions were bound on their short side and each page had double columns of text. After V-J Day, ASEs, like *The Chicago Cubs,* were printed in upright format. The front cover of each ASE had a thumbnail image of the hardcover edition, the back cover described the book, and the inside back cover included a list of that month's titles.

Some servicemen were eager to read *Strange Fruit* and *Forever Amber,* as they contained sex scenes considered so indecent that they were banned in Boston. "If you've ever seen books that were completely worn out by reading," one serviceman said, "it was the copies of *Forever Amber.*"

Betty Smith's *A Tree Grows in Brooklyn* and Rosemary Taylor's *Chicken Every Sunday* were beloved for their wholesome accounts of American life. They were compared to taking a leave or receiving a good letter from home.

Soldiers wrote heartfelt letters to Betty Smith, crediting her book with instilling a sense of purpose, helping them survive battles, and just plain cheering them up. Smith responded to most of her fan letters, even sending autographed photographs upon request.

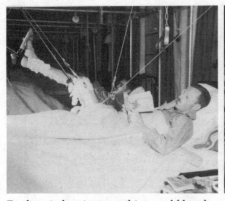

For hospital patients, nothing could break the monotony of spending days in bed like a book. Paperbacks were in high demand, since they could be held comfortably for hours while a soldier was flat on his back convalescing.

On LSTs, the stress of imminent battle could be suffocating. Books were a godsend when it came to distraction.

Once an area was secured, libraries were established. In Italy, this mobile library is housed in a tent, and soldiers recline in folding lounge chairs as they read.

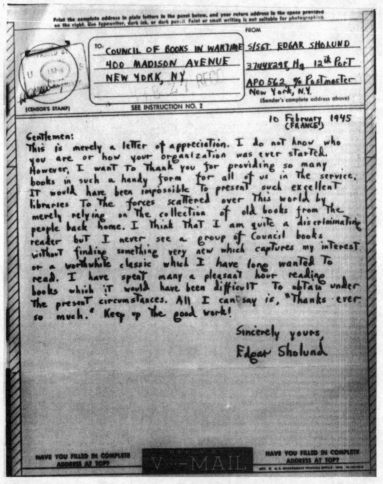

10 February 1945
(FRANCE)

Gentlemen:

This is merely a letter of appreciation. I do not know who you are or how your organization was ever started. However, I want to thank you for providing so many books in such a handy form for all of us in the service. It would have been impossible to present such excellent libraries to the forces scattered over this world by merely relying on the collection of old books from the people back home. I think that I am quite a discriminating reader but I never see a group of Council books without finding something very new which captures my interest or a worthwhile classic which I have long wanted to read. I have spent many a pleasant hour reading books which it would have been difficult to obtain under the present circumstances. All I can say is, "Thanks ever so much." Keep up the good work!

Sincerely yours,
Edgar Sholund

Publishers and authors received bags of mail from grateful servicemen. ASEs were the most reliable form of amusement; they helped a generation get through the war.

The *Chicago Sun* suggested the public not kid itself about the true nature of the act and Title V: it was a Republican move to deprive Roosevelt of a fourth term. "Congress in its wisdom has decreed that fighting men should be insulated from political 'propaganda.' The idea was to protect these innocent young men from nefarious attempts to sway them for a F - - - th T - - m." After considering the books being banned under Title V, the *Sun* remarked that not one of them had "any remote bearing on the F - - - th T - - m," and that if they did have any political content, it was "in the same sense that the Constitution or a history of the United States might have it." The whole episode seemed patently absurd, and the *Sun* said that the council "does well to protest this silly ban in the strongest terms."

One of the most exasperating repercussions of Title V was the fact that best-selling books with no apparent political agenda were swept up in the ban. That Catherine Drinker Bowen's *Yankee from Olympus,* Charles Beard's *The Republic,* and E. B. White's *One Man's Meat* were somehow going to sway the upcoming federal election was nonsensical. After the *Rochester Times Union* carefully inspected every page of *Yankee from Olympus,* it concluded that the only portion of the book that could have triggered the ban was a description of a conversation between the chief justice and President Roosevelt that was confined to a single page and did not go beyond an exchange of pleasantries. "If this is 'political propaganda,' then so's your 'World Almanac,'" the *Times Union* said. Similarly, a Michigan newspaper scoured Charles Beard's *The Republic,* only to find no political partisanship; the book, however, did contain an "excellent discussion of how the fundamental principles of American government evolved from the Constitutional convention." A favorite anomaly covered by the newspapers was the ban on E. B. White's *One Man's Meat* — a collection of whimsical essays about life in New England that originally appeared in the *New Yorker* and other periodicals; the very same essays were readily available to the fighting forces in the magazines they received. (White, himself, once admitted that he never understood why *One Man's Meat* was banned, but he liked that it was. "It shows somebody read it," he said.)

The council's media campaign generated an avalanche of letters to the editors of newspapers and opinion pieces slamming the Soldier Voting Act and demanding its repeal. Democracy on the home front was thriving: people were speaking their minds and criticizing their government. The backlash concerning Title V also showed that the public understood that books were not mere stories; they contained vital information that helped soldiers understand why they were fighting and risking their lives. Books were intertwined with the values at stake in the war, and Americans would not tolerate any restriction on their reading materials.

On symbol-laden Fourth of July, the War Department made an announcement that, due to the Soldier's Voting Act, it was forced to withdraw several textbooks used in Army education courses. These textbooks, which had been used in teaching history and economics to soldiers for years, had fallen into disrepute because they made at least a passing comment on politics or government. A few days later, *Time* magazine reported that the Army newspaper *Stars and Stripes* was forced to censor its news stories in order to avoid offending Title V. For example, when the Rome edition of *Stars and Stripes* published a story about the Republican candidate for president, Thomas E. Dewey, it was forced to omit Dewey's criticisms of the Roosevelt administration. Another report said that the Mediterranean edition of *Stars and Stripes* was forbidden to print Associated Press articles on politics. The U.S. Air Force Institute was compelled to stop offering four of its correspondence courses because certain textbooks fell under the ban. *Time* commented that these books were "likely to be saved from Congressional book-burning only by the waste-paper salvage campaign." It seemed incomprehensible that such actions were being taken in order to comply with American legislation. The *Saturday Review of Literature* diagnosed Congress with a bad case of "censoritis"; the only known cure was repeal of Title V.

On July 3 and 5, 1944, the council met with the Writers' War Board to strategize their next move. The two organizations agreed that they would personally contact Senator Robert Taft, Title V's sponsor, to pressure him to support amending or repealing the law. A special committee of council members joined members of the Writers' War Board, the Authors' League, and the writers' organization PEN to draft a formal letter to Senator Taft. The missive began by mentioning the recent publicity that Title V had received, noting that "all of it [was] sympathetic to our point of view." Striking a conciliatory tone, the letter insisted that no one believed it was Taft's intent to prevent the distribution of books that fell under a literal interpretation of the bill. Yet best-selling books containing no political propaganda were subject to the ban. The council warned that it would use the press and radio, at home and overseas, to inform the public and servicemen about Title V, and its "implication that the men overseas cannot be trusted with the same reading matter available at home." The alternative: Taft could meet with the council to come up with a solution.

Lieutenant Colonel Trautman soon informed the council that, after a recent meeting with five Army generals, a decision had been made that the bill would be interpreted even more strictly than before, causing additional books to fall within the scope of the ban. The Army's position effectively was to dou-

ble down its support for the council's attack on the bill. A draft
of the council's meeting minutes reveals that Philip Van Doren
Stern "reported that the Army had told him unofficially that
they will continue to interpret the bill literally in the hopes that
it will force a repeal or revision" of Title V. Stern's remark was
omitted from the final version of the council's minutes.

Senator Taft, a scion of Ohio's powerful Taft family, a son
of a president himself, and a perennial contender for the White
House, was not prone to avoiding battles. Within days of receiving the council's letter demanding amendment of Title V,
the senator sent an unapologetic response, insisting that the
council did not seem to understand the act. After noting that
any book could be privately purchased and sent to those in the
services, Taft emphasized that it was only books purchased with
government funds that were affected. Taft smugly noted that
"no one can question the wisdom of the provision which pro-
hibits the expenditure of government money to print and distribute books containing political argument and political propaganda just before the 1944 election." Taft faulted the Army for
reading the act much too strictly and added he did not see how
The Republic or *Yankee from Olympus* contained political argument or propaganda. Yet the senator did agree to travel to New
York to discuss the legislation and possible revisions to it.

On July 20, Senator Taft met with several members of the
council, Lieutenant Colonel Trautman and several other Army
representatives, Norman Cousins of the *Saturday Review of Literature,* and Carl Carmer of the Writers' War Board. The group
met at the Rockefeller Lunch Club in Manhattan, where Taft
spoke for roughly fifteen minutes, explaining that it was not the
intention of Congress, nor was it his purpose, to limit the supply of printed matter to those fighting the war. He expressed
willingness to sponsor amendments to the act that would ame-

liorate the problems that had arisen. In response, the council and its supporters offered the senator three options: repeal, removal of the criminal punishment clause (making violation of the law practically meaningless), or amendment of the law to prohibit only those books that, when considered in their entirety, were obvious political propaganda.

A representative from the Army spoke next on how Title V had hampered the Army's massive program of information and education. To avoid violating the law, the Army had adopted the motto "Leave it out when in doubt." Educational courses were dismantled, and individual books were removed from library shelves. "We believe that the best soldier is an informed soldier," an Army spokesperson said. "We believe that we can fight a better war and end it sooner with men who know what is happening in the world." But the recent limitations on books and educational courses had thwarted the Army's objectives.

Despite his tenaciousness, Senator Taft was in a sensitive political position. He did not want to be seen as supporting censorship of servicemen's reading materials. Nor did he want to be called out for backtracking on his own legislation. Thus, after meeting with the council, Taft issued a statement, reiterating his long-standing belief that "the general principle of prohibiting government funds for political propaganda is admitted by all, but the provisions of the act are somewhat too strict and make administration by the Army too difficult." He openly criticized the Army's interpretation of the law, but conceded that he would sponsor amendments to the act in order to increase its flexibility.

Before Congress took any action, the situation only became worse for Senator Taft. A group of well-respected journalists who covered the July 20 meeting had overheard Taft state that 75 percent of the servicemen would vote for Roosevelt if given a chance, and that he was opposed to soldier voting because those serving overseas "were out of touch with the country, lacking knowledge of issues and candidates, and would quite naturally vote for their Commander-in-Chief." The journalists who heard these comments published them. As word spread, Taft's colleagues began to distance themselves from him. For example, Illinois senator Scott Lucas said: "Senator Taft apparently does not yet realize that this is a global war and that our men fighting and flying all over the world may have a better idea than we at home as to what the true issues for America will be in the 1944 election."

The Army continued to publicize the asinine consequences of Title V. On August 9, news broke that even more censorship was in store for the soldiers when the War Department announced that servicemen were barred from viewing the movie *Wilson,* a biography of the late president, and the film *Heavenly Days,* a comedy about a couple who visit Washington, D.C., starring the popular radio duo Fibber McGee and Molly (a film so anodyne, it has been long forgotten). The War Department also confirmed the rumor that all British newspapers were banned from circulation to American troops because these papers would undoubtedly take sides in the election. Two days later, the Army hammered the final nail into Title V's coffin when it announced that it was forced to prohibit the sale and distribution of the *Official Guide to the Army Air Force* because it contained a picture of President Roosevelt labeled commander in chief. This was an Army that knew how to win wars at home. Congress had little choice but to act immediately.

By August 15, Senator Theodore Green of the Committee on Privileges and Elections submitted a report stating that amendment of Title V was vital because members of the armed services needed access to a variety of reading materials to sustain morale and offset enemy propaganda. According to Green, the law's intent was "not to shut off from members of the Army and Navy the news and information accessible generally to civilians in the United States." In a reference to Senator Taft's fondness for blaming the Army for too strictly interpreting the law, Senator Green said that "the cure for the situation is certainly not to have the services loosely interpret the law"; rather, Congress had an obligation to correct the law itself. Senator Green recommended that Congress eliminate Title V's prohibition on materials containing a reference to politics and amend the law to permit distribution of books, magazines, and newspapers that were generally available on the home front. Under the amended law, the only acceptable limitation on the distribution of reading materials would be if "difficulties of transportation or other exigencies of war" prevented books from making their way to the various fronts. It wasn't just an amendment, it was a full retreat.

With uncharacteristic speed, the proposed amendment to the Soldier Voting Act was passed unanimously by the Senate on August 15, 1944. The following day, the House approved the amendment and sent the final bill to the White House for the president's signature. By August 24, 1944, the council proudly announced that three of the books that had been previously banned under Title V would be published in ASE format: Catherine Drinker Bowen's *Yankee from Olympus;* Charles A. Beard's *The Republic;* and E. B. White's *One Man's Meat.* The council also printed *Slogum House* and *Strange Fruit,* Bostonians notwithstanding.

The council's victory in the battle over Title V was one of its greatest achievements. By galvanizing the media to report the issue and inspiring Americans to exercise their freedom of speech to criticize a ludicrous law, the nation proved its democratic mettle. In the words of the council's executive director, Archibald Ogden, "it is a refreshing example of democracy in action to bring a complete turn-about in both the Senate and the House within the space of less than two months."

Perhaps the droves of soldiers who voted for Roosevelt in the 1944 election did so because he was the only candidate whose name they could recall and record on their bobtailed ballots. Perhaps the Title V fiasco left such a bitter aftertaste that many Americans were driven to side with Roosevelt rather than censorship-promoting Republicans. Or maybe the nation felt most confident with the man who had led them for twelve years, and the troops supported their commander. Whatever their reasons, in November 1944 voters elected Roosevelt to a fourth term as president by a relatively slim margin of approximately 3 million votes. An estimated 3.4 million votes were cast by absentee ballots under the mechanism provided by the Soldier Voting Act, and that may well have made the difference. When Harvard University issued its 1944 *Alumni Bulletin,* it drily reported: "Franklin D. Roosevelt, Grad. '03–'04 ... No change of address."

NINE

Germany's Surrender and the Godforsaken Islands

There were people who cared for him and people who didn't, and those who didn't hate him were out to get him ... But they couldn't touch him ... because he was Tarzan, Mandrake, Flash Gordon. He was Bill Shakespeare. He was Cain, Ulysses, the Flying Dutchman; he was Lot in Sodom, Deidre of the Sorrows, Sweeney in the nightingales among trees.

— JOSEPH HELLER, *CATCH-22*

A S AMERICANS TAUNTED death and marched toward victory in Europe in 1945, they were carrying tens of thousands of copies of titles that were forbidden in the lands they walked on. Many authors outlawed by Germany made an appearance by way of the ASEs. American servicemen toted Ernest Hemingway's *Selected Short Stories*; Jack London's *Sea-Wolf, White Fang, The Cruise of the Snark*, and *The Call of the Wild*; and Voltaire's *Candide*. Later editions of ASEs included Thomas Mann's *Selected Short Stories*; Stefan Zweig's *The Royal Game*; H. G. Wells's *The Time Machine, The Island of Dr. Moreau, The War of the Worlds*, and *The Food of*

151

the Giants; and Erich Maria Remarque's *The Arch of Triumph*. What weapons could be more fitting for the liberation of a continent than the very books that had been banned and burned there?

But the council did not end its work with the distribution of hundreds of thousands of ASEs in occupied Europe. It also considered what role it might play in the reintroduction of prohibited books in European nations that had been shackled by Nazi restrictions on their printing presses and bookshops. For years, books that fell within Germany's ban were confiscated and destroyed, with no remuneration to publishers or store owners. Bookshelves were emptied of all works deemed antagonistic to Germany. Libraries were purged, and cherished books disappeared. The Nazis seized control of European printing presses and carefully monitored what was being printed. The sale or distribution of books published in the United States and Britain was forbidden. By 1944, an independent publishing industry was practically nonexistent in Europe — or, in the words of the United States Office of War Information (OWI), it was "shot to pieces."

Knowing the emaciated state of European publishing and book buying, the council considered the necessity of printing books for regions that had been deprived of American books since as early as 1939. In 1944, council members Stanley Rinehart of Farrar & Rinehart, William Sloane of Henry Holt & Co., and Marshall Best of the Viking Press had approached the OWI to inquire whether it had any interest in financing a project to translate American books and distribute them in Europe as soon as nations were freed from Nazi control. The OWI was receptive to collaborating with the council on this project, and the council assembled a list of one hundred of its ASE titles that had universal appeal. As the OWI would provide special funding for the creation of these "Overseas Editions" (OEs), the project had to be kept completely separate from the ASEs. Thus, a new branch of the council was formed — the Overseas Editions, Inc. (OEI).

The OEs got off to a bumpy start. First, although the OWI approved the Overseas Editions in theory, it could not guarantee funding, so the project languished for months. When funds became available in August 1944, the project only sank deeper into a logistical morass. Many books needed to be translated into French and Italian — a step in production that proved incredibly time-consuming. Plus, to keep production costs to a minimum, the entire series had to be printed in one fell swoop. Thus, printing could not begin for the entire project until every last translation had been completed. When the manuscripts were finally ready to be printed, another problem arose regarding publication rights: publishers were uncertain whether their contracts with authors included the right to publish books for overseas use. At the eleventh hour, individual contracts were tweaked to account for overseas distribution.

Finally, by February 1945, the first batch of OEs was shipped to Europe. They were compact (measuring four and three-quarters by six and three-eighths inches — about the same size as the larger ASEs) and rather bland-looking, but they nourished a book-starved Europe. The OWI was so pleased with the first batch of OEs that, in March 1945, it requested that the council print additional titles in German, Chinese, and Japanese. Funding problems once again plagued the project, resulting in no Chinese or Japanese translations. In the end, however, a total of seventy-two titles were printed and sold, including twenty-two in English, twenty-two in French, twenty-three in German, and five in Italian. Titles tended to center on an American perspective — Stephen Vincent Benét's *America,* Catherine Drinker

Bowen's *Yankee from Olympus,* and J. C. Furnas's *How America Lives* were among those printed.

A total of 3,636,074 OEs were distributed in France, Belgium, Holland, Norway, Denmark, Romania, Czechoslovakia, Poland, Yugoslavia, Hungary, Italy, North Africa, Syria, Turkey, Austria, and Greece. Although 3.6 million books were a drop in the bucket when compared to the estimated destruction of more than 100 million books in Europe by the Nazis, the production of the OEs at least began the reintroduction of American books in countries that had been deprived of them for years.

It was not only the nations that fell under Nazi rule that reeled from a lack of books. Britain's publishing industry had been decimated by the war, resulting in book shortages that kept shelves in book stores empty and rendered distribution of free reading material to members of the Royal Army and Navy impossible. Like their Yank counterparts, British soldiers yearned for books. As one U.S. Army lieutenant recalled, when his unit was stationed on a British troop transport and the Americans carried their library onboard — "a crate of ASE's mounted on two oil drums" — the British troops gaped at the books and begged for the privilege of reading them. The lieutenant's unit shared their ASEs, and "many of the English fellows shook their heads and marveled at how well taken care of the American soldier is." Many British soldiers were left wondering: Why didn't their government care for their morale needs by supplying paperback books?

The main culprits were the early bombing of Britain's publishing industry followed by severe paper rationing. The two strangled Britain's printing capacity. Throughout 1940 and 1941, Germany had bombed Britain with abandon; residential neighborhoods, farmland, business districts — no place was immune. When German planes flew over London on December 29, 1940, they released their bomb loads on the warehouses and offices of Britain's publishing companies, which were tucked together, "cheek by jowl, in a small area of the city, with Paternoster Row at its heart." Seventeen firms were completely destroyed. Over one million books served as kindling for flames that stubbornly burned for hours. Overnight, London's book world was obliterated.

Next, paper rationing further constricted publishers, reducing their paper allotment to 37.5 percent of what they had used in 1938. Books grew scarce as demand soared. Bookshops could not keep books in stock. Publishers frantically scrapped traditional layouts, margin sizes, paper weight, typography, and binding: books were reconstructed to require the least amount of materials. Despite these measures, British publishers could not print enough books to sate the public's hunger. The reason the Royal Army and Navy lacked books was because there simply were not enough of them to go around. Although Britain organized a book drive similar to the VBC, it collected an inadequate quantity of clunky hardcovers that were unsuitable for overseas service.

The ASEs left a deep impression on the British servicemen who encountered them. One member of the Royal Air Force reported that the best stint of his lengthy military service occurred when he was stationed with an American fighting squadron. Each evening, he would "stroll into the mess, have a delicious chat or two, . . . and, of course, come away with one or two . . . 'super' Service editions in my pocket, pressed upon me by one or three of my American friends with the exhortation to pass it on to the 'Boys' when I had finished." The ASEs were one of the only things that had given his unit "many hours of deep satisfaction and cheer," he said. He marveled at the council's "superb piece of printing and distribution work; a thing, which, so far as I have seen since being overseas for nearly three years, doesn't exist . . . from our own side."

Hospitals that cared for American and British soldiers were hotbeds of ASE generosity. One wounded British soldier recalled suffering from depression and uncertainty as he convalesced in a Burmese field hospital. "Humour was always at a premium in those gloomy days," he said. Several injured Merrill's Marauders (a U.S. Army special operations unit) in his ward, taking note of his dour spirit, passed Max Schulman's *The Feather Merchants* down to his bed and urged him to read it. This book's protagonist returns to the home front, expecting a hero's welcome, only to be driven home on black-market gasoline and treated to a meal of hoarded foods. Even worse, his desk job did not make him a "real hero" in the eyes of his girlfriend. The book tells a hilarious story of everything going wrong. The British soldier could not help but chuckle and smile as he read it.

British soldiers were desperate for ASEs, and British publishing firms heard an earful about how popular the Americans' little paperbacks were. Already struggling to produce large numbers of books, publishers found the idea of printing miniature books like the ASEs irresistible. They would not be distributed free to British fighting forces, but in 1945, British publishers began *selling* paperback books that bore an uncanny resemblance to the ASE format. Costing as little as twopence, Bear, Hudson, Ltd., of London published Bear Pocket Books, and the W. H. Allen Company of London printed Allen Super Hurricanes. At a glance, the Bears and Hurricanes could easily be mistaken for ASEs — they were the same size, their front covers had a thumbnail image of the original cover design, they were bound by staples, their interior pages had two columns of text, and they were printed on lightweight paper. While the Bear Pocket Books were geared toward the British public, and their miniature size was attributed to rationing and supply shortages, the Hurricanes advertised their suitability for "those in the services — because they are well produced, handy in size," and were "designed with the object of fitting the reader's pocket — in two senses." The council was gratified that its model had helped the floundering British book trade get back on its feet. Paper rationing in Britain would not be lifted until 1949.

During the spring of 1945, the Allies crept closer to Berlin and spirits soared on the home front as victory in Europe seemed a certainty. But on April 12, 1945, Franklin Delano Roosevelt died after a severe decline in health, which had been largely kept from public knowledge. This loss was felt around the world. As Corporal Frank Slechta, an armorer with the Eighth Air Force, said, "It wasn't like just another politician dying; it was like losing a friend." "We've lost a great leader," seconded Corporal Louis F. Schier, of an armored field artillery unit, "and I know what that is from combat." He explained: "When I was in France, there was a major in charge of the task force that we all respected and followed. I was just a hundred yards away from him when he was killed by a machine-pistol, and after that it was pretty tough getting ourselves together. It's the same case with FDR." Private Morris Kravitz, a rifleman with the Twenty-Eighth Division, said: "I've seen men die at the front, and it just didn't affect me like this." As they mourned, the tragedy inspired a sense of resilience and purpose. In the words of First Lieutenant Walter J. Hinton, "I suppose the Nazis were glad to hear of his death, but we will fight all the harder to show them how we feel about it."

On the heels of FDR's death came the news that Joseph Goebbels and Adolf Hitler had committed suicide. Despite the collapse of its leadership and the destruction of its cities by intense Allied bombings, Germany's soldiers continued fighting. It took days before President Harry S. Truman was able to announce, on May 8, 1945, that Germany had officially surrendered and the "flags of freedom fly all over Europe." But he reminded Americans that the victory was only half won, for while the "West is free . . . the East is still in bondage to the treacherous tyranny of the Japanese."

While it might seem obvious that the Allied soldiers in Europe would be shipped to the Pacific when Germany surrendered, many Americans who served in Europe operated under the illusion that they would be discharged upon V-E Day. Publications such as *Yank, the Army Weekly* had published stories throughout 1944 discussing the Army and Navy's post-victory demobilization plans. These articles created the false hope of an imminent homecoming. The harsh reality was that much of the Army in Europe would return home only after paying the Japanese a visit. Instead of demobilization, the armed forces in Europe faced redeployment.

On May 10, the Army announced that, of its 3.5 million men in Europe, 3.1 million were destined for the Pacific, and the remaining 400,000 would stay in Europe as reoccupation forces. Only a minority of those in the Army would be discharged. The Navy announced that it expected virtually no reduction of forces. As an Army spokesperson explained, to discharge those who fought in Europe rather than redeploy them to the Pacific would be like fighting with one hand. To defeat Japan, the Allies would need to unleash their full force on the Pacific to issue a final, decisive blow.

The Army and Navy tried to soften the news of redeployment by offering rest periods in the Pacific or furloughs in the

United States between engagements, but these promises had little impact on the bitter feelings many servicemen harbored. As Private First Class Justin Gray explained in *Yank:* "Relief periods in the Pacific have meant little more than being stuck on some God-forsaken island far from anything that resembles Western civilization." In fact, he knew of one unlucky unit that was sent to a "rest camp" only to find themselves "in coconut groves, [with] tents and lumber" and orders to build the rest area. They did not complete construction before being called back to the front. "Just like that old favorite of ours, 'Sad Sack,' we'll just wait for rest until we get back to our foxholes," a sergeant griped. The home front shared a gloomy outlook on redeployment. "Those who are to be shipped directly to the Pacific will not relish the thought," one newspaper explained. "They have fought one war; they think their job is done." Servicemen who were permitted to return home before being redeployed fared no better. They would enjoy a happy homecoming only to be wrested from their families two or three weeks later so they could serve another tour of duty. Besides, having cheated death once in Europe, many lost hope of being lucky enough to do it again, especially in the Pacific.

Reading of island warfare in their newspapers and magazines, soldiers in Europe were well aware of the notorious reputation of the Pacific battles. As the Allies' island-hopping campaign drew closer to Japan, the fighting seemed to only grow more intense. Preferring death to surrender, Japanese soldiers fought to the last man. This prolonged even the most futile battles and sent casualty rates skyward. The fight for Iwo Jima, which ended just before Germany's surrender, was described as the bitterest battle in Marine Corps history, and co-commander Lieutenant General Holland M. Smith said that never in the 168 years' history of the Marines had their motto, *Semper Fidelis* (always faithful), "been tried or challenged so greatly." It was the only Marine battle in which American casualties exceeded Japan's. As redeployment loomed, the fight for Okinawa raged. Engaged in "hand-to-hand fighting, blasting the Japanese out of caves with grenades or burning them out with flame-throwers," the "going was tough and slow," the *New York Times* reported. While Americans adopted rhyming mantras for when they expected to return home, those who served in the Pacific kept pushing the date back. "Home alive in '45" turned into "Out of the sticks in '46," and then to "Hell to Heaven in '47," only to be followed by "Golden Gate in '48." Others were not hopeful that they would ever return home.

Although morale was severely challenged in the island battles, the Pacific theater, especially in the later years of the war, was not devoid of amusements for those out of the line of fire. Few newspapers and magazines gave credit to the important work done by the Special Services Division on behalf of the servicemen deployed in these remote regions. Once an area was secured, servicemen were given wide latitude to Americanize the islands to the extent possible. They built baseball diamonds "set in jungle glades to the specifications of Abner Doubleday," and signs were posted next to ponds or lakes used for swimming, reading "Jones Beach," or "Old Swimmin' Hole." By 1944, Guadalcanal was unrecognizable to those who had landed there in 1942: vegetables grew on former battlefields, an ice-cream factory churned out two hundred quarts of ice cream a day, hundreds of musical instruments were available for playing, 150 movie theaters (consisting of "coconut logs or oil drums in front of an outdoor screen") showed C-grade films, and athletic venues hosted boxing matches and other sports contests. Across the Mariana Islands, theater stages were built, volleyball and basketball courts were erected, boxing rings were installed, and thousands of radios were distributed.

But radio was a double-edged sword. It allowed the men to listen to their favorite music and hear the news, but just as Europe had Axis Sally, the Pacific had its own favorite propagandist: Tokyo Rose, a persona attributed to Iva Toguri, an American citizen living in Japan. Rose's broadcasts were rarely of the caliber of Axis Sally's hauntingly accurate and unsettling pronouncements, but she had her moments. She always seemed to have credible information on American casualties, and her manner of delivering this news was cruel. "Well, you boys in Moresby, how did you like that ack-ack last night over Rabaul?" she asked during one broadcast. "Your communiqué didn't say anything about losing those two Fortresses, did it? But you fellows know, don't you? You know what did not come back," she taunted.

Regardless of whether men were stationed on secured islands or were fighting for the next one, they all turned to books and magazines. Even on the remotest islands men could rely on receiving their reading ration. War correspondents who reported on the Pacific theater were often amazed at how zealously men read. "In these South Sea isles and waters, known principally to Americans from the books of Melville and Stevenson, it seems fitting that reading is the universal pastime of all the services," Major Frederick Simpich Jr. reported in an article for *National Geographic*. "What they read and how much is limited only by the pile of books and magazines available," he said. Stranded on an island with little to do, men who had avoided reading as civilians found themselves poring over anything they could get their hands on. When one dubious Marine was given Herman Melville's *Typee,* he reluctantly started reading it out of sheer boredom. Once he started, he was hooked.

His review: "Hot stuff. That guy wrote about three islands I'd been on!"

As disgruntlement over redeployment spread throughout the services, the Army and Navy turned to the council for help. They faced a morale crisis of serious proportions, and there was only one surefire way of dealing with it: books.

In 1945, Lieutenant Colonel Trautman attended the council's annual meeting and stressed just how badly more books were needed. Though thankful for the council's increase in ASE output over the prior year—from twenty million to fifty million volumes—Trautman insisted that there still were not enough. "There should have been 5 times as many to really go around," he said. "When a soldier with a monthly pay of $55 is willing to pay 500 francs or 10 American dollars for the privilege of being next in line to read a particular Council Book they are pretty scarce."

To make his point, Trautman described his experiences in Europe. One thing that impressed him was how quickly the ASEs fell apart under combat conditions. "A man reads a book to death very quickly while standing in the rain or snow without any shelter to keep the pages dry." When there were more men than ASEs, it was "not unusual for a man to tear off the portion of a book he had finished to give it to the next man who doesn't have a book to read saying—'I'll save my pages for you.'" Trautman had intended to bring examples of books in "a state of combat exhaustion" to show to the council, but the servicemen had resisted. "'You wouldn't take our books away, would you? We can still read them,'" the men had said to Trautman. "So I haven't any examples of book casualties to show you," Trautman unapologetically remarked to council members.

During his tour of the European theater, Trautman saw the

ASEs everywhere. On Christmas Day at a Belgian hospital, he spotted an ASE on the floor of the operating room — it had blood on the cover and red smudges on nearly every page for two-thirds of the book. On a visit to a platoon of combat engineers who had gotten separated from the rest of their company, Trautman noticed a pile of about ten ASEs; they were all the books the unit had. They were considered so precious that the platoon commander had ordered the men to read in groups to reduce the wear and tear of multiple handlings. In Nazi prison camps, Trautman watched as ASEs were distributed through the International YMCA; they were one of the most important items in making life bearable for prisoners, he said. While on a tour through Holland, Trautman discussed how he cautiously parked his vehicle near a military police station for safekeeping. Overnight, his car was burglarized anyway. Of all the valuables inside, the only thing that had been taken was a carton of thirty-two ASEs. Although it seemed that the books had reached units in every cranny of the world, and were treasured by the men who read them, Trautman said there was one resounding complaint: "There just aren't enough of them."

Joining Trautman's plea for more books were the soldiers stationed in the Pacific. For example, a member of the United States Infantry wrote the council in May 1945, stating that the ASEs had provided "many hours of precious relaxation not easily obtainable by servicemen stranded in a foreign country with a military unit." At the time he wrote, he was "enjoying somewhat of a respite before once again plunging into the routine of war." But "off-duty pleasures remain pretty much a personal problem with the individual soldier," he said. Under the circumstances, the men hungered for books and other reading materials. "Our appetite is unquenchable," he declared. "Our recreational problem is at present extraordinary," and if the council saw fit "to answer this request with a supply of books, I promise you they will be distributed equitably throughout the company, in whose behalf I am writing."

Another source of pressure for more books was the Special Services Division. Burdened with the responsibility of providing morale-boosting reading material to Americans stationed around the world, Special Services officers feared they would not be able to meet the demand for books as servicemen faced redeployment. At a 1945 meeting of two hundred Special Services officers, it was estimated that more books were needed to the scale of one new book per man per month in combat areas. In the words of General Joseph Byron, who headed the division, ASEs were "*the* most important morale work done by the Special Services Division." One Special Services officer who had worked with combat troops for over two years grew so worried about the men he supplied that he wrote the council begging for more books. He insisted there just "never seems to be enough," and that combat troops were "STARVED" for titles by Thorne Smith, Ernest Hemingway, John Steinbeck, H. Allen Smith, Tiffany Thayer, Sinclair Lewis, and Lloyd Douglas. The men also never stopped asking for *A Tree Grows in Brooklyn, Chicken Every Sunday, Forever Amber,* and *Strange Fruit.*

Even letters from servicemen's family members emphasized that troops in the Pacific needed books more than ever. In one particularly frank letter, a woman pleaded with the council to help her brother and his entire unit; their sanity hung in the balance. Her brother and his Marine battalion had just finished some very tough fighting and a recent letter from him stressed how desperate they were for good books. "You see," she said, "my kid brother has been fighting for 14 mos . . . and right now things are quieting down for them." But, "they had just received the bad news that they must spend 24 to 30 mos. in [the Pacific] before they can be replaced and it seems as though the boys are pretty depressed and clamoring for some good reading matter." She closed: "P.S. If you make it a practice to send out different books at regular intervals, please keep these fellows on the mailing list. These 'Leathernecks' are fighting not only Japs, but the elements and disease and believe me, if they don't get something to take their minds off their surroundings, they'll most surely crack up."

In early 1945 Philip Van Doren Stern met with Army officers to brainstorm. How could more books be produced? Stern reported back to the council that the Army was considering asking the War Production Board to compel printers to manufacture ASEs. While the government was contractually obligated to supply the council with paper for ASEs, when Stern learned of an opportunity to buy 141 tons of paper outside the amount provided by the government, the executive committee authorized Stern to make the purchase. The U.S. Army and Special Services Division also worked to drum up resources to ensure that the maximum number of books could be produced.

Despite these efforts, there was one missing ingredient to bolster production: money. In May 1945, Lieutenant Colonel Trautman reported that the Army had no funds to pay for any additional production costs for council books; the only way to print more ASEs would be to somehow reduce the cost of each book. "If enough funds were available," Trautman told the council's executive board, "the Army could increase their order for ASE books by about one third or approximately 160,000 to 175,000 books" per month. But Trautman was out of ideas on how to secure the funding he needed. After he left the meeting, the executive board had a discussion about trimming all waste from the production cost, including the controversial one-cent royalty factored into the price of each ASE. From the beginning, some authors and publishing companies opposed receiving any royalty from the ASEs, but the council insisted on keeping its contracts uniform, binding all authors and publishing companies to identical terms to avoid drafting hundreds of individual contracts tailored to the whims and preferences of each party. Now, with the need for ASEs greater than ever, the council reversed itself, reasoning that the benefits flowing from the elimination of the royalty outweighed the need for uniform contracts. Authors and publishing companies would be given the option of waiving the one-cent royalty.

There was an additional supply-side problem, however. The council's editorial committee complained to Philip Van Doren Stern that they were "scraping the bottom of the barrel to secure new titles." They wanted to reduce the number of books in each series — from forty to twenty-eight — to avoid recommending lackluster titles. Although Stern opposed this idea, he was sympathetic to the committee's dilemma. Because of the war, the number of titles being published for the civilian market each year had dwindled. In 1942 there was a 10 percent decline when compared to 1941, and the number continued to fall each ensuing year. At the same time, the number of manuscripts submitted to publishing companies drastically fell. Many established and aspiring authors had joined the services or devoted themselves to war work — they were not writing books. As one newspaper remarked, "even if the adage about the comparative mights of pen and sword is still true, the draft boards find nothing about it in their rules of procedure."

Ultimately, Stern offered a compromise. At an executive committee meeting, he proposed that the council increase the number of reprints each month. The committee endorsed Stern's plan — it was recommended that twenty-eight of each month's titles be new (meaning, never before printed as ASEs);

the remaining titles could be composed of reprints or "made" books (the latter referred to council compilations of stories, radio scripts, poems, and the like). In the end, ninety-nine titles were reprinted and seventy-three books were made, which helped alleviate the burden on the editorial committee. Examples of the council's made books include *The New Yorker Reporter at Large, Five Western Stories, The Dunwich Horror and Other Weird Tales, Love Poems,* Eugene O'Neill's *Selected Plays,* and Edna St. Vincent Millay's *Lyrics and Sonnets.*

Even while fighting his frontline battles with economics and supply and demand, Stern faced a rearguard action with one formidable ally: Isabel DuBois, the head of the Library Section of the Navy. Just as with the VBC, DuBois had strong opinions about the council's work and never restrained herself from voicing them. Throughout June 1945, she penned countless letters to "My dear Mr. Stern," grumbling about various mundane issues with the ASEs. She loathed titles that began with the word "Selected," that is, " 'Selected Short Stories of _____,' or 'Selected Poems of _____.' " She thought they sounded dull. DuBois also complained about the T-series of ASEs because "not any of them have the staples through the covers"; they were glued together. In private memoranda, council members grew increasingly annoyed with DuBois. As one publisher said, she had an amazing penchant for making "a huge issue of a triviality which no one else ever troubled about."

Stern, whose greatest virtue must have been patience, responded to each of DuBois's concerns. DuBois was assured that the council would try to avoid "selected" titles in later editions. In the matter of staples versus glue, Stern explained to DuBois that, in the beginning, when there were print runs of only 50,000 copies of each book, stapling the books was possible. However, as the project ballooned to print runs of 155,000, printers had become overly burdened, and adding staples had become an impossibility. Stern added that the council had "not received one single complaint from overseas after the distribution of more than fifty million books," which suggested "the water-proof glued on covers must be working satisfactorily." Stern's boldness was a tactical mistake. DuBois made sure to get in the last word. She clarified that her prior letter "should be taken as a complaint," and she believed ASE covers *were* prone to becoming detached and "steps should be taken to make the covers . . . more secure."

Even the council's printers seemed to resent working with the Navy. When the council was forced to change the packaging for the ASEs out of necessity, some naval inspectors threw a fit and took out their frustration on the printing companies that delivered these packages. The situation grew so heated at the Street & Smith printing firm that its manager threatened to "no longer print any books for the Navy because of the general attitude" of one cantankerous inspector. The council had to intervene to pacify all parties involved. Through the professionalism of Stern, these headaches and complaints never slowed the production of the ASEs.

As the council intensified its efforts to print books for the Pacific, its ASEs in Europe continued to make an impact. In the summer and fall of 1945, preparations were made for the prosecution of dozens of Nazi Germany's most prominent political and military leaders at Nuremberg. They were charged with conspiring against peace, planning and waging a war of aggression, and committing war crimes and crimes against humanity. The men charged included Hermann Göring, a senior Nazi official, and Joachim von Ribbentrop, Nazi Germany's minister of foreign affairs.

After spending several weeks interrogating war criminals with a copy of Henry Hough's *Country Editor* tucked in his pocket, one major, who was a veteran of both world wars, finally had a chance to write to Hough in September 1945. Whenever he had a chance, he would read a few pages about Hough's life as an editor and contributor to a small newspaper on Martha's Vineyard. He cherished every page. "When one is far from home and from a past which treasured a boyhood in an old Massachusetts town, the years roll back easily and a mere closing of the eyes brings it all near again." He especially appreciated being reminded of simpler times, considering the historic task he had just completed.

> Just two weeks ago at Nuremberg where I was interrogating some of those men who brought suffering to millions of innocent people, von Ribbentrop asked if I were finished with it. Those men are reading books of this type given them by the Red Cross. I wish every one of them there could read *Country Editor*. It tells more eloquently than a recitation of America's strength and greatness — the simple formula that has made us the envied nation of the whole world. The obese and irritable man next door in a plain cell room in marked contrast to his former homes was reading the Bible. Because Göring wears glasses, a guard was in his cell to take them from him when he finished reading.

Reflecting on his war experiences and then Nuremberg, this major found himself pondering the question "What makes America great?" He gave his answer to Hough: it was "because there are the people such as you write about in the *Country Editor.*"

TEN

Peace at Last

My old division was one of several whose only rest seemed to come when they were waiting for boats to carry them to other lands where the language was different but the war was the same. These amphibious creatures have seen so much action that when they land back in the States they will, just from force of habit, come off shooting and establish a beachhead around Coney Island. There they will probably dig in and fight until demobilization thins their ranks and allows the local partisans to push the survivors back into the sea.

— BILL MAULDIN

WITH ONE FRONT collapsed, and the full strength of the Allies bearing down on Japan, those serving in the armed forces began to think about their futures. Over time, the war had stolen from them the details of what home was like, and some men wondered whether it would measure up to the ideals they had projected onto it. As one serviceman explained: "Home had faded from us. Home had become an irreality, a blurred recollection where the names, the faces and voices of all but the closest and dearest ones were lost. They were forced from us by the guns, the planes, the mines and bombs." The one place that should have felt familiar did not. Where would they live after the war? What would home be like? Would it be difficult to become a civilian again?

Finding a job was a major concern. When they had joined the Army or Navy, the economy still had not fully recovered from the Great Depression. As late as 1940, unemployment lingered at an estimated 15 percent. Plus, during the war, women and minorities had entered the workforce, taking jobs that were traditionally filled by white men. There was concern that if these new workers remained employed, there would be few jobs for returning veterans. Some soldiers also wondered whether they could find employment that utilized the skills they had developed while at war. In the course of training, many servicemen enrolled in educational courses and spent long hours studying mathematics, science, and technical books to pass examinations and climb the ranks. They did not want this knowledge to go to waste.

The council began to include in each monthly ASE series practical nonfiction for those mulling over their futures. Several titles that were selected for this purpose were ultimately published after the war ended. Darrel and Frances Huff's *Twenty Careers of Tomorrow* discussed how the war affected employment, and provided information about a range of occupations — including working in plastics, fabrics, recycling, aviation, refrigeration, publishing, television and radio, education, medicine, market research, and the automobile industry. Another useful title printed at the behest of the Army was *You and Your Future Job,* by William G. Campbell and James H. Bedford. This book provided information on how to choose a vocation, with specific advice for those who had become disabled during the war, people who were over forty years of age, and women. For those looking for pointers on how to make money no matter what profession they chose, there was John Wharton's *The Theory and Practice of Earning a Living.*

Almost every soldier on the frontlines was aware of life-saving advances made in the field of medicine. Sulfanilamide, a substance that could be sprinkled on wounds and consumed to ward off infection, was carried by every man. Stories abounded of gravely wounded men who were saved because they used their "sulfa." ASEs such as *The Story of Penicillin, Miracles of Military Medicine,* and *Burma Surgeon* inspired some men to think about a medical career.

Others dreamed of joining the legal profession. Arthur Train's ASEs about the fictitious lawyer Ephraim Tutt — who was forever rescuing clients from the clutches of a legal conundrum through some novel scheme — inspired many servicemen to go to law school. Still others decided to practice law after reading Bellamy Partridge's *Country Lawyer,* which romanticized the small-town law practice of a likable attorney. For those who wanted to fight crime rather than prosecute or defend criminals, John Floherty's *Inside the FBI* was a book worth tracking down.

Men who studied science and math (such as assault engineers) might enjoy *A Treasury of Science, Science Remakes the World, This Chemical Age,* and *Mathematics and the Imagination,* to name a few. Those who felt an entrepreneurial spirit and dreamed of opening a business might consult *A Small Store & Independence: A Guide to Retailing.* For those interested in making a living through agriculture, M. G. Kains's *Five Acres and Independence: Selecting and Managing the Small Farm* was indispensable, as it provided advice ranging from how to select fertile land to the nuances of keeping honeybees. Meyer Berger's story of a New York correspondent in *The Eight Million,* Ernie Pyle's books describing his experiences as a war correspondent, and Oliver Gramling's *AP: The Story of News* were just a few of the titles that appealed to men who were considering careers in journalism.

It is no exaggeration to say that the ASEs helped create an entire new cohort of readers. The flip side of a new universe of readers, however, is that almost everyone thinks he can be a writer. Ironically, council publishers were soon besieged with book proposals as countless men expressed a desire to publish their war stories. One such man, a private in the Army, wrote a colorful letter brimming with enthusiasm to publish a book about his experiences as an infantryman. He described his life on the front as a tumult of "death, plus rain, bugs, flies, mud, and mosquitoes," and joked that his line of work (running a women's millinery store in Connecticut) had not prepared him for life in artillery. But he insisted that there was a humor and beauty to the hardships he faced, even in the monotony of digging his 1,054th foxhole (from which he claimed to be writing). Inspired by the ASEs he read by Ernie Pyle, this private hoped to write about his experiences in "a Pyle-ish manner": "descriptive, frank and human, seasoned with a bit of sympathy and emotion and flavored with humanity." With his "writing pad soaking wet," he wrote his letter on sheets cut from a paper bag; he had to "steam" his package of envelopes in order to dry one enough to mail his letter. "War is hell, isn't it?" he stated.

The summer of 1945 brought "the most intensive bombardment campaign in the history of war." With complete devotion to destroying a single enemy, the Allies delivered blow after blow to Japan's navy and its cities. The Allied bases secured in Guam, Saipan, and the Mariana Islands, could now be used to full advantage. As many as eight hundred to a thousand B-29s stood ready from the Marianas alone. Despite the destruction that rained down from these airplanes (as of June 1945, it was estimated that 50 percent of Tokyo had been destroyed, and many of Japan's industrial centers had been neutralized by Allied bombs), a significant portion of Japan's war industry remained unscathed.

In addition to bombs, America's B-29s daily dropped 750,000 pamphlets on Japanese cities, urging an end to the conflict and Japan's unconditional surrender. Premier Kantaro Suzuki defiantly declared in early June that the Japanese would fight to the finish and confidently predicted that Japan "will smash the enemy in a decisive battle on our homeland, which will be quite different from battles on islands." Yet on June 9, Japan's grip on the Philippines was all but lost, and the Philippine Congress met for its first session since 1941.

In the end, Okinawa was the last major battle in the Pacific war. Although plans to invade the Japanese mainland were already in place, and Marine units were preparing for what would surely be a deadly fight, on August 6, 1945, an American B-29 closed in on Hiroshima, an important Japanese port and military center, and dropped a four-hundred-pound atomic bomb. Unprepared for the power of this new weapon, members of the B-29 crew could hardly believe what fury it unleashed. One recalled: "There was a terrific flash of light, even in the daytime . . . a couple of sharp slaps against the airplane," and then white smoke billowed into a mushroom-shaped cloud that rose twenty thousand feet. Four square miles, or 60 percent of the city, were completely leveled; houses and other buildings outside this radius were damaged beyond repair.

Shortly after the bombing of Hiroshima, President Truman warned that if Japanese leaders did not immediately accept the Allies' terms of surrender, "they may expect a rain of ruin from the air, the like of which has never been seen on this earth." Yet Japan remained undeterred. Its official news agency, Dōmei, beamed a radio transmission to the United States stating that America's "desire for an early conclusion of the present war of Greater East [A]sia is mere wishful thinking." Seventy-five hours after chaos poured down on Hiroshima, a second atomic bomb was dropped. This weapon wholly destroyed 30 percent of Nagasaki and left large swaths of the city in ruins. On August 10, President Truman again warned Japan that unless it surrendered, "we shall use the atomic bomb . . . relentlessly" and "bombs will have to be dropped on war industries and, unfortunately, thousands of civilian lives will be lost." After waiting for five agonizing days, an official announcement was made at 7:03 p.m. (Eastern Standard Time) on August 14 that Japan had unconditionally surrendered. At long last, the war was over. V-J Day had arrived.

Around the world, celebrations erupted. In New York City, signs in Times Square advertised the news, and a "victory roar" swelled and continued for over twenty minutes as emotions exploded "with atomic force." According to the *New York Times,* "Restraint was thrown to the winds. Those in the crowds in the streets tossed hats, boxes, and flags into the air. From those leaning perilously out of the windows of office buildings and hotels came a shower of paper, confetti, streamers. Men and women embraced — there were no strangers." In London, American and British soldiers formed a conga line that snaked through the city; they grabbed a partner and danced and celebrated for hours. In Paris, soldiers and WACs ran into the streets, shaking hands with the French and forming an impromptu parade down the Champs Élysées. A truck driver caught in the ruckus was out to deliver the Army newspaper *Stars and Stripes*—the headline read "Stimson Says He'll Recheck to See if Army Can Be Cut." "He goddam well better," the driver bellowed. A war correspondent in Berlin reported that the GIs there were jubilant as peace in the Pacific would save them from more fighting and might speed demobilization. The GIs in Okinawa, who had believed it would be years before they made it home, "slapped each others backs, danced, cheered and shouted: 'To hell with Golden Gate by '48, we'll be home by September 8.'" In Tinian, where B-29 pilots were being briefed for their thirty-fifth mission—their last one before going home—a group leader interrupted to inform the men that their mission had been canceled. Pure and unadulterated joy swelled as the three hundred men who were about to risk their lives in a difficult daylight mission stood down. In Guam, the news prompted shouting and the shooting of all manner of weapons into the air in celebration; bottles of whiskey that had been squirreled away in hiding places were passed around as the men toasted peace. Back in Hawaii, where the first bombs dropped on the United States had claimed thousands of young lives, pedestrians on the ground tipped their hats as low-flying B-29s passed overhead. It was finally over. On September 2, 1945, Japan signed official documents of surrender aboard the USS *Missouri*.

The council, like so many other wartime organizations, began to wind down. At an August 1945 executive committee meeting, some members urged that the association immediately dissolve; others felt that there would be a continued need for ASEs during demobilization and that the council should continue its work for a brief period. The Army estimated that demobilization of an anticipated six million men would not be completed until July 1, 1946, or later. In addition, it announced that occupation forces were needed to the tune of five hundred thousand men in Europe, nine hundred thousand in the Pacific, and another six hundred thousand for overseeing the first year of peace. The council and War Department settled on the view that there remained a need for ASEs. Production of the books continued through the first half of 1946 at a rate of 110,000 copies of each title; beginning in June 1946, the project was scaled back to 80,000 copies of each title per month.

Many publishers expressed relief that the council would not yet disband, and hoped to continue the collaborative effort in some new fashion. As William W. Norton said at one council meeting, "it would be short sighted to dissolve so successful a cooperative enterprise of the publishing industry." Norton even endorsed the idea of creating a "larger peacetime book organization [for] which the Council could be instrumental in laying the groundwork."

In December 1945, Philip Van Doren Stern left his post as manager of the ASEs and returned to full-time work at Pocket Books. He was succeeded by Stahley Thompson, who helped design the ASEs at the outset of the project and had just returned to the United States after completing a term of military service with *Yank*. Up to this time, the council had generally expected that its ASE branch would be liquidated in the summer of 1946, since the last contract between the council and the government provided that the printing of ASEs would not continue for more than one year after hostilities had ceased. However, Paul E. Postell, who had succeeded Lieutenant Colonel Trautman as chief of the Army's Library Section, believed that the half million or more occupation troops who would remain overseas after the summer of 1946 would still need books. These men would largely serve in isolated constabulary units, which could not be easily served through regular library service.

Thompson, fresh from a stint of service overseas, insisted there was still an unsated hunger for reading materials. The war might have ended, but the need for pocket-sized paperbacks had not. The Army and Navy hoped that the council would continue its work a little longer.

But as the size of the Army and Navy dramatically decreased, orders for new books also fell. In December 1945, the Army estimated that its monthly book needs would consist of a maximum of twenty thousand sets of twelve or fifteen books each, and the Navy hoped to secure approximately five thousand sets. This precipitous reduction in the scope of the project (to about 15 percent of the amount demanded at the height of ASE production) created problems. Fewer books meant higher prices. The council debated whether the War Department should simply purchase domestic editions of paperback books, as Pocket Books and other publishers sold paperbacks for as little as twenty-five cents. But they were still too expensive compared to ASEs, which cost as little as five cents apiece. Negotiations between Postell, Thompson, and the ASE management continued during the early months of 1946, with Thompson proposing a number of ideas on how to reduce costs. In the end, by adopting the methods used by Pocket Books and lowering production expenses by utilizing modern printing technology, the council was able to print runs of twenty-five thousand books that cost eighteen cents apiece. The council entered a contract with the Army and Navy to print series II through TT, for distribution from October 1946 through September 1947. Using the J. W. Clement Company of Buffalo for the printing, ASEs continued to be churned out at the pace of twelve titles per month, or about three hundred thousand books.

Unlike the earlier series, the ASEs in series II to TT took on the appearance of ordinary paperback books — they were bound on their long edge and were thus taller than they were wide. Rather than two columns of text per page, they had a single column. No longer were there two sizes of ASEs; the new upright-format books were all four and a quarter by six and a half inches. However, some features remained the same. The cover of each ASE continued to display a thumbnail image of the dust jacket from the hardcover edition, the back cover provided a short summary of the book, and the inside back cover listed the titles printed for the servicemen that month.

Midway through the contract for series II to TT, the Army informed the council that its budget had been cut and that it could no longer pay for the ASEs it had ordered. The Navy also faced a lack of funding for ASEs. Both services insisted they wanted the books they had contracted to buy, but payment was a financial impossibility. At a special meeting of the council's directors held in January 1947, Malcolm Johnson, the man who had first proposed the creation of the ASEs, suggested that the council examine its finances and determine if the books could still be printed. After discovering a surplus of funds, Johnson suggested that the council enter a new contract with the Army and Navy to print books through September 1947 by expending this surplus. The directors passed a resolution: the Army and Navy would each remit payment of one dollar in exchange for the council's production of series NN through TT — a total of 1.5 million ASEs. The council would cover the rest.

The ASE program finally came to an end in September 1947, when the final batch of ASEs was delivered to the Army and Navy. Among these titles were Max Brand's *The False Rider* (a western), Bob Feller's *Strikeout Story* (an autobiography), Thomas B. Costain's *The Moneyman* (historical fiction), Budd Schulberg's *The Harder They Fall* (a boxing novel), and Craig

Rice's *Los Angeles Murders* (a mystery). The last ASE to be printed was Ernie Pyle's *Home Country,* a nod to America's favorite war correspondent, who was killed by a Japanese sniper in the Pacific.

As it wound down its affairs, the council received a flood of mail from servicemen who realized how much they would miss their monthly book ration. In the words of one captain, the ASEs "followed me through combat and now in the occupation phase. Needless to say, they have been a tremendous morale factor." "I treasure them to such an extent," he said, "that I should like to have them in my home in the future months when I return." The council responded that production had ended; there would be no new titles and all books had been distributed. But the ASEs continued on anyway. Some servicemen brought a book or two home to keep as war souvenirs or for future reading. Others grabbed a single volume to swap with others for the long ride back to the States. Those who remained overseas as occupation forces hoarded small collections of ASEs for their leisure hours. Some ASEs made their way into overseas military libraries — with call numbers added to their spines and circulation tabs kept on them. Some even survived long enough to serve the men who fought in America's "forgotten war," Korea. Although new ASEs would not be printed, the profound impact they made on all those fortunate enough to experience them did not fade. As millions of veterans returned home, many would bring with them a love of reading that they did not have when they first went off to war.

And the government had one more inspired idea by which books would help veterans as they prepared to resume their civilian lives.

ELEVEN

Damned Average Raisers

We have taught our youth how to wage war; we
must also teach them how to live useful and happy
lives in freedom, justice, and decency.

— MESSAGE TO CONGRESS FROM PRESIDENT
ROOSEVELT, 1943

WELL BEFORE THE war ended, the U.S. government contemplated the likely problems that
would arise from mass demobilization. One major concern was employment. It was difficult to comprehend
how there would be enough jobs for the wartime labor force *plus*
the fifteen million men and women (more than one in ten of the
nation's population) who were returning home after completing
their service to the country. Policymakers fretted over the "political consequences of massive unemployment, when hordes of
young men, skilled in firearms, would begin to roam the streets,
angry over their inability to regain a foothold in the civilian
world." Another concern on the home front was that veterans
would return home harboring all manner of psychological issues: 2.5 million individuals had been discharged from military
service on the basis of psychological maladies. Eradicating cases

of soldier maladjustment was deemed a pressing matter of national security. To say the least, it did not do the servicemen any good when they heard that they were being compared to "psycho" killers back home. In the words of one veteran, "This prevailing tendency to regard a man who has been in uniform as a potential criminal lunatic is probably the most depressing phase of a veteran's homecoming and thoughts of home."

The servicemen had their own anxieties. The Army's research branch conducted surveys revealing that many soldiers worried they would have "difficulty in settling down, getting over restlessness, adjusting to a steady job, or getting over the mental effects of the war." Others feared they would not easily adjust to life as a civilian, or that they would feel unfamiliar with their friends and family. Those who well remembered the lasting effects of the Great Depression when they entered military service wondered whether there would be a shortage of jobs when they returned to the States. The research branch learned that some servicemen envisioned "a future of ditch digging and bread lines"; others predicted the nation would fall into another economic depression, and still others imagined an army of eleven million apple salesmen pounding the pavement to make a postwar living.

Concern about how the domestic economy would absorb the incredible influx of veterans had been the source of debate and controversy even before Japan surrendered. A mini scandal erupted over a well-publicized statement by Major General Lewis B. Hershey, the national director of Selective Service, who said in 1944 that it would be "cheaper to keep men in the Army than . . . to set up an agency to take care of them when they are released." Hershey added that the economy might not be able to handle both the eleven million men in the armed services and the seventeen to eighteen million Americans who joined the workforce to serve the war industries. Hershey's statements, which millions of servicemen read in *Yank,* touched a nerve. "This plan would be quite feasible if it concerned a herd of cattle," Sergeant Louis Doyle commented, as cattle "can assuredly be maintained more cheaply as a group than if given a measure of individual, free life . . . I would, however, remind Washington officials that we are human beings, not cattle, and claim a right to return to the society which we are at present bending every effort to maintain." The government rejected Hershey's view; instead, it focused on how it could provide for the diverse needs of the returning servicemen.

President Roosevelt had spurred the New Deal to help America dig itself out of the Great Depression. During the war, he championed legislation to benefit the returning veteran. As early as 1943, Roosevelt called on Congress to draft a bill ensuring that honorably discharged servicemen would return home with the promise that they could attend college and secure vocational training on the government's dime. "During the war we have seen to it that they have received the best training and equipment, the best food, shelter and medical attention, the best protection and care which planning, ingenuity, physical resources and money could furnish in time of war," Roosevelt said in a message to Congress in 1943. Similarly, he believed the nation had an obligation to provide its veterans with the very best training and equipment after the war.

Roosevelt envisioned a law that would provide each man with a handsome sum of mustering-out pay, money that would tide them over as they searched for employment and readjusted to civilian life. Since some members of the armed forces might not immediately find a job, Roosevelt called for unemployment benefits to fill the breach until they could be absorbed by private industry. Some men and women had interrupted their education in order to serve the nation, and President Roosevelt asked Congress to provide veterans with the opportunity to attend college or apply for technical training after their discharge — at the government's cost. And Roosevelt wanted Congress to act without delay. "Nothing," the president said, would be "more conducive to the maintenance of high morale in our troops than the knowledge that steps are being taken now to give them education and technical training when the fighting is over."

At the time President Roosevelt announced these goals, a college education was largely outside the grasp of most working-class families. Placing a college degree within reach of every qualified veteran was extraordinary. In 1940 the average worker earned less than $1,000 each year, and the annual cost of a college education fell anywhere between $453 at state colleges to $979 at private universities. Under Roosevelt's plan, higher education would be doled out irrespective of social class or wealth for the first time in American history. This democratization of education for veterans was a fitting conclusion to a war fought in the name of democracy and freedom.

The American Legion, a veterans' organization, took up the task of drafting a bill that would encompass President Roosevelt's vision. After months of hashing out language, the omnibus veterans' relief bill, which became the Serviceman's Readjustment Act of 1944, was presented to Congress. Believing this title had "all the political sex of a castrated mule," the Legion's publicity director urged calling it simply the "GI Bill of Rights." This catchier name stuck. The GI Bill promised servicemen and servicewomen in the Army and Navy access to counseling, disability and unemployment benefits, low-interest loans for homes and businesses, and two years of college or job training. After the bill was unanimously passed in the House and Senate, President Roosevelt hosted a public ceremony on June 22, 1944, to celebrate his signing it into law. Roosevelt said that the GI Bill gave "emphatic notice to the men and women in our armed forces that the American people do not intend to let them down."

Although politicians believed that veterans would enthusiastically take advantage of the panoply of benefits provided under the GI Bill, the law, at least initially, was grossly underutilized. While officials were relieved that veterans did not need to rely on the full scope of unemployment benefits, they were dismayed at the apparent failure of the GI Bill's education provision. As of February 1, 1945, only 12,844 of the 1.5 million who had been discharged from service — less than 1 percent — sought an education. That Army officials were disappointed was said to be "the understatement of the decade." The *Saturday Evening Post* investigated, concluding that the average soldier "has no patience for books; he is becoming increasingly fed up with regimentation." Men would rather obtain employment than an education, the *Post* said.

The *Post* was wrong. Overseas, men were eager to sign up for a free education, many just did not qualify for one. The most problematic provision of the bill was its age requirement: only those under twenty-five could receive more than one year of education. Many thousands of servicepeople were automatically excluded. "I would rather have had the Bill not passed at all," one man who was over twenty-five years old said. "The smug assurances of our country's generosity constantly dinned into our ears . . . becomes sickening after a time when one realizes the full (and feeble) effects the Bill will have."

The federal government took note of both the sluggish application rate and the complaints about the bill's exclusion of a large number of veterans who wanted an education. In late 1945, with the war finally over, Congress enhanced the law significantly. The maximum length of government-paid study increased from two to four years, restrictions that hampered the ease with which GIs could qualify for an education were dropped, and subsistence allowances were increased to help pay for expenses incurred outside of college tuition — such as groceries, rent, and books. Gone was the twenty-five-year-old age limitation that had excluded older veterans. Also, men were given more time to begin and complete their education; before the amendments, there was a seven-year window to finish one's schooling, but after the amendments, this period was extended to nine years. Numerous pamphlets were issued to help publicize, in easy-to-understand terms, what benefits the GIs could expect when they returned home. Every person in the military was given a pocket-sized booklet — similar to the standard ASE — entitled *Going Back to Civilian Life*. It provided information on where veterans could turn for help with personal problems stemming from their separation from military service, and how they could seek reemployment at an old job, obtain new employment, or work for the government. The booklet also provided a general explanation of the GI Bill of Rights, including information on education, unemployment compensation, and veterans' entitlement to a guarantee of loans for a home or business.

Librarians once again rose to action, and domestic libraries entered their own readjustment stage. Just as librarians prepared and educated their patrons as the United States transitioned to a nation at war (helping with everything from what plants would grow best in a local victory garden to assembling reading lists of books that would foster an understanding of why the world was at war), librarians assisted the nation as it demobilized. Many librarians established programs, with the cooperation of the Veterans Administration and the Red Cross, to help veterans learn more about the GI Bill of Rights. Librarians doled out advice about everything from reemployment and vocational rehabilitation to how a veteran could go about obtaining a loan, insurance, or an education. Some libraries secured films on readjustment and hosted movie nights; many libraries created reading lists that highlighted books that might help families deal with the problems demobilization posed. Still other libraries offered counseling services to assist veterans in signing up for the benefits being offered, and apprising them of what programs might interest them.

Between August 1945 and January 1946, 5.4 million Americans who served in the Army and Navy were discharged from service. As these veterans learned of the benefits available under the amended GI Bill, they turned out in droves to register for a college education. Enrollment reached its pinnacle in 1948, when 900,000 veterans signed up for college classes. Over the course of nine years, approximately 7.8 million veterans pursued education or training under the GI Bill, with a total of 2.2 million enrolling in college-level studies. From 1947 to 1948, 50 percent of college students in the United States were veterans, and the overall number of people attending colleges and universities was higher than ever before. Although some early critics believed that veterans did not want to learn, had no interest in reading books, and were inclined to pursue immediate employment rather than an education, veterans quickly earned reputations as mature, serious students; they attended classes, took meticulous notes, studied hard, and earned top grades. Non-veteran students began to resent having veterans in their classes because former GIs' high marks wreaked havoc on grading curves. Civilian students at the University of California began to refer to veteran students by the acronym DARs — Damned Average Raisers. "It's books, books, books all the time," one exasperated student at Lehigh University in Pennsylvania said about his veteran classmates. "They study so hard we have to slave to keep up with them."

Across the country, veterans outperformed the expectations colleges had for them; they had lower dropout rates than non-veteran students, and exhibited a work ethic that surprised many instructors. As one professor said, the veterans had "one priceless quality which is the answer of every teacher's prayer: they want to learn." Not only did veterans exhibit a zeal for their classes, they pursued demanding courses of study, "gravitating especially toward business administration, followed by professional fields such as law, medicine, dentistry, and teaching, and then, in almost equal numbers, engineering, architecture, the physical sciences, the humanities, and the social sciences." Even early opponents of the GI Bill were forced to admit that veterans made excellent students. Harvard president James Bryant Conant marveled at the quality of students ushered into universities through the GI Bill. He declared in 1946 that the legislation was "a heartening sign that the democratic process of social mobility is energetically at work, piercing the class barriers which, even in America, have tended to keep a college education the prerogative of the few." Many grateful veterans openly acknowledged that the GI Bill had changed their lives.

Sadly, not all veterans had equal access to an education, even under the GI Bill's amendments. Although no provision prevented African American and female veterans from securing an education under the bill, these veterans returned to a nation that still endorsed segregated schools and largely believed a woman's place was in the home. For African American veterans, educational opportunities were limited. In the words of historian Christopher P. Loss, "Legalized segregation denied most black veterans admission into the nation's elite, overwhelmingly white universities, and insufficient capacity at the all-black schools they could attend failed to match black veterans' demand." The number of African American students at U.S. colleges and universities tripled between 1940 and 1950, but many prospective students were turned away because of their race. For those African Americans who did earn a degree under the GI Bill, employment discrimination prevented them from gaining positions commensurate with their education. Many African American college graduates were offered low-level jobs that they could have secured without any education. Almost a decade elapsed between V-J Day and the Supreme Court's landmark decision in *Brown v. Board of Education,* which struck down segregated schools. It would take another decade after *Brown* for the civil rights movement to fully develop and for public schools to make significant strides in integrating.

As for female veterans, societal pressures caused many to forgo educational and other opportunities under the GI Bill in favor of serving a traditional domestic role. Policymakers and labor unions that had eagerly urged women to fill positions in the war industries while millions of men served overseas changed their tune after the war. Facing a "back to the kitchen" movement, women were implored to leave the workforce to make way for male veterans. Barriers were raised as employers favored men over women to fill positions. Under these circumstances, women, like African Americans, faced the prospect of gaining an education under the GI Bill only to be robbed of the chance of putting their degree to full use. It would take time for policymakers to discover that male veterans could be absorbed into the workforce without sending the domestic economy spiraling toward depression. And it would take until the 1970s before higher education became fully "co-ed."

· · ·

If it had not been for the mountains of books that were sent to the training camps and overseas units during the war, many men may never have developed an interest in reading, studying, or returning to school. Thanks to the council's troop-friendly format and carefully curated selections for each month's reading ration, books became an irresistible pleasure — even to those who eschewed books before the war. As even the *New Republic,* which had expressed doubts about the ASE program back in 1943, observed in 1945: "If 'Editions for the Armed Services' did no more than provide good reading matter, and plenty of it, for those who already had the habit when they went into the army, this would be a sound and useful enterprise. In fact, however, it goes far beyond this; it is teaching literally millions of Americans to read books, many of them good books, who never read anything but newspapers, and in them chiefly the comic strips." The council and the Victory Book Campaign were responsible for showing men that they could thrive at book learning and studying after the war. As the *New York Post* boasted in the spring of 1945, America had "the best read army in the world."

Many ASE authors witnessed the postwar impact of the program firsthand. Wallace Stegner, author of *The Big Rock Candy Mountain,* recalled the "flood of GI students" who enrolled in his classes at Stanford University. "I found that a lot of them had read N-32 in the South Pacific or the European theater." He was humbled that so many men had read his book while at war. "The book gave us a bond," he said. It "gave them a certain confidence in me, and me a lot of respect for them." Other authors maintained correspondence with veterans, and were updated on their progress after the war. Helen MacInnes, author of *While Still We Live,* would never forget one young soldier who insisted that her ASE "got him *enjoying* literature." This man began to read constantly and developed an interest in attending college after the war. Years later, when he completed his PhD dissertation, he sent a copy to MacInnes, for he had dedicated it to her: "the writer of the novel that started his reading."

By the time this generation of veterans returned home, many had already tackled Plato, Shakespeare, and Dickens from the frontlines. Others had read about history, business, mathematics, science, journalism, and law. When faced with the opportunity to earn a college degree, these men had already proven that they could apply their energies to an activity as scholarly as reading and thrive. After all, if they could read and learn burrowed in a foxhole between shell bursts, surely they could handle a course of study in a classroom.

Just as the GI Bill granted all veterans access to an education — irrespective of wealth and class — books underwent the same democratization during the war, thanks to the paperback revolution. Before the war, Pocket Books and Penguin Books were the only companies experimenting with the softcover trade. Now there were Avon, Popular Library, Dell, Bantam, Ballantine Books, New American Library, and others. These companies produced classics as well as modern fiction and nonfiction. As more publishing firms jumped onto the paperback bandwagon, sales skyrocketed, from 40 million in 1943 to 95 million in 1947. In 1952, sales leapt to 270 million, and in 1959 paperback sales exceeded hardcovers for the first time in American publishing history. Paperbacks were no longer quarantined to drugstores and five-and-dimes. They were sold everywhere, from traditional bookstores to newsstands, variety stores, tobacconists, and railroad stations. The servicemen would no longer have Armed Services Editions, but the booming paperback trade ensured they would have an endless supply of pocket-sized softcovers.

Afterword

Today, a memorial in Berlin's Bebelplatz commemorates the Nazi book burnings of 1933. Set into the plaza's cobblestones is a glass plate covering a subterranean room lined with empty bookshelves. Visitors may peer downward and consider the tens of thousands of volumes that were destroyed in that square because of the ideas they contained. No parallel monument has been erected in the United States to commemorate the number of books collected and produced to combat the Nazi's war of ideas. Perhaps this book may serve as a memorial to those efforts.

Books have always housed the world's most powerful thoughts and ideas. It was not until World War II, however, that these repositories of knowledge were refashioned into indomitable weapons of warfare. On one side, *Mein Kampf* spread Nazi ideology and propaganda, hatred and devastation. On the other, books spread ideas in the face of their very destruction, stimulated thought about the terms of a lasting peace, and built understanding. As Hitler waged total war, America fought back not just with men and bullets, but with books. Despite the many advances in modern warfare — from airplanes to the atomic bomb — books proved to be one of the most formidable weapons of them all.

It is estimated that more than 100 million books perished over the course of the war. This figure includes books that were destroyed by air raids and bombs as well as by book burnings. Through the efforts of the Council on Books in Wartime, over 123 million Armed Services Editions were printed. The Victory Book Campaign added 18 million donated books to the total number distributed to American troops. More books were given to the American armed services than Hitler destroyed.

Acknowledgments

I was first introduced to the Armed Services Editions while digging through the archives of Charles Scribner's Sons publishing company, researching my first book. There, I found countless letters from servicemen extending their sincerest thanks to Scribner's for participating in the Council on Books in Wartime and providing free, miniature paperback editions to brighten their days at war. I was immediately intrigued and fascinated by these letters, and was eager to learn more about the ASEs. It was a fortuitous discovery. Telling the story of how books helped win World War II became a passion of mine.

I have been extremely fortunate to have had the help and support of a wonderful group of people along the way. Writing a book is a massive undertaking, and I am thankful for the many family members who have cheered me on over the years, with special thanks to my mother, Nancy Anne Guptill, for being a constant source of support. She has been such an extraordinary example, and I am blessed to have her as a role model. My husband, Christopher Manning, helped me work through ideas, reviewed early drafts, and believed in this book as much as I did. Thank goodness for his patience, kindness, and ability to know just when I needed a dose of encouragement. I am so lucky to be married to him.

Two of my talented colleagues, Ilana Drescher and John Mulvaney, read several drafts of the manuscript and provided great advice and ideas on how to make the story shine. Ilana, your enthusiasm and poignant insight were incredibly useful and I appreciate your wonderful suggestions. John, your advice was spot-on, and our "book lunches" were a highlight for me — your excitement for the topic was infectious and your careful edits were especially helpful.

I owe special thanks to Professor Richard Hamm, a favorite college professor, thesis advisor, and friend. Over a decade ago, he helped seal my love of history in the classroom, and I continue to learn from him today. There aren't words to describe how much I appreciate his invaluable advice and suggestions. I am so grateful for the help he gave me, and for his encouragement through the book-writing process.

ASE expert Brian Anderson was also a tremendous help. I was not sure if anyone could love ASEs as much as I do, and then I met Brian. I have learned so much from him, and have thoroughly enjoyed our discussions about the ASEs and many other novelties of World War II publishing. I am so thankful for his careful review of my manuscript, keen editorial eye, and wonderful ideas. I especially enjoyed his ability to infuse humor into his comments in the margins. I have never laughed so hard while reading an edited document.

A group of fantastic researchers helped me find source material, and I am deeply grateful for their help. Amanda Lawrence helped me understand the character and wit of Althea Warren thanks to her careful review of the Althea Warren Papers at the University of Illinois at Urbana-Champaign. Maryellen Tinsley found what became some of my favorite letters from servicemen in the Betty Smith Papers at the Wilson Library, University of North Carolina at Chapel Hill. And Peggy Ann Brown discovered the needle in a haystack I was searching for in the papers of Katherine Anne Porter at the University of Maryland at College Park. When it comes to source material, I must also thank James Dourgarian, the quintessential bookman, for tracking down documents and ASEs that I needed for this book.

Once I felt the manuscript was ready, I had the good fortune of working with E. J. McCarthy, an extraordinary agent. I cannot thank him enough for being so passionate about this book. I feel fortunate to have had his expert guidance through the publishing process and excellent suggestions and advice. His meticulous edits and profound knowledge of World War II were immensely helpful. It has been such a joy working with him, and I hope this is the beginning of a long friendship and writing partnership.

When I first spoke with Bruce Nichols, of Houghton Mifflin Harcourt, I knew my book had landed in the right hands. He seemed to know exactly what I wanted this book to be, and thanks to his thoughtful edits and inspired ideas, he refined and polished the manuscript into the book it is today. It has been a true pleasure working with him. I also wish to thank Ben Hyman, of Houghton Mifflin Harcourt, for his willingness to answer my many questions about the publishing process and for guiding me closer and closer to publication. I'm also grateful to Melissa Dobson, who carefully copyedited my manuscript.

Appendix A
Banned Authors

The authors listed below, in random order, represent a fraction of the ten thousand whose books were banned in Germany and all German-occupied countries during World War II.

Ernest Hemingway

Walter Rathenau

Émile Zola

Thomas Mann

Michael Gold

Helen Keller

Lion Feuchtwanger

Arthur Schnitzler

Heinrich Heine

Emile Vandervelde

Leon Trotsky

Karl Marx

Ernst Toller

Henri Barbusse

Georges Duhamel

David Lloyd George

Alfred Döblin

Walter Hasenclever

Alfred Schirokauer

John Dos Passos

H. R. Knickerbocker

Nevile Henderson

Arthur Eloesser

Joseph Kallinikow

Ludwig Renn

Kurt Tucholsky

Joseph Roth

Erich Muhsam

Carl Einstein

Rudolf Olden

Arthur Holitscher

Leonhard Frank

Albrecht Schaeffer

Hermann Broch

Erika Mann

Bruno Frank

Rudolf Leonhard

Alfred Neumann

Georg Bernhard

Ernst Bloch

Kurt Kersten

Bodo Uhse

Adam Scharrer

Annette Kolb

Erich Weinert

Georg Hermann

Maria Leitner

Franz Weiskopf

Max Raphaël

Bruno Frei

Paul Zech

Heinz Pol

Max Osborn

Sigrid Undset

Franz Werfel

August Bebel

Gina Kaus

Karel Čapek

Otto Strasser

H. G. Wells

Maxim Gorki

Alfred Kerr

Heinrich Mann

Stephen Zweig

C. G. Jung

Jakob Wassermann

Albert Einstein

Arnold Zweig

Theodore Dreiser

John Gunther

G. K. Chesterton

Albert Ehrenstein

Heinrich Eduard Jacob

Ernest Ottwalt

Upton Sinclair

John Reed

Max Brod

Jaroslav Hašek

Richard Beer-Hofmann

Anatoly Lunacharsky

Karl Tschuppik

Werner Hegemann

Franz Hessel

Walter Benjamin

Robert Musil

Anna Seghers

Carl Zuckmayer

Alfred Polgar

Arthur Koestler

Klaus Mann

Alfred Wolfenstein

Martin Gumpert

Willi Bredel

O. M. Graf

Julius Hay

Fritz Brügel

Hans Sahl

Georg Kaiser

Franz Blei

Leo Lania

Gustav Regler

Wilhelm Herzog

Carl Sternheim

Paul Tillich

Karin Michaëlis

Jules Romains

Geneviève Tabouis

Romain Rolland

Jean-Jacques Rousseau

Konrad Heiden

Sholem Asch

Voltaire

Sigmund Freud

Jack London

Benedict Spinoza

Ignazio Silone

Emil Ludwig

Erich Maria Remarque

André Malraux

Louis Fischer

Bertolt Brecht

Egon Kisch

Theodore Plievier

Ludwig Renn

Louis Aragon

Vicki Baum

Winston Churchill

Ilya Ehrenburg

Kurt Pinthus

Paul Levy

Otto Bauer

Carl von Ossietzky

Theodor Lessing

Ernst Weiss

René Schickele

Helmut von Gerlach

Alfons Goldschmidt

Fritz von Unruh

Paul Stefan

Walter Mehring

Balder Olden

Hans Siemsen

Theodor Wolff

Johannes R. Becher

Paul Westheim

Hans Marchwitza

Alfred Kantorowicz

Friedrich Wolf

Maria Gleit

Alexander Roda Roda

Hermynia Zur Mühlen

Max Werner

Ferdinand Bruckner

Wieland Herzfelde

Martin Andersen Nexø

André Maurois

Henri de Kérillis

Appendix B
Armed Services Editions

B-33 Robert Frost,
      *Come In, and
      Other Poems*

B-34 Edith Wharton,
      Ethan Frome

B-35 Mary Lasswell,
      Suds In Your Eye

B-36 Peter Field, *Fight
      for Powder Valley!*

B-37 Cornelia Otis
      Skinner and Emily
      Kimbrough,
      *Our Hearts Were
      Young and Gay*

B-38 MacKinlay Kantor,
      Gentle Annie

B-39 R. Benchley,
      *Benchley Beside
      Himself*

B-40 William Sloane,
      To Walk the Night

B-41 Edmund Gilligan,
      The Gaunt Woman

B-42 Alan LeMay,
      Winter Range

B-43 Arthur Henry
      Gooden, *Painted
      Buttes*

B-44 Rosemary Taylor,
      *Chicken Every
      Sunday*

B-45 P. Lowe, *Father
      and Glorious
      Descendant*

B-46 H. Allen Smith,
      *Life in a Putty
      Knife Factory*

B-47 Archie Binns,
      Lightship

B-48 Hartzell Spence,
      *Get Thee
      Behind Me*

B-49 Mary O' Hara,
      My Friend Flicka

B-50 Henry C. Cassidy,
      Moscow Dateline

B-51 Dorothy Macardle,
      The Uninvited

B-52 Walter D.
      Edmonds, *Rome
      Haul*

B-53 Struthers Burt,
      Powder River

B-54 Louis Adamic, *The
      Native's Return*

B-55 Majorie Kinnan
      Rawlings,
      The Yearling

B-56 Stefan Heym,
      Hostages

B-57 Hubert Herring,
      Good Neighbors

B-58 Merrill Denison,
      Klondike Mike

B-59 Marcus Goodrich,
      Delilah

B-60 Peter Freuchen,
      Arctic Adventure

C-Series,
November 1943

C-61 Alan H. Brodrick,
      North Africa

C-62 Conrad Richter,
      The Sea of Grass

C-63 J. H. Robinson,
      *The Mind in the
      Making*

C-64 Voltaire, *Candide*

C-65 Stewart Edward
      White, *The Forest*

C-66 Nelson C. Nye,
      Pistols for Hire

C-67 Max Beerbohm,
      Seven Men

C-68 Vereen Bell,
      Swamp Water

C-69 Charles Courtney,
      *Unlocking
      Adventure*

C-70 Booth Tarkington,
      Penrod

C-71 W. H. Hudson,
      Green Mansions

C-72 Clarence E.
      Mulford, *Hopalong
      Cassidy Serves a
      Writ*

C-73 Walter Lippmann,
      U.S. Foreign Policy

C-74 DuBose Heyward,
      *Star Spangled
      Virgin*

C-75 J. B. Priestley,
      *Black-Out in
      Gretley*

C-76 Mark Twain,
      *The Adventures
      of Tom Sawyer*

C-77 Stephen Vincent
      Benét, *Short Stories*

C-78 Betty Wason,
      Miracle in Hellas

C-79 Frank Meier,
      Fathoms Below

C-80 Ernestine Hill,
      Australian Frontier

C-81 George R. Stewart,
      Storm

C-82 Gontran De
Poncins, *Kabloona*

C-83 Hervey Allen,
*The Forest and
the Fort*

C-84 Herbert Quick,
The Hawkeye

C-85 J. W. Thomason,
*. . . And a Few
Marines*

C-86 John Selby,
Starbuck

C-87 Edison Marshall,
Great Smith

C-88 Esther Forbes, *Paul
Revere and the
World He Lived In*

C-89 Manuel Komroff,
Coronet

C-90 John Steinbeck,
*The Grapes of
Wrath*

D-Series,
December 1943

D-91 James Hilton, *The
Story of Dr. Wassell*

D-92 Charles Spalding
and Otis Carney,
Love at First Flight

D-93 Stewart E. White,
Blazed Trail Stories

D-94 W. C. Tuttle,
*Tumbling River
Range*

D-95 Berry Fleming,
*Colonel Effingham's
Raid*

D-96 Martha Albrand,
Without Orders

D-97 Willa Cather,
*Death Comes for
the Archbishop*

D-98 Conrad Richter,
The Trees

D-99 Mark Van Doren,
ed., *The Night
of the Summer
Solstice*

D-100 C. B. Kelland,
Valley of the Sun

D-101 Elizabeth Daly,
*Evidence of
Things Seen*

D-102 Joseph
Hergesheimer,
Java Head

D-103 George S. Bryan,
Mystery Ship

D-104 Gordon S.
Seagrave, *Burma
Surgeon*

D-105 Harry Emerson
Fosdick, *On
Being a Real
Person*

D-106 Hans Zinsser,
*Rats, Lice, and
History*

D-107 Charles Allen
Smart, *R. F. D.*

D-108 Joseph Mitchell,
*McSorley's
Wonderful Saloon*

D-109 Bellamy Partridge,
Country Lawyer

D-110 Mark Twain, *The
Adventures of
Huckleberry Finn*

D-111 Joseph Shearing,
Blanche Fury

D-112 Marjorie Kinnan
Rawlings,
Cross Creek

D-113 A. J. Cronin,
*The Keys of
the Kingdom*

D-114 John T. Whitaker,
*We Cannot Escape
History*

D-115 William Wister
Haines, *Slim*

D-116 Martha Foley,
ed., *The Best
American Short
Stories, 1942*

D-117 Betty Smith,
*A Tree Grows
in Brooklyn*

D-118 Lloyd C. Douglas,
The Robe

D-119 F. van Wyck
Mason, *Rivers
of Glory*

D-120 John P.
Marquand,
So Little Time

E-Series,
January 1944

E-121 Phil Stong,
State Fair

E-122 Ralph Waldo
Emerson,
Seven Essays

E-123 W. C. Tuttle,
Ghost Trails

E-124 Arthur H.
Gooden,
*The Range
Hawk*

E-125 Frank H. Spearman, *The Mountain Divide*

E-126 Bertha Damon, *A Sense of Humus*

E-127 Alexandre Pernikoff, *"Bushido": The Anatomy of Terror*

E-128 W. Somerset Maugham, *The Moon and Sixpence*

E-129 Ernest Haycox, *Saddle and Ride*

E-130 Earl Derr Biggers, *Seven Keys to Baldpate*

E-131 J. D. Ratcliff, ed., *Science Yearbook of 1943*

E-132 Julian Duguid, *Green Hell*

E-133 C. S. Forester, *Ship of the Line*

E-134 George R. Stewart, *Ordeal by Hunger*

E-135 Myron Brinig, *The Gambler Takes a Wife*

E-136 Charles Grayson, ed., *Stories for Men*

E-137 Daphne du Maurier, *Jamaica Inn*

E-138 James Hilton, *Random Harvest*

E-139 Mark Twain, *A Connecticut Yankee in King Arthur's Court*

E-140 Edna Ferber, *Cimarron*

E-141 Osa Johnson, *I Married Adventure*

E-142 Mary Ellen Chase, *Windswept*

E-143 Louise R. Pierson, *Roughly Speaking*

E-144 Comm. Edward Ellsberg, *Hell on Ice*

E-145 James T. Flexner, *Doctors on Horseback*

E-146 John P. Marquand, *The Late George Apley*

E-147 Stephen Crane, *Short Stories*

E-148 David Lavender, *One Man's West*

E-149 Walter D. Edmonds, *Drums Along the Mohawk*

E-150 Henry Bellamann, *King's Row*

F-Series, February 1944

F-151 Donn Byrne, *Messer Marco Polo*

F-152 Antoine de Saint-Exupéry, *Night Flight*

F-153 Abraham Lincoln, *The Selected Writings of Abraham Lincoln*

F-154 John Vandercook, *Black Majesty*

F-155 Negley Farson, *Going Fishing*

F-156 Eric Knight, *Lassie Come-Home*

F-157 C. S. Forester, *Flying Colours*

F-158 Joseph Bromley, *Clear the Tracks*

F-159 H. L. Mencken, *Happy Days*

F-160 William McLeod Raine, *Border Breed*

F-161 William Beebe, *Jungle Peace*

F-162 Bret Harte, *Selected Short Stories of Bret Harte*

F-163 Clarence E. Mulford, *The Bar 20 Rides Again*

F-164 Ernest Haycox, *Border Trumpet*

F-165 Edna Ferber, *So Big*

F-166 Beryl Markham, *West with the Night*

F-167 Agnes Keith, *Land Below the Wind*

F-168 Roy Chapman Andrews, *Under a Lucky Star*

F-169 A. E. Hertzler, *The Horse and Buggy Doctor*

F-170 Ernie Pyle, *Here Is Your War*

F-171   Stewart Edward White, *The Blazed Trail*

F-172   Ring Lardner, *Round Up*

F-173   Mari Sandoz, *Old Jules*

F-174   Mark Twain, *Life on the Mississippi*

F-175   Charles Lamb, *The Essays of Charles Lamb*

F-176   E. B. White and K. S. White, *A Subtreasury of American Humor*

F-177   Philip Guedalla, *Wellington*

F-178   William McFee, *Casuals of the Sea*

F-179   James Norman Hall, *Dr. Dogbody's Leg*

F-180   Jack London, *The Sea-Wolf*

G-Series, March 1944

G-181   Thorne Smith, *The Glorious Pool*

G-182   Jack London, *White Fang*

G-183   H. Allen Smith, *Low Man on a Totem Pole*

G-184   William MacLeod Raine, *Trail's End*

G-185   Willa Cather, *My Ántonia*

G-186   Alexander Woollcott, *Long, Long Ago*

G-187   Eric Knight, *Sam Small Flies Again*

G-188   Jesse Stuart, *Taps for Private Tussie*

G-189   Homer W. Smith, *Kamongo*

G-190   Eugene Manlove Rhodes, *The Trusty Knaves*

G-191   W. R. Burnett, *Little Caesar*

G-192   Robert Benchley, *Inside Benchley*

G-193   Robert H. Thouless, *How to Think Straight*

G-194   Joseph Conrad, *The Mirror of the Sea*

G-195   Luke Short, *Raiders of the Rimrock*

G-196   W. H. Hudson, *A Crystal Age*

G-197   Stephen Leacock, *Laugh with Leacock*

G-198   Rudyard Kipling, *Kim*

G-199   Donald Culross Peattie, *Journey into America*

G-200   Gladys Hasty Carroll, *As the Earth Turns*

G-201   T. R. Ybarra, *Young Man of Caracas*

G-202   MacKinlay Kantor, *Arouse and Beware*

G-203   William Haynes, *This Chemical Age*

G-204   Mary O'Hara, *Thunderhead*

G-205   Carl D. Lane, *The Fleet in the Forest*

G-206   Martha Foley, ed., *The Best American Short Stories of 1943*

G-207   Harry Harrison Kroll, *Rogues' Company*

G-208   John P. Marquand, *H. M. Pulham, Esq.*

G-209   Herman Melville, *Moby-Dick*

G-210   George R. Stewart, *East of the Giants*

H-Series, April 1944

H-211   Corporal Thomas R. St. George, *C/O Postmaster*

H-212   Eugene Manlove Rhodes, *Beyond the Desert*

H-213   C. S. Forester, *Payment Deferred*

H-214   Arnold Bennett, *Buried Alive*

H-215   Stephen Vincent Benét, *Western Star*

H-216 Oliver La Farge, *Laughing Boy*

H-217 I. A. Richards, ed., *The Republic of Plato*

H-218 Donald Culross Peattie, *Forward the Nation*

H-219 Carl Glick, *Three Times I Bow*

H-220 Cora Jarrett, *Night over Fitch's Pond*

H-221 Jack London, *The Cruise of the Snark*

H-222 Eugene Cunningham, *Riders of the Night*

H-223 Michael MacDougall, *Danger in the Cards*

H-224 Stewart H. Holbrook, *Burning an Empire*

H-225 Richard Dempewolff, *Animal Reveille*

H-226 Clark McMeekin, *Red Raskall*

H-227 Clarence E. Mulford, *Corson of the J. C.*

H-228 Kenneth Roberts, *Captain Caution*

H-229 Grace Zaring Stone (Ethel Vance), *The Cold Journey*

H-230 Thorne Smith, *The Bishop's Jaegers*

H-231 Franklin P. Adams, ed., *Innocent Merriment*

H-232 Frank H. Spearman, *Carmen of the Rancho*

H-233 Robert W. Chambers, *Cardigan*

H-234 Marjorie Barrows and George Eaton, *Box Office*

H-235 Felix Risenberg, *The Pacific Ocean*

H-236 Manuel Komroff, *The Travels of Marco Polo*

H-237 Edmund Gilligan, *The Ringed Horizon*

H-238 Charles Nordhoff and James Norman Hall, *Botany Bay*

H-239 Richard Llewellyn, *How Green Was My Valley*

H-240 Walter D. Edmonds, *Chad Hanna*

I-Series, May 1944

I-241 Kay Boyle, *Avalanche*

I-242 Keith Ayling, *Semper Fidelis*

I-243 Isabel Scott Rorick, *Mr. and Mrs. Cugat*

I-244 Roark Bradford, *Ol' Man Adam an' His Chillun*

I-245 W. C. Tuttle, *The Mystery of the Red Triangle*

I-246 Emily Kimbrough, *We Followed Our Hearts to Hollywood*

I-247 Paul B. Sears, *Deserts on the March*

I-248 Geoffrey Household, *Rogue Male*

I-249 William Wister Haines, *High Tension*

I-250 Bruce Barton, *The Book Nobody Knows*

I-251 Harry Sinclair Drago, *Stagecoach Kingdom*

I-252 J. Middleton Murry, ed., *Stories by Katherine Mansfield: A Selection*

I-253 James Thurber, *The Middle-Aged Man on the Flying Trapeze*

I-254 Ernest Haycox, *Deep West*

I-255 Clarence Budington Kelland, *Arizona*

I-256 Jesse James Benton, *Cow by the Tail*

I-257 Clarence E. Mulford, *Hopalong Cassidy's Protégé*

I-258 Karl Baarslag, *Coast Guard to the Rescue*

I-259 Commander Edward Ellsberg, *On the Bottom*

I-260 W. Somerset Maugham, *Ashenden*

I-261 Lytton Strachey, *Queen Victoria*

I-262 Francis Griswold, *Tides of Malvern*

I-263 Alexander Johnston, *Ten . . . and Out!*

I-264 Joseph Conrad, *Victory*

I-265 Louis Bromfield, *Mrs. Parkington*

I-266 Rafael Sabatini, *The Sea Hawk*

I-267 H. L. Davis, *Honey in the Horn*

I-268 Charlotte Brontë, *Jane Eyre*

I-269 Esther Forbes, *Paradise*

I-270 Howard Spring, *My Son, My Son!*

J-Series, June 1944

J-271 Eugene Manlove Rhodes, *The Proud Sheriff*

J-272 William Saroyan, *My Name Is Aram*

J-273 Joseph Conrad, *The Shadow Line*

J-274 Bob Davis, *Tree Toad*

J-275 Frederick R. Bechdolt, *Riot at Red Water*

J-276 Charles J. Finney, *Past the End of the Pavement*

J-277 Frank Graham, *Lou Gehrig*

J-278 Ring Lardner, *You Know Me, Al*

J-279 George Agnew Chamberlain, *The Phantom Filly*

J-280 Charles Snow, *Sheriff of Yavisa*

J-281 Constance Rourke, *Davy Crockett*

J-282 Richard Hughes, *A High Wind in Jamaica*

J-283 Harvey Smith, *The Gang's All Here*

J-284 Thorne Smith, *Skin and Bones*

J-285 James Gould Cozzens, *The Last Adam*

J-286 Max Brand, *South of Rio Grande*

J-287 Ward Morehouse, *George M. Cohan*

J-288 Norah Lofts, *The Golden Fleece*

J-289 Ward Weaver, *End of Track*

J-290 Paul Gallico, *Selected Stories*

J-291 Victoria Lincoln, *February Hill*

J-292 H. M. Tomlinson, *The Sea and the Jungle*

J-293 Agnes Morley Cleaveland, *No Life for a Lady*

J-294 Harnett T. Kane, *The Bayous of Louisiana*

J-295 Irene D. Paden, *The Wake of the Prairie Schooner*

J-296 William Makepeace Thackeray, *Vanity Fair*

J-297 Edgar Allan Poe, *Selected Stories*

J-298 Walter D. Edmonds, *Young Ames*

J-299 Sholem Asch, *The Apostle*

J-300 Gene Fowler, *Good Night, Sweet Prince*

J-301 Archer Butler Hulbert, *Forty-Niners*

J-302 Carolyn Thomas Foreman, *Indians Abroad*

K-Series, July 1944

K-1 Clarence Day, *This Simian World*

K-2 Don Marquis, *The Old Soak*

K-3 Jack London, *The Call of the Wild*

K-4 G. B. Stern, *The Dark Gentleman*

K-5 Max Brand, *The Secret of Dr. Kildare*

K-6 MacKinlay Kantor, *The Noise of Their Wings*

K-7 Walter Beebe Wilder, *Bounty of the Wayside*

K-8 Eugene Manlove Rhodes, *Stepsons of Light*

K-9 Ernest Hemingway, *Short Stories*

K-10 Robert Bright, *The Life and Death of Little Jo*

K-11 Charles H. Snow, *Rebel of Ronde Valley*

K-12 Henry Beston, *The St. Lawrence*

K-13 Stewart H. Holbrook, *Ethan Allan*

K-14 Ernest Haycox, *The Wild Bunch*

K-15 Thorne Smith, *The Stray Lamb*

K-16 O'Henry, *Short Stories*

K-17 Meyer Berger, *The Eight Million*

K-18 Willard Robertson, *Moon Tide*

K-19 Antonio de Fierro Blanco, *The Journey of the Flame*

K-20 T. R. Ybarra, *Young Man of the World*

K-21 Mildred Walker, *Winter Wheat*

K-22 Henry Seidel Canby, *Walt Whitman*

K-23 Marquis James, *Andrew Jackson: The Border Captain*

K-24 Sinclair Lewis, *Babbitt*

K-25 Arthur Train, *Yankee Lawyer: The Autobiography of Ephraim Tutt*

K-26 Herbert Asbury, *Sucker's Progress*

K-27 Lloyd C. Douglas, *The Robe*

K-28 Betty Smith, *A Tree Grows in Brooklyn*

K-29 Oliver Gramling, *AP: The Story of News*

K-30 Carl Van Doren, *Benjamin Franklin*

K-31 Laurence Sterne, *Tristram Shandy*

K-32 Albert Spalding, *Rise to Follow*

L-Series, August 1944

L-1 Rosemary Benét and Stephen Vincent Benét, *A Book of Americans*

L-2 James Thurber, *My Life and Hard Times*

L-3 Henry G. Lamond, *Kilgour's Mare*

L-4 James Stephens, *Etched in Moonlight*

L-5 DuBose Heyward, *Porgy*

L-6 Louis Untermeyer, ed., *Great Poems from Chaucer to Whitman*

L-7 Louis Bromfield, *What Became of Anna Bolton*

L-8 Evan Evans, *Montana Rides Again*

L-9 William MacLeod Raine, *The Sheriff's Son*

L-10 Stephen Leacock, *Happy Stories Just to Laugh At*

L-11 Arthur Henry Gooden, *Roaring River Range*

L-12 Frances Eisenberg, *There's One in Every Family*

L-13 Max Brand, *The King Bird Rides*

L-14 Evelyn Eaton, *The Sea Is So Wide*

L-15 Herman Melville, *Omoo*

L-16 George Sessions Perry, *Hackberry Cavalier*

L-17 Thorne Smith, *Turnabout*

L-18 Carl Crow, *400 Million Customers*

L-19 Philip Wylie, *Fish and Tin Fish*

L-20 Lytton Strachey, *Eminent Victorians*

L-21 Homer Croy, *Country Cured*

L-22 George W. Gray, *Science at War*

L-23 Hervey Allen, *Bedford Village*

L-24 Joseph Shearing, *The Lady and the Arsenic*

L-25 Bram Stoker, *Dracula*

L-26 John P. Marquand, *Wickford Point*

L-27 Robert Graves, *I, Claudius*

L-28 Thomas Mann, *Selected Short Stories*

L-29 Irving Stone, *Lust for Life*

L-30 W. Somerset Maugham, *Of Human Bondage*

L-31 Archie Binns, *The Land Is Bright*

L-32 Osa Johnson, *Four Years in Paradise*

M-Series, September 1944

M-1 A. E. Housman, *Selected Poems*

M-2 James Thurber and E. B. White, *Is Sex Necessary?*

M-3 Saki (H. H. Munro), *Selected Short Stories*

M-4 Robert Benchley, *20,000 Leagues Under the Sea; or, David Copperfield*

M-5 Agnes Repplier, *Père Marquette*

M-6 Eugene Manlove Rhodes, *Copper Streak Trail*

M-7 Edwin Way Teale, *Dune Boy*

M-8 James Stevens, *Paul Bunyan*

M-9 John D. Ratcliff, ed., *Science Yearbook of 1944*

M-10 Barry Benefield, *The Chicken-Wagon Family*

M-11 Philip Wylie, *The Big Ones Get Away*

M-12 Angus McDonald, *Old McDonald Had a Farm*

M-13 Ernest Haycox, *Action by Night*

M-14 Max Brand, *The Border Kid*

M-15 Dane Coolidge, *Fighting Men of the West*

M-16 Edgar Rice Burroughs, *Tarzan of the Apes*

M-17 Harry Bedwell, *The Boomer*

M-18 Robert J. Casey, *Such Interesting People*

M-19 Eva Bruce, *Call Her Rosie*

M-20 A. R. Beverly-Giddings, *Larrish Hundred*

M-21 Henry B. Hough, *Country Editor*

M-22 David Cornel DeJong, *With a Dutch Accent*

M-23 Hellman, Thurber and Nugent, Chodorov and Fields, and Kingsley, *Four Modern American Plays*

M-24 M. Lincoln Schuster, ed., *A Treasury of the World's Great Letters*

M-25 Christine Weston, *Indigo*

M-26 M. R. Werner, *Barnum*

M-27 Clark McMeekin, *Show Me a Land*

M-28 Captain Charles Grayson, ed., *New Stories for Men*

M-29 Wilkie Collins, *The Moonstone*

M-30 Konrad Heiden, *Der Fuehrer*

M-31 F. van Wyck Mason, *Stars on the Sea*

M-32 Helen MacInnes, *While Still We Live*

N-Series, October 1944

N-1 Mark Twain, *The Mysterious Stranger*

N-2 S. J. Perelman, *The Dream Department*

N-3 Stephen Vincent Benét, *America*

N-4 Bruce Barton, *The Man Nobody Knows*

N-5 James Stephens, *The Crock of Gold*

N-6 Carl Sandburg, *Selected Poems*

N-7 James Thurber, *Let Your Mind Alone*

N-8 E. C. Abbott and Helena Huntington Smith, *We Pointed Them North*

N-9 Ernest Haycox, *Rim of the Desert*

N-10 Alan LeMay, *Useless Cowboy*

N-11 Dorothy B. Hughes, *The Fallen Sparrow*

N-12 Donald Hough, *Snow Above Town*

N-13 Robert Louis Stevenson, *Kidnapped*

N-14 W. Somerset Maugham, *The Summing Up*

N-15 Max Brand, *The Iron Trail*

N-16 Charles A. Siringo, *Riata and Spurs*

N-17 Niven Busch, *Duel in the Sun*

N-18 Theodore Pratt, *Thunder Mountain*

N-19 Lt. H. E. Riesenberg, *I Dive for Treasure*

N-20 Jack Iams, *Prophet by Experience*

N-21 Donn Byrne, *Hangman's House*

N-22 Clyde Brion Davis, *The Great American Novel*

N-23 Constance Robertson, *Fire Bell in the Night*

N-24 Robert Standish, *Bonin*

N-25 James Newman and Edward Kasner, *Mathematics and the Imagination*

N-26 Eric Linklater, *Magnus Merriman*

N-27 Leslie T. White, *Look Away, Look Away*

N-28 Jack London, *Martin Eden*

N-29 Stuart Cloete, *The Turning Wheels*

N-30 C. M. Sublette and Harry Harrison Kroll, *Perilous Journey*

N-31 Charles Dickens, *David Copperfield*

N-32 Wallace Stegner, *The Big Rock Candy Mountain*

O-Series, November 1944

O-1 Percy Bysshe Shelley, *Selected Poems*

O-2 Kahlil Gibran, *The Prophet*

O-3 John Mulholland, *The Art of Illusion*

O-4 Harry Grayson, *They Played the Game*

O-5 W. H. Hudson, *Tales of the Pampas*

O-6 Edward H. Faulkner, *Plowman's Folly*

O-7 Guy Gilpatric, *Mr. Glencannon Ignores the War*

O-8 Arthur Kober, *My Dear Bella*

O-9 Curt Siodmak, *Donovan's Brain*

O-10 Nelson C. Nye, *Wild Horse Shorty*

O-11 Cornelia Goodhue, *Journey into the Fog*

O-12 C. S. Forester, *The African Queen*

O-13 Anne Terry White, *Lost Worlds*

O-14 Bob Hope, *I Never Left Home*

O-15 Ernest K. Gann, *Island in the Sky*

O-16 Charles L. McNichols, *Crazy Weather*

O-17 W. R. Burnett, *Nobody Lives Forever*

O-18 Damon Runyon, *Runyon à la Carte*

O-19 Charles Jackson, *The Lost Weekend*

O-20 John Russell, *Selected Short Stories*

O-21 Georges Simenon, *On the Danger Line*

O-22 Edgar Rice Burroughs, *The Return of Tarzan*

O-23 Robert Sturgis, *Men Like Gods*

O-24 Joseph Hergesheimer, *The Three Black Pennys*

O-25 Frank Spearman, *Selwood of Sleepy Cat*

O-26 Constance Helmericks, *We Live in Alaska*

O-27 Frances Gaither, *The Red Cock Crows*

O-28 M. R. James, *Selected Ghost Stories*

O-29 Ben Ames Williams, *Leave Her to Heaven*

O-30 Zofia Kossak, *Blessed Are the Meek*

O-31 Thomas Wolfe, *Look Homeward, Angel*

O-32 Le Grand Cannon, *Look to the Mountain*

P-Series, December 1944

P-1 David Garnett, *Lady into Fox*

P-2 Commander William Chambliss, *Boomerang*

P-3 John R. Tunis, *Rookie of the Year*

P-4 Ludwig Bemelmans, *Hotel Splendide*

P-5 James Norman Hall, *Lost Island*

P-6 Rex Stout, *Not Quite Dead Enough*

P-7 Will Cuppy, *The Great Bustard and Other People*

P-8 Max Brand, *The Fighting Four*

P-9 Hobert D. Skidmore, *Valley of the Sky*

P-10 Benny Goodman and Irving Kolodin, *The Kingdom of Swing*

P-11 H. R. Hays, *Lie Down in Darkness*

P-12 James Oliver Curwood, *The Valley of Silent Men*

P-13 Miriam Young, *Mother Wore Tights*

P-14 Frederick Way Jr., *Pilotin' Comes Natural*

P-15 Tom Gill, *Starlight Pass*

P-16 Ernest Haycox, *Trail Town*

P-17 Hilda Lawrence, *Blood upon the Snow*

P-18   Arthur Loveridge,
        *Many Happy Days
        I've Squandered*

P-19   Erskine Caldwell,
        *Stories by Erskine
        Caldwell*

P-20   Captain John D.
        Craig, *Danger Is
        My Business*

P-21   William Hazlett
        Upson, *Botts in
        War, Botts in Peace*

P-22   Irvin S. Cobb,
        ed., *World's Great
        Humorous Stories*

P-23   Joseph Shearing,
        Aunt Beardie

P-24   Clyde Brion Davis,
        *Rebellion of Leo
        McGuire*

P-25   Herschel Brickell,
        ed., *O. Henry
        Memorial Award
        Prize Short Stories
        for 1943*

P-26   E. B. White,
        One Man's Meat

P-27   Anya Seton,
        Dragonwyck

P-28   Mari Sandoz,
        Slogum House

P-29   Charles A. Beard,
        The Republic

P-30   Ernie Pyle,
        Brave Men

P-31   Harlow Shapley,
        ed., *A Treasury of
        Science*

P-32   Catherine Drinker
        Bowen, *Yankee
        from Olympus*

Q-Series,
January 1945

Q-1   Cornelia Otis
        Skinner, *Excuse It,
        Please!*

Q-2   James M. Cain,
        *The Postman
        Always Rings Twice*

Q-3   David Ewen,
        *The Story of
        George Gershwin*

Q-4   Hugh Gray and
        Lillian R. Lieber,
        *The Education of
        T. C. Mits*

Q-5   Max Shulman,
        *The Feather
        Merchants*

Q-6   Mel Heimer,
        *The World Ends
        at Hoboken*

Q-7   Mary Lasswell,
        High Time

Q-8   John R. Tunis,
        Keystone Kids

Q-9   Sherwood
        Anderson, *Selected
        Short Stories
        of Sherwood
        Anderson*

Q-10   A. A. Fair,
        Give 'Em the Ax

Q-11   E. E. Halleran,
        Prairie Guns

Q-12   Theodore Naidish,
        *Watch Out for
        Willie Carter*

Q-13   Thorne Smith,
        *The Passionate
        Witch*

Q-14   Lord Dunsany,
        Guerilla

Q-15   R. A. J. Walling,
        *The Corpse
        Without a Clue*

Q-16   Ernest Haycox,
        Man in the Saddle

Q-17   Frances Crane, *The
        Amethyst Spectacles*

Q-18   C. S. Forester,
        Beat to Quarters

Q-19   Zane Grey,
        *The Heritage of
        the Desert*

Q-20   John Hawkins and
        Ward Hawkins,
        Devil on His Trail

Q-21   Philip Wylie,
        Salt Water Daffy

Q-22   Mary Reisner, *The
        House of Cobwebs*

Q-23   Donal Hamilton
        Haines, *Luck in
        All Weathers*

Q-24   Max Brand,
        Happy Jack

Q-25   Mac Gardner,
        Mom Counted Six

Q-26   Margaret Case
        Harriman, *Take
        Them Up Tenderly*

Q-27   A. J. Cronin,
        The Green Years

Q-28   Ross McLaury
        Taylor, *The Saddle
        and the Plow*

Q-29   Kenneth Roberts,
        The Lively Lady

Q-30   Clark McMeekin,
        *Reckon with
        the River*

Q-31 W. Somerset Maugham, *The Razor's Edge*

Q-32 Lillian Smith, *Strange Fruit*

Q-33 Anna Seghers, *The Seventh Cross*

Q-34 Louis Bromfield, *Wild Is the River*

Q-35 Eugene O'Neill, *Selected Plays of Eugene O'Neill*

Q-36 John Jennings, *The Shadow and the Glory*

Q-37 Rachel Field, *Time Out of Mind*

Q-38 Alexander Laing, *The Sea Witch*

Q-39 Ben Ames Williams, *The Strange Woman*

Q-40 Henry Adams, *The Education of Henry Adams*

R-Series, February 1945

R-1 G. B. Stern, *The Ugly Dachshund*

R-2 John Keats, *Selected Poems of John Keats*

R-3 Robert Nathan, *One More Spring*

R-4 Dorothy Parker, *Selected Short Stories of Dorothy Parker*

R-5 Robert Benchley, *After 1903 — What?*

R-6 William H. Roberts, *Psychology You Can Use*

R-7 Norman Corwin, *Selected Radio Plays of Norman Corwin*

R-8 Colonel Stoopnagle, *You Wouldn't Know Me from Adam*

R-9 Jacland Marmur, *Sea Duty*

R-10 Samuel Michael Fuller, *The Dark Page*

R-11 Luke Short, *War on the Cimarron*

R-12 Roderick Peattie, *Geography in Human Destiny*

R-13 David Garth, *Bermuda Calling*

R-14 Sir William Cecil Dampier, *A Shorter History of Science*

R-15 George Sanders, *Crime on My Hands*

R-16 D. W. Brogan, *The American Character*

R-17 Emily Kimbrough and Cornelia Otis Skinner, *Our Hearts Were Young and Gay*

R-18 Alan Le May, *Winter Range*

R-19 Edmund Gilligan, *The Gaunt Woman*

R-20 Arthur Harry Gooden, *Painted Buttes*

R-21 Katherine Anne Porter, *Selected Short Stories of Katherine Anne Porter*

R-22 Margery Sharp, *Cluny Brown*

R-23 Deems Taylor, *Of Men and Music*

R-24 Max Brand, *The Long Chance*

R-25 Christopher Morley, *Kitty Foyle*

R-26 David L. Cohn, *Combustion on Wheels*

R-27 Gwethalyn Graham, *Earth and High Heaven*

R-28 Herbert Best, *Young 'Un*

R-29 Clifford Dowdey, *Gamble's Hundred*

R-30 Sigrid Undset, *The Bridal Wreath*

R-31 Bennett Cerf, *Try and Stop Me*

R-32 Rafael Sabatini, *Captain Blood*

R-33 August Derleth, ed., *Sleep No More*

R-34 Stefan Heym, *Of Smiling Peace*

R-35 Sumner Welles,
*The Time for
Decision*

R-36 Thomas B.
Costain, *For My
Great Folly*

R-37 Lloyd C. Douglas,
Disputed Passage

R-38 W. E. Woodward,
*The Way Our
People Lived*

R-39 Henrietta
Buckmaster,
Deep River

R-40 Samuel Hopkins
Adams, *Canal
Town*

S-Series,
March 1945

S-1 Major William
A. Aiken, ed.,
*A Wartime
Whitman*

S-2 William Saroyan,
Dear Baby

S-3 Ludwig
Bemelmans,
*I Love You, I Love
You, I Love You*

S-4 James Gould
Cozzens, *Castaway*

S-5 James Thurber,
*My World and
Welcome to It*

S-6 Frank Gruber,
Peace Marshal

S-7 Richard Sale,
*Not Too Narrow,
Not Too Deep*

S-8 Philip Wylie,
*Selected Short
Stories of Philip
Wylie*

S-9 Mark Twain,
*Selected Short
Stories of Mark
Twain*

S-10 Dorothy Baker,
*Young Man with
a Horn*

S-11 Frank Sullivan,
*A Pearl in Every
Oyster*

S-12 Eric Hatch,
Unexpected Uncle

S-13 Thomas Beer,
The Mauve Decade

S-14 Evelyn Eaton,
In What Torn Ship

S-15 Alexander Laing,
Clipper Ship Men

S-16 Virginia Perdue,
*Alarum and
Excursion*

S-17 Donald Hough,
Captain Retread

S-18 William MacLeod
Raine, *Guns of the
Frontier*

S-19 Joe E. Brown, *Your
Kids and Mine*

S-20 William Irish,
After-Dinner Story

S-21 Erle Stanley
Gardner, *The Case
of the Black-Eyed
Blonde*

S-22 H. Allen Smith,
*Lost in the Horse
Latitudes*

S-23 Max Brand,
Hunted Riders

S-24 Walter Van
Tilburg Clark,
*The Ox-Bow
Incident*

S-25 Frederick G. Lieb,
*The St. Louis
Cardinals*

S-26 Algernon
Blackwood,
*Selected Short
Stories of Algernon
Blackwood*

S-27 Donald Culross
Peattie, *An
Almanac for
Moderns*

S-28 Thorne Smith,
*The Night Life of
the Gods*

S-29 Edgar Snow, *People
on Our Side*

S-30 Harlan Hatcher,
The Great Lakes

S-31 Louis Bromfield,
The Farm

S-32 Marguerite F.
Bayliss, *The
Bolinvars*

S-33 Marjorie Kinnan
Rawlings,
The Yearling

S-34 Merrill Denison,
Klondike Mike

S-35 William
Makepeace
Thackeray, *Henry
Esmond*

S-36 Joseph Stanley
Pennell,

*The History of
Rome Hanks*

S-37 Francis Hackett,
Henry the Eighth

S-38 Kenneth Roberts,
Arundel

S-39 Elizabeth Goudge,
*Green Dolphin
Street*

S-40 Jean Stafford,
Boston Adventure

T-Series, April 1945

T-1 Cornelia Otis
Skinner, *Dithers
and Jitters*

T-2 H. G. Wells, *The
Time Machine*

T-3 George Papashvily
and Helen
Papashvily,
*Anything Can
Happen*

T-4 David Ewen,
*Men of Popular
Music*

T-5 John Steinbeck,
Cannery Row

T-6 Timothy Fuller,
*This Is Murder,
Mr. Jones*

T-7 Oscar Levant,
*A Smattering of
Ignorance*

T-8 Louis Untermeyer,
ed., *The Fireside
Book of Verse*

T-9 Ezra Stone and
Weldon Melick,
Coming, Major!

T-10 Charles Nordhoff
and James Norman
Hall, *Men Against
the Sea*

T-11 Henry Tetlow,
*We Farm for a
Hobby and Make
It Pay*

T-12 Margery Sharp,
*The Stone of
Chastity*

T-13 Robert Benchley,
*Benchley Beside
Himself*

T-14 MacKinlay Kantor,
Gentle Annie

T-15 Robert M. Coates,
The Outlaw Years

T-16 Charles Alden
Seltzer, *The Range
Boss*

T-17 Patrick Quentin,
Puzzle for Puppets

T-18 Henry James,
*Daisy Miller and
Other Stories*

T-19 Rosemary Taylor,
Ridin' the Rainbow

T-20 Eugene
Cunningham,
Pistol Passport

T-21 Max Brand, *Riders
of the Plain*

T-22 David Rame,
Tunnel from Calais

T-23 William Sloane,
*The Edge of
Running Water*

T-24 Frank Graham,
*The New York
Yankees*

T-25 Burns Mantle, ed.,
*The Best Plays of
1943–1944*

T-26 Howard Fast,
Freedom Road

T-27 Ben Lucien
Burman, *Blow for
a Landing*

T-28 Foster, Nafziger,
Shaw, and Ranger,
*Wolf Law and
Three Other Stories
of the West*

T-29 Esther Forbes,
*The General's
Lady*

T-30 Carl Carmer,
Genesee Fever

T-31 Commander
Walter Karig
and Lieutenant
Welbourne Kelley,
Battle Report

T-32 Louis Bromfield,
*The World We
Live In*

T-33 A. J. Cronin,
The Citadel

T-34 Maritta M. Wolff,
Whistle Stop

T-35 Iola Fuller, *Loon
Feather*

T-36 Daphne du
Maurier,
Rebecca

T-37 Marcus Goodrich,
Delilah

T-38 Peter Freuchen,
Arctic Adventure

T-39 Kathleen Winsor,
Forever Amber

T-40 Margaret Landon,
*Anna and the
King of Siam*

U-Series, May 1945

655 Robert Nathan,
Portrait of Jenny

656 George Lowther,
*Adventures of
Superman*

657 Max Shulman,
*Barefoot Boy with
Cheek*

658 Alfred Lord
Tennyson,
*The Charge of the
Light Brigade and
Other Poems*

659 Joseph Dunninger,
*What's on Your
Mind?*

660 Henry Beston,
*The Outermost
House*

661 Roderick Peattie,
*Look to the
Frontiers*

662 John P. Sousa III,
*My Family, Right
or Wrong*

663 Brett Halliday,
*Murder and the
Married Virgin*

664 George Sessions
Perry and Israel
Leighton, *Where
Away*

665 J. B. Priestley,
*The Old Dark
House*

666 Vera Caspary,
Laura

667 Ernest
Hemingway,
*To Have and
Have Not*

668 Thomas Beer,
*Mrs. Egg and
Other Barbarians*

669 Guy de
Maupassant,
*Mademoiselle
Fifi and Other
Stories*

670 Luke Short,
Gunman's Chance

671 Thorne Smith,
The Glorious Pool

672 Jack London,
White Fang

673 H. Allen Smith,
*Low Man on a
Totem Pole*

674 William MacLeod
Raine, *Trail's End*

675 Dorothy Cameron
Disney, *The 17th
Letter*

676 Paul Eduard
Miller, ed.,
*Esquire's Jazz Book
(1944)*

677 Walter D.
Edmonds,
*Selected Short
Stories*

678 Zane Grey,
Western Union

679 C. S. Forester,
*The Captain from
Connecticut*

680 Ellery Queen,
Calamity Town

681 Elliot Arnold,
*Tomorrow Will
Sing*

682 James Stokley,
*Science Remakes
the World*

683 Ernest Haycox,
*Bugles in the
Afternoon*

684 John J. O'Neill,
*Prodigal Genius:
The Life and Times
of Nikola Tesla*

685 Alexander Laing,
*The Cadaver of
Gideon Wyck*

686 William Targ,
ed., *Western Story
Omnibus*

687 Isak Dinesen,
Seven Gothic Tales

688 Ellen Glasgow,
Barren Ground

689 Edison Marshall,
Great Smith

690 John Steinbeck,
*The Grapes
of Wrath*

691 Charles Dickens,
Pickwick Papers

692 Douglas Rigby and
Elizabeth Rigby,
*Lock, Stock and
Barrel*

693 Irving Stone,
Immortal Wife

694 Martin Flavin,
*Journey in the
Dark*

V-Series, June 1945

695   Ruth McKenney,
      *The McKenneys
      Carry On*

696   E. B. White,
      Quo Vadimus?

697   Arthur Kober,
      *Thunder over
      the Bronx*

698   H. G. Wells,
      *The Island of
      Dr. Moreau*

699   Sally Benson, *Meet
      Me in St. Louis*

700   Frederic F. Van de
      Water, *A Home in
      the Country*

701   Rose Franken,
      Another Claudia

702   Earl Wilson, *I Am
      Gazing Into My
      8-Ball*

703   John Steinbeck,
      *The Pastures of
      Heaven*

704   Henry Wadsworth
      Longfellow, *Paul
      Revere's Ride and
      Other Poems*

705   James Thurber,
      *The Middle-Aged
      Man on the Flying
      Trapeze*

706   Ernest Haycox,
      Deep West

707   Clarence
      Budington
      Kelland, *Arizona*

708   Jesse James
      Benton, *Cow
      by the Tail*

709   C. S. Forester,
      To the Indies

710   Barry Benefield,
      *Eddie and the
      Archangel Mike*

711   Mignon G.
      Eberhart, *Wings
      of Fear*

712   William Colt
      MacDonald,
      *The Three
      Mesquiteers*

713   Vardis Fisher,
      The Golden Rooms

714   Albert Payson
      Terhune, *Lad:
      A Dog*

715   Max Brand,
      Gunman's Gold

716   Walter Blair,
      Tell Tale America

717   *Webster's New
      Handy Dictionary*

718   *Webster's New
      Handy Dictionary*

719   Sgt. George Baker,
      The Sad Sack

720   Edmund Gilligan,
      *Voyage of the
      Golden Hind*

721   W. H. Hudson,
      The Purple Land

722   Zane Grey,
      Sunset Pass

723   J. H. Wallis,
      *The Woman in the
      Window*

724   Marjorie Kinnan
      Rawlings, *South
      Moon Under*

725   Charles Nordhoff

and James Norman
Hall, *Pitcairn's
Island*

726   Frederic Ramsey
      Jr. and Charles
      Edward Smith,
      Jazzmen

727   Ngaio Marsh,
      *Death and the
      Dancing Footman*

728   Paul Gallico,
      Farewell to Sport

729   William Howells,
      Mankind So Far

730   H. P. Lovecraft,
      *The Dunwich
      Horror and Other
      Weird Tales*

731   Colonel John W.
      Thomason Jr., . . .
      And a Few Marines

732   John Selby,
      Starbuck

733   Albert Maltz,
      *The Cross and
      the Arrow*

734   Edward Kasner,
      Lower Than Angels

W-Series, July 1945

735   Gerald Johnson,
      *A Little Night
      Music*

736   William
      Wordsworth, *My
      Heart Leaps Up
      and Other Poems*

737   Robert Nathan,
      *The Enchanted
      Voyage*

738 Gustav Eckstein, *Lives*

739 *Soldier Art* (distributed to Army only)

740 Sgt. Frank Brandt, ed., *Cartoons for Fighters*

741 John O'Hara, *Pipe Night*

742 Morton Thompson, *Joe, the Wounded Tennis Player*

743 Vereen Bell, *Brag Dog and Other Stories*

744 Timothy Fuller, *Harvard Has a Homicide*

745 H. G. Wells, *The War of the Worlds*

746 Francis Wallace, *Kid Galahad*

747 Frances Lockridge and Richard Lockridge, *Death on the Aisle*

748 Ernest Haycox, *Starlight Rider*

749 Joseph Wechsberg, *Looking for a Bluebird*

750 John Steinbeck, *Cup of Gold*

751 Raymond Chandler, *The Big Sleep*

752 Arthur Henry Gooden, *The Valley of Dry Bones*

753 Eugene Cunningham, *Diamond River Man*

754 Paul Gallico, *Adventures of Hiram Holliday*

755 James Thurber, *Let Your Mind Alone*

756 E. C. Abbott and Helena Huntington Smith, *We Pointed Them North*

757 Meyer Berger, *The Eight Million*

758 Willard Robertson, *Moon Tide*

759 Clarence E. Mulford, *Buck Peters, Ranchman*

760 Ngaio Marsh, *Died in the Wool*

761 William Hazlett Upson, *Keep 'Em Crawling*

762 Rhoda Truax, *Joseph Lister*

763 Carl Carmer, *Listen for a Lonesome Drum*

764 Frederick Prokosch, *The Asiatics*

765 William McFee, ed., *World's Great Tales of the Sea*

766 James M. Cain, *Double Indemnity and Two Other Short Novels*

767 Edgar Allan Poe, *Selected Stories of Edgar Allan Poe*

768 Walter D. Edmonds, *Young Ames*

769 Clarence Day, *Life with Father and Mother*

770 Evelyn Eaton, *Quietly My Captain Waits*

771 Lloyd Lewis, *Myths after Lincoln*

772 Virginia Woolf, *The Years*

773 Gene Fowler, *Timber Line*

774 Philip Wylie, *Night unto Night*

X-Series, August 1945

775 William March, *Some Like Them Short*

776 Rupert Brooke, *Collected Poems of Rupert Brooke*

777 Gustav Eckstein, *Canary*

778 Hiram Percy Maxim, *A Genius in the Family*

779 Lawrence Edward Watkin, *On Borrowed Time*

780 Bliss Lomax, *Horsethief Creek*

781 Frank Graham, *Lou Gehrig*

782   Ring Lardner,
      You Know Me, Al

783   George
      Chamberlain,
      The Phantom Filly

784   Charles H. Snow,
      Sheriff of Yavisa

785   Dorothy B.
      Hughes, *The So
      Blue Marble*

786   Baynard Kendrick,
      Blind Man's Bluff

787   Howard Fast,
      *Patrick Henry and
      the Frigate's Keel*

788   Edward L.
      McKenna,
      The Bruiser

789   Frances Lockridge
      and Richard
      Lockridge, *Payoff
      for the Banker*

790   Paul B. Sears,
      This Is Our World

791   Ernest Haycox,
      Trail Smoke

792   Glenway Wescott,
      *Apartment
      in Athens*

793   Theodore Pratt,
      *The Barefoot
      Mountain*

794   John Steinbeck,
      The Long Valley

795   H. Rider Haggard,
      *King Solomon's
      Mines*

796   Arthur Train, *Mr.
      Tutt Finds a Way*

797   Zane Grey, *Forlorn
      River*

798   Ione Sandberg
      Shriber, *Pattern
      for Murder*

799   John O'Hara,
      Butterfield 8

800   Robert Nathan,
      *The Bishop's Wife
      and Two Other
      Novels*

801   Edwin Balmer
      and Philip Wylie,
      *When Worlds
      Collide*

802   Isak Dinesen,
      Winter's Tales

803   Coburn, Foster,
      Ranger, McCulley,
      and Wilson, *Five
      Western Stories*

804   C. S. Forester,
      *Commodore
      Hornblower*

805   Eric Baume,
      Yankee Woman

806   Carl Carmer,
      The Hudson

807   Monte Barrett,
      Sun in Their Eyes

808   Paul de Kruif, *Men
      Against Death*

809   Bernard Jaffe,
      *Men of Science in
      America*

810   Herbert V.
      Prochnow, ed.,
      *Great Stories from
      Great Lives*

811   Louis Bromfield,
      Mrs. Parkington

812   Rafael Sabatini,
      The Sea Hawk

813   MacKinlay Kantor,
      Author's Choice

814   Thomas B.
      Costain, *Ride
      with Me*

Y-Series,
September 1945

815   John van Drutten,
      *The Voice of the
      Turtle*

816   Richard Harding
      Davis, *In the Fog*

817   John O'Hara,
      Pal Joey

818   Joel Sayre,
      Rackety Rax

819   *The New Yorker's
      Baedeker*

820   John Masefield,
      *Selected Poems of
      John Masefield*

821   Richard Shattuck,
      *The Half-Haunted
      Saloon*

822   Bill Mauldin,
      Up Front

823   Willa Cather,
      O Pioneers!

824   John Mills,
      *Electronics
      Today and
      Tomorrow*

825   William Faulkner,
      *A Rose for Emily
      and Other Stories*

826   Margaret Mead,
      *Coming of Age in
      Samoa*

827   Frances Crane,

The Indigo Necklace

828 Dorothy B. Hughes, *The Delicate Ape*

829 C. S. Forester, *Payment Deferred*

830 Arnold Bennett, *Buried Alive*

831 Tom Powers, *Virgin with Butterflies*

832 Thomas L. Stix, ed., *The Sporting Gesture*

833 Charles Alden Seltzer, *Square Deal Sanderson*

834 Clarence E. Mulford, *Bar-20 Days*

835 Ira Wolfert, *American Guerrilla in the Philippines*

836 Rose Franken, *Claudia and David*

837 Ernest Haycox, *Sundown Jim*

838 Raymond Chandler, *The Lady in the Lake*

839 Harry Hamilton, *River Song*

840 James Street, *The Biscuit Eater and Other Stories*

841 Edison Marshall, *The Upstart*

842 Zane Grey, *Twin Sombreros*

843 Margaret Irwin, *Young Bess*

844 Booth Tarkington, *Little Orvie*

845 Louis Bromfield, *Pleasant Valley*

846 Frank Graham, *McGraw of the Giants*

847 Ralph Temple, *Cuckoo Time*

848 Whit Burnett, ed., *Time to Be Young*

849 Hervey Allen, *Bedford Village*

850 Joseph Shearing, *The Lady and the Arsenic*

851 Bram Stoker, *Dracula*

852 John P. Marquand, *Wickford Point*

853 Adria Locke Langley, *A Lion Is in the Streets*

854 Samuel Shellabarger, *Captain from Castile*

Z-Series, October 1945

855 Rosemary Benét and Stephen Vincent Benét, *A Book of Americans*

856 James Thurber, *My Life and Hard Times*

857 Edna St. Vincent Millay, *Lyrics and*

Sonnets

858 Maude Smith Delavan, *The Rumelhearts of Rampler Avenue*

859 Conrad Richter, *Tacey Cromwell*

860 Stefan Zweig, *The Royal Game*

861 Charles Nordhoff, *The Pearl Lagooon*

862 F. Scott Fitzgerald, *The Great Gatsby*

863 Nathaniel Hawthorne, *The Gray Champion and Other Tales*

864 André Maurois, *Ariel: The Life of Shelley*

865 Robert Benchley, *My Ten Years in a Quandary*

866 Erskine Caldwell, *Tragic Ground*

867 Ernest Haycox, *Rim of the Desert*

868 Alan Le May, *Useless Cowboy*

869 Dorothy B. Hughes, *The Fallen Sparrow*

870 Donald Hough, *Snow Above Town*

871 John Collier, *Green Thoughts and Other Strange Tales*

872 S. J. Perelman, *Crazy Like a Fox*

873 Graham Greene,

919 William Maxwell,
     The Folded Leaf
920 Robert Goffin,
     Jazz
921 Ben Hecht,
     *Concerning a
     Woman of Sin and
     Other Stories*
922 Thorne Smith,
     *Rain in the
     Doorway*
923 Joseph Shearing,
     Aunt Beardie
924 Clyde Brion Davis,
     *Rebellion of Leo
     McGuire*
925 Homer, *The
     Odyssey* (Trans. by
     T. E. Shaw)
926 Aldous Huxley,
     *The Gioconda
     Smile and Other
     Stories*
927 Elliot Paul,
     *The Last Time
     I Saw Paris*
928 Hugh Walpole,
     Fortitude
929 George R. Stewart,
     Names on the Land
930 Leonard Ehrlich,
     God's Angry Men
931 Samuel Hopkins
     Adams,
     *A. Woollcott: His
     Life and His World*
932 Hugh MacLennan,
     Two Solitudes
933 *The Bedside Tales*
     (introduction by
     Peter Arno)

934 *The Best from
     Yank, the Army
     Weekly*

**BB-Series,
December 1945**

935 Norman Krasna,
     Dear Ruth
936 Joe (The Markee)
     Madden, *Set
     'Em Up!*
937 Rufus King,
     *The Deadly
     Dove*
938 Francis Russell
     Hart, *Admirals
     of the Caribbean*
939 Robert Browning
     and Elizabeth
     Barrett Browning,
     Love Poems
940 Arthur Machen,
     *The Great God
     Pan and Other
     Weird Stories*
941 Harry Brown,
     *Artie Greengroin,
     Pfc.*
942 Bruce Marshall,
     *The World, the
     Flesh, and Father
     Smith*
943 Vera Caspary,
     Bedelia
944 O. Henry,
     *The Ransom of
     Red Chief and
     Other Stories*
945 Erskine Caldwell,
     God's Little Acre

946 James Gunn,
     *Deadlier Than
     the Male*
947 E. B. Mann,
     Comanche Kid
948 Marione
     Derrickson, ed.,
     Laugh It Off
949 Charles Alden
     Seltzer, *The Boss
     of the Lazy Y*
950 Frances Lockridge
     and Richard
     Lockridge,
     Killing the Goose
951 E. E. Halleran,
     Prairie Guns
952 Theodore Naidish,
     *Watch Out for
     Willie Carter*
953 Thorne Smith,
     *The Passionate
     Witch*
954 Lord Dunsany,
     Guerrilla
955 *The New Yorker
     Profiles*
956 William Colt
     MacDonald,
     Cartridge Carnival
957 Ronald
     Kirkbridge,
     *Winds, Blow
     Gently*
958 H. G. Wells,
     *The Food of the
     Gods*
959 Edna Ferber,
     Great Son
960 Herbert S. Zim,
     Rockets and Jets

961   Phil Stong,
      Marta of Muscovy

962   John D. Ratcliff,
      ed., *Science
      Yearbook of 1945*

963   Frank Graham,
      *The Brooklyn
      Dodgers*

964   Dillon Ripley,
      *Trail of the
      Money Bird*

965   Herb Graffis, ed.,
      *Esquire's First
      Sports Reader*

966   James Hilton,
      *So Well
      Remembered*

967   Jack Gaver and
      Dave Stanley,
      *There's Laughter
      in the Air!*

968   Lau Shaw,
      Rickshaw Boy

969   Sinclair Lewis,
      Cass Timberlane

970   James Thurber,
      *The Thurber
      Carnival*

971   W. Somerset
      Maugham,
      The Razor's Edge

972   Lillian Smith,
      Strange Fruit

973   Stuart Cloete,
      *Against These
      Three*

974   Walter Van
      Tilburg Clark,
      *The City of
      Trembling
      Leaves*

*CC-Series,
January 1946*

975   Herbert Clyde
      Lewis, *Gentleman
      Overboard*

976   Stephen Leacock,
      *My Remarkable
      Uncle and Other
      Sketches*

977   Paul Corey,
      Buy an Acre

978   C. B. F. Macauley,
      *The Helicopters
      Are Coming*

979   John O'Hara,
      *The Doctor's Son
      and Other Stories*

980   Robert Trumbull,
      Silversides

981   Ogden Nash,
      *I'm a Stranger
      Here Myself*

982   Max Brand,
      Silvertip's Search

983   Oliver Weld
      Bayer, *An Eye for
      an Eye*

984   G. K. Chesterton,
      *The Man Who
      Was Thursday*

985   Archie Robertson,
      *Slow Train to
      Yesterday*

986   Irving Crump,
      *Our United States
      Secret Service*

987   Charles Alden
      Seltzer, *"Beau"
      Rand*

988   Richard Powell,

*Lay That Pistol
Down*

989   William MacLeod
      Raine, *Who Wants
      to Live Forever?*

990   Donald
      Henderson Clarke,
      Louis Beretti

991   Carter Dickson,
      *The Curse of the
      Bronze Lamp*

992   Sewell Peaslee
      Wright, ed.,
      Chicago Murders

993   Stanley Frank, ed.,
      Sports Extra

994   John Erskine,
      *The Private Life
      of Helen of Troy*

995   Frances Crane,
      *The Amethyst
      Spectacles*

996   C. S. Forester,
      Beat to Quarters

997   Zane Grey,
      *The Heritage
      of the Desert*

998   John Hawkins and
      Ward Hawkins,
      Devil on His Trail

999   Ben Lucien
      Burman, *Rooster
      Crows for Day*

1000 Paul Eduard
      Miller, ed.,
      *Esquire's 1945
      Jazz Book*

1001 Clark McMeekin,
      Black Moon

1002 Darrell Huff and
      Frances Huff,

Twenty Careers of Tomorrow

1003 Edgcumb Pinchon, *Dan Sickles*

1004 Bellamy Partridge, *January Thaw*

1005 George Bernard Shaw, *Arms and the Man and Two Other Plays*

1006 Rafael Sabatini, *The Birth of Mischief*

1007 Thomas Bell, *All Brides Are Beautiful*

1008 George Russell Harrison, *Atoms in Action*

1009 A. J. Cronin, *The Green Years*

1010 Ross McLaury Taylor, *The Saddle and the Plow*

1011 Jack London, *Best Short Stories of Jack London*

1012 Sophie Tucker, *Some of These Days*

1013 Thomas Wolfe, *Of Time and the River*

1014 Kenneth Roberts, *Northwest Passage*

DD-Series, February 1946

1015 A. E. Housman, *Selected Poems of A. E. Housman*

1016 James Thurber and E. B. White, *Is Sex Necessary?*

1017 Fred Russell, *I'll Try Anything Twice*

1018 John Paul Andrews, *Your Personal Plane*

1019 S. J. Perelman and Q. J. Reynolds, *Parlor, Bedlam, and Bath*

1020 Thomas Bell, *Till I Come Back to You*

1021 W. C. Tuttle, *The Wolf Pack of Lobo Butte*

1022 Bliss Lomax, *Rusty Guns*

1023 Virgil Thomson, *The State of Music*

1024 Mark Van Doren, *Liberal Education*

1025 Clarence Budington Kelland, *Dreamland*

1026 Francis Bonnamy, *The King Is Dead on Queen Street*

1027 Earl Schenck Miers, *Big Ben*

1028 T. S. Stribling, *Red Sand*

1029 George Price, *Is It Anyone We Know?*

1030 Charles Alden Seltzer, *"Drag" Harlan*

1031 Nicholas Blake, *The Corpse in the Snowman*

1032 Douglas E. Lurton, *Make the Most of Your Life*

1033 Esther Forbes, *O Genteel Lady!*

1034 Helen McCloy, *Panic*

1035 Alfredo Segre, *Mahogany*

1036 Eugene Cunningham, *Buckaroo*

1037 Arch Ward, *Frank Leahy and the Fighting Irish*

1038 Manning Coles, *They Tell No Tales*

1039 Erle Stanley Gardner, *The Case of the Half-Wakened Wife*

1040 John F. Embree, *The Japanese Nation*

1041 Charles Jackson, *The Lost Weekend*

1042 John Russell, *Selected Short Stories of John Russell*

1043 F. Scott Fitzgerald, *The Diamond as Big as the Ritz and Other Stories*

1044 Harland Manchester, *New World of Machines*

1045 George R. Stewart, *Storm*

1046 Gontran de Poncins, *Kabloona*

1047 Josephine Pinckey,
      *Three O'Clock
      Dinner*
1048 Margaret
      Armstrong,
      Trelawny
1049 Alice Tisdale
      Hobart, *Oil for the
      Lamps of China*
1050 Bennett Cerf, ed.,
      *Modern American
      Short Stories*
1051 D. B. Steinman,
      *The Builders of
      the Bridge*
1052 George F.
      Willison, *Saints
      and Strangers*
1053 James Ramsey
      Ullman, *The
      White Tower*
1054 A. J. Cronin,
      *The Stars Look
      Down*

**EE-Series,
March 1946**

1055 Edmund Gilligan,
      *Hunter's Moon and
      Other Stories*
1056 Robert Herrick,
      *The Love Poems
      of Robert Herrick*
1057 Cornelia Otis
      Skinner, *Excuse
      It, Please!*
1058 James M. Cain,
      *The Postman
      Always Rings Twice*
1059 David Ewen,

      *The Story of
      George Gershwin*
1060 Hugh Gray and
      Lillian R. Lieber,
      *The Education of
      T. C. Mits*
1061 Sally Carrighar,
      *One Day on Beetle
      Rock*
1062 Nicolas
      Kalashnikoff,
      Jumper
1063 David Dietz,
      *Atomic Energy in
      the Coming Era*
1064 George S. Brooks,
      *Block That Bride
      and Other Stories*
1065 James Oliver
      Curwood, *Kazan*
1066 *The New Yorker
      Reporter at
      Large*
1067 George Sessions
      Perry, *Hold
      Autumn in Your
      Hand*
1068 John J. Floherty,
      Inside the F.B.I.
1069 Carter Dickson,
      *The Department of
      Queer Complaints*
1070 Dorothy Caruso,
      Enrico Caruso
1071 Charles Alden
      Seltzer, *The
      Vengeance of
      Jefferson Gawne*
1072 Clarence E.
      Mulford, *The Man
      from Bar-20*

1073 James B. Hendryx,
      *Gold and Guns on
      Halfaday Creek*
1074 Craig Rice,
      *The Sunday Pigeon
      Murders*
1075 Hulbert Footner,
      *The Murder That
      Had Everything*
1076 R. N. Linscott,
      Comic Relief
1077 Louise Dickinson
      Rich, *We Took to
      the Woods*
1078 Darwin L. Teilhet,
      My True Love
1079 Carroll Lane
      Fenton and
      Mildred Adams
      Fenton,
      *The Story of the
      Great Geologists*
1080 Leo Tolstoy,
      Tales by Tolstoy
1081 William G.
      Campbell and
      James H. Bedford,
      *You and Your
      Future Job*
1082 Thomas B.
      Costain,
      The Black Rose

**FF-Series,
April 1946**

1083 *Walt Tulley's
      Baseball Recorder*
1084 John P. Marquand,
      Repent in Haste
1085 Lawrence Lariar,

ed., *Best Cartoons of the Year 1945*

1086 J. Storer Clouston, *The Lunatic at Large*

1087 George Gamow, *Biography of the Earth*

1088 Roy Huggins, *The Double Take*

1089 Ladd Haystead, *If the Prospect Pleases*

1090 Robert S. Dowst, *Straight, Place and Show*

1091 H. G. Wells, *The War of the Worlds*

1092 Francis Wallace, *Kid Galahad*

1093 Frances Lockridge and Richard Lockridge, *Death on the Aisle*

1094 Ernest Haycox, *Starlight Rider*

1095 David B. Greenberg and Henry Schindall, *A Small Store and Independence*

1096 Ben Lucien Burman, *Steamboat Round the Bend*

1097 Baynard Kendrick, *Out of Control*

1098 Lawrence Treat, *V as in Victim*

1099 Joseph Conrad, *Typhoon* and *The End of the Tether*

1100 Betty MacDonald, *The Egg and I*

1101 Charles Alden Seltzer, *The Ranchman*

1102 Captain Harry C. Butcher, U.S.N.R., *My Three Years with Eisenhower*

1103 Deems Taylor, *The Well-Tempered Listener*

1104 Nancy Bruff, *The Manatee*

1105 John F. Wharton, *The Theory and Practice of Earning a Living*

1106 Craig Rice, *The Big Midget Murders*

1107 Zane Grey, *The Border Legion*

1108 Walter Noble Burns, *The Saga of Billy the Kid*

1109 Douglass Welch, *Mr. Digby*

1110 Richard C. Gill, *White Water and Black Magic*

1111 Edna Ferber, *Saratoga Trunk*

1112 Orrin E. Dunlap Jr., *Radio's 100 Men of Science*

1113 Konstantine Simonov, *Days and Nights*

1114 Stephen Vincent Benét, *John Brown's Body*

GG-Series, May 1946

1115 Christopher Isherwood, *Prater Violet*

1116 Sgt. Leonard Sansone, *The Wolf*

1117 H. Vernor Dixon, *Come In Like a Yankee and Other Stories*

1118 Margery Miller, *Joe Louis: American*

1119 Max Shulman, *The Zebra Derby*

1120 Henry G. Lamond, *Dingo*

1121 James Stephens, *The Crock of Gold*

1122 Carl Sandburg, *Selected Poems of Carl Sandburg*

1123 Kathleen Moore Knight, *Port of Seven Strangers*

1124 Martin Johnson, *Safari*

1125 Grace Zaring Stone (Ethel Vance), *The Bitter Tea of General Yen*

1126 Carl Crow, *The Great American Customer*

1127 Barry Benefield, *Valiant Is the Word for Carrie*

1128 John P. Carmichael,

*My Greatest Day
in Baseball*

1129 William MacLeod
Raine, *Courage
Stout*

1130 W. Barber and
R. Schabelitz, *The
Noose Is Drawn*

1131 Erle Stanley
Gardner, *The Case
of the Black-Eyed
Blonde*

1132 H. Allen Smith,
*Lost in the Horse
Latitudes*

1133 Max Brand,
Hunted Riders

1134 Walter Van
Tilburg Clark, *The
Ox-Bow Incident*

1135 Forbes Parkhill,
Troopers West

1136 George Harmon
Coxe, *Woman
at Bay*

1137 Ed Fitzgerald, ed.,
Tales for Males

1138 Robert Standish,
The Small General

1139 Ivan T. Sanderson,
*Caribbean
Treasure*

1140 Norman V.
Carlisle and
Frank B. Latham,
Miracles Ahead

1141 Clarence E.
Mulford,
The Bar-20 Three

1142 Mark Van Doren,
Shakespeare

1143 Lee R.Steiner,
*Where Do People
Take Their
Troubles?*

1144 Marquis James,
The Cherokee Ship

1145 Christina Stead
and William Blake,
eds., *Modern
Women in Love*

1146 Wilbur Daniel
Steele, *That Girl
from Memphis*

HH-Series,
June 1946

1147 John O'Hara,
Pal Joey

1148 Joel Sayre,
Rackety Rax

1149 George Papashvily
and Helen
Papashvily,
*Anything Can
Happen*

1150 David Ewen, *Men
of Popular Music*

1151 Ogden Nash,
*Many Long
Years Ago*

1152 Grace Zaring
Stone (Ethel
Vance), *Winter
Meeting*

1153 M. M. Musselman,
*Wheels in His
Head*

1154 Peter Field,
*The End of the
Trail*

1155 Margaret Scherf,
*The Owl in the
Cellar*

1156 *The Dark Ship and
Other Selections
from the New
Yorker*

1157 Clyde Fisher, *The
Story of the Moon*

1158 W. H. B. Kent,
The Tenderfoot

1159 Russell Maloney,
It's Still Maloney

1160 Roy Chapman
Andrews, *Meet
Your Ancestors*

1161 W. R. Burnett,
*Tomorrow's
Another Day*

1162 Frances Lockridge
and Richard
Lockridge, *Murder
within Murder*

1163 Tom Gill,
Starlight Pass

1164 Ernest Haycox,
Trail Town

1165 Geoffrey
Household,
*The Salvation of
Pisco Gabar and
Other Stories*

1166 Patricia
Wentworth,
She Came Back

1167 Walter S. Landis,
*Your Servant the
Molecule*

1168 Commander
Edward Ellsberg,
Treasure Below

1169 William Sloane, *The Edge of Running Water*

1170 Frank Graham, *The New York Yankees*

1171 Harold Hart, ed., *Top Stuff*

1172 J. Roy Stockton, *The Gashouse Gang*

1173 William Irish, *I Wouldn't Be in Your Shoes*

1174 Peter W. Rainier, *Green Fire*

1175 B. D. Zevin, ed., *Cobb's Cavalcade*

1176 Daphne du Maurier, *The King's General*

1177 Erich Maria Remarque, *Arch of Triumph*

1178 Jack Goodman, ed., *While You Were Gone*

Beginning with the II-Series, the ASEs were printed in smaller batches for occupation troops.

II-Series, July 1946

1179 Ernie Pyle, *Last Chapter*

1180 John McNulty, *Third Avenue, New York*

1181 Peter Field, *Ravaged Range*

1182 Gore Vidal, *Williwaw*

1183 Will Ermine, *Outlaw on Horseback*

1184 Luke Short, *Coroner Creek*

1185 Dorothy Macardle, *The Unforeseen*

1186 Lucy Cores, *Let's Kill George*

1187 C. S. Forester, *Lord Hornblower*

1188 Alice Campbell, *With Bated Breath*

1189 Gene Fowler, *A Solo in Tom-Toms*

1190 Ben Hibbs, ed., *The Saturday Evening Post Stories, 1942–1945*

JJ-Series, August 1946

1191 Lee Casey, ed., *Denver Murders*

1192 Curtis Bishop, *By Way of Wyoming*

1193 Frank Sullivan, *A Rock in Every Snowball*

1194 Jonathan Stagge, *Death's Old Sweet Song*

1195 Rex Beach, *The World in His Arms*

1196 William MacLeod Raine, *Clattering Hoofs*

1197 Warren Brown, *The Chicago Cubs*

1198 Jim Corbett, *Man-Eater of Kumaon*

1199 Stanley Vestal, *Jim Bridger*

1200 Ernest K. Gann, *Blaze of Noon*

1201 Robert Penn Warren, *All the King's Men*

1202 Willa Gibbs, *Tell Your Sons*

KK-Series, September 1946

1203 Thomas Heggen, *Mister Roberts*

1204 Arthur Sampson, *Football Coach*

1205 Richard Sale, *Benefit Performance*

1206 E. E. Halleran, *Double Cross Trail*

1207 Earl Wilson, *Pikes Peek or Bust*

1208 William Colt MacDonald, *Thunderbird Trail*

1209 Vera Caspary, *Stranger Than Truth*

1210 George Tabori, *Companions of the Left Hand*

1211 Mary O'Hara,
       *Green Grass of
       Wyoming*

1212 Theodora C.
       Stanwell-Fletcher,
       Driftwood Valley

1213 Wilbur Daniel
       Steele, *The Best
       Stories of Wilbur
       Daniel Steele*

1214 Commander
       Edward Ellsberg,
       *Under the Red
       Sea Sun*

LL-Series,
October 1946

1215 Kenneth Fearing,
       The Big Clock

1216 Max Brand,
       Mountain Riders

1217 Pat Frank,
       Mr. Adam

1218 Erle Stanley
       Gardner, *The Case
       of the Borrowed
       Brunette*

1219 Christopher
       La Farge,
       *The Sudden
       Guest*

1220 Peter Freuchen,
       White Man

1221 Jonathan Daniels,
       *Frontier on the
       Potomac*

1222 Stout Rex,
       The Silent Speaker

1223 Joseph A.
       Margolies, ed.,

*Strange and
Fantastic Stories*

1224 Odell Shepard and
       Willard Shepard,
       Holdfast Gaines

1225 John P. Marquand,
       B.F.'s Daughter

1226 John Jennings,
       The Salem Frigate

MM-Series,
November 1946

1227 Ralph G. Martin,
       Boy from Nebraska

1228 David Stern,
       Francis

1229 Willis George,
       *Surreptitious
       Entry*

1230 James B. Hendryx,
       *Courage of the
       North*

1231 Frances Lockridge
       and Richard
       Lockridge, *Death
       of a Tall Man*

1232 John Steinbeck,
       The Wayward Bus

1233 MacKinlay Kantor,
       *But Look, the
       Morn*

1234 Van Wyck Mason,
       Saigon Singer

1235 Fred Gipson,
       Fabulous Empire

1236 Frank Waters,
       The Colorado

1237 Ed Ainsworth
       (Edward M.),
       Eagles Fly West

1238 Inglis Fletcher,
       Toil of the Brave

NN-Series,
December 1946

1239 Les Savage Jr.,
       *Treasure of the
       Brasada*

1240 Tom West, *Six
       Gun Showdown*

1241 Helen Reilly,
       *The Silver
       Leopard*

1242 Luther Whiteman,
       *The Face of the
       Clam*

1243 William Wister
       Haines, *Command
       Decision*

1244 Arthur Henry
       Gooden,
       *The Shadowed
       Trail*

1245 Bergen Evans,
       *The Natural
       History of
       Nonsense*

1246 Carter Dickson,
       My Late Wives

1247 Mildred Walker,
       The Quarry

1248 James A.
       Michener, *Tales of
       the South Pacific*

1249 Holger Cahill,
       *Look South to
       the Polar Star*

1250 Eric Sevareid,
       *Not So Wild a
       Dream*

Nancy Freedman,
Mrs. Mike

1296 Annemarie Ewing,
Little Gate

1297 A. B. Guthrie Jr.,
The Big Sky

1298 Raymond T. Bond,
ed., *Famous Stories
of Code & Cipher*

SS-Series, May 1947

1299 Allan R.
Bosworth, *Hang
and Rattle*

1300 Peter Field, *Trail
from Needle Rock*

1301 George Milburn,
Flannigan's Folly

1302 Erle Stanley
Gardner, *The Case
of the Fan-Dancer's
Horse*

1303 Francis Rufus
Bellamy, *Blood
Money*

1304 William Colt
MacDonald,
Master of the Mesa

1305 Arthur Loveridge,
*Tomorrow's a
Holiday*

1306 John Jennings,
*Boston: Cradle
of Liberty*

1307 Michael Leigh,
Comrade Forest

1308 Robert
McLaughlin,

*The Side of the
Angels*

1309 Herbert Krause,
The Thresher

1310 Idwal Jones,
Vermilion

TT-Series, June 1947

1311 Max Brand,
The False Rider

1312 Kathleen Moore
Knight, *The Blue
Horse of Taxco*

1313 Craig Rice, ed., *Los
Angeles Murders*

1314 Elliot Merrick,
Passing By

1315 Richard Phenix,
On My Way Home

1316 Bob Feller,
Strikeout Story

1317 Budd Schulberg,
*The Harder They
Fall*

1318 Charles E.
Gillham, *Raw
North*

1319 Natalie Anderson
Scott, *The Story of
Mrs. Murphy*

1320 Thomas B.
Costain, *The
Moneyman*

1321 Samuel
Shellabarger,
Prince of Foxes

1322 Ernie Pyle, *Home
Country*

2002–3

The Armed Services Editions reappeared in 2002 and 2003, when Andrew Carroll's Legacy Project distributed 100,000 copies of seven titles to Americans serving in the armed forces around the world. These modern ASEs had the same dimensions and appearance as the 1940s ASEs.

Allen Mikaelian,
Medal of Honor

William Shakespeare,
Henry V

Sun Tzu,
The Art of War

Andrew Carroll, ed.,
War Letters

Christopher Buckley,
Wry Martinis

Dr. John A. Gable, ed.,
The Man in the Arena

Geraldine
McCaughrean,
*One Thousand and
One Arabian Nights*

Notes

Introduction

page

xi *"Were you ever"*: Letter from D. C. to "Mrs. Jones," May 20, 1944, Council on Books in Wartime Records, 1942–1947, Coll. No. MC038, 20th Century Public Policy Papers, Seeley G. Mudd Manuscript Library, Department of Rare Books and Special Collections, Princeton University Library (hereinafter Council Records).

xii *"have breakfast with"*: Letter from "somewhere in the Philippines," February 2, 1945, Council Records.

xiii *"God-damned infantry"*: Ernie Pyle, *Here Is Your War* (New York: Pocket Books, 1944), 255.

    ducks in a shooting: James J. Fahey, *Pacific War Diary* (New York: Zebra Books, 1963), 63.

xiv *"out of uniform"*: Letter from B. T. C., October 17, 1944, Council Records.

    "To heave one": Letter from "Sidney" from "somewhere at sea" (undated), Council Records.

1. A Phoenix Will Rise

1 *Even the misty:* Frederick T. Birchall, "Nazi Book-Burning Fails to Stir Berlin," *New York Times,* May 11, 1933.

2 *"the Jew, who is powerful"*: Ibid.

    "literary rascality": Ibid.

3 *Goebbels oversaw:* A. J. Ryder, *Twentieth-Century Germany: From Bismarck to Brandt* (New York: Columbia University Press, 1973), 357–58.

    "Jewish intellectualism": Birchall, "Nazi Book-Burning Fails to Stir Berlin."

4 *ninety-three additional:* Jan-Pieter Barbian, *The Politics of Literature in Nazi Germany: Books in the Media Dictatorship,* trans. Kate Sturge (New York: Bloomsbury Academic, 2013), 23–25.

    one hundred massive volumes: "100 Volumes Burned in Munich," *New York Times,* May 11, 1933.

"as you watch": "Bibliocaust," *Time,* May 22, 1933.

"really clean": Jonathan Rose, ed., *The Holocaust and the Book: Destruction and Preservation* (Amherst: University of Massachusetts Press, 2001), 17.

among the authors: Writers' War Board List of Banned Authors, Council Records.

"History has taught": "Helen Keller Warns Germany's Students; Says Burning of Books Cannot Kill Ideas," *New York Times,* May 10, 1933.

5 *"noblest books produced":* "Nazis Pile Books for Bonfires Today," *New York Times,* May 10, 1933.

"had never yet destroyed": "H. G. Wells Scores Nazis as 'Louts,'" *New York Times,* September 22, 1933.

Library of Burned: "Paris Library for Banned Books Opens on First Anniversary of Nazi Bonfire," *New York Times,* May 11, 1934.

6 *chief glory:* Editorial, "Enlightenment," *New York Times,* April 30, 1933.

"such an exhibition": "Book-Burning Day," *New York Times,* May 11, 1933.

"bibliocaust": "Bibliocaust," *Time,* May 22, 1933.

state-sanctioned reading: Abraham Foxman, introduction to *Mein Kampf,* trans. Ralph Manheim (Boston: Houghton Mifflin, 1999), xxi.

The führer's involvement: Steven Kasher, "The Art of Hitler," *October* 59 (Winter 1992), 52, 65.

7 *"everything concerning":* "Nazis Pile Books for Bonfires," *New York Times.*

vacancies ran: Ryder, *Twentieth-Century Germany,* 364.

exploited radio: Kasher, "The Art of Hitler."

8 *wielded enormous power:* Richard Lucas, *Axis Sally: The American Voice of Nazi Germany* (Philadelphia: Casemate, 2010), 46.

banned eighteen categories: Christopher P. Loss, "Reading Between Enemy Lines: Armed Services Editions and World War II," *Journal of Military History* 67, no. 3 (July 2003), 817.

books to people: Lucas, *Axis Sally,* 53.

violent anti-Jewish: "Berlin Raids Reply to Death of Envoy," *New York Times,* November 10, 1938.

9 *By the following day:* Otto D. Tolischus, "Nazis Defend Wave of Terror," *New York Times,* November 12, 1938; Lucas, *Axis Sally,* 53.

"openly sanctioned": Tolischus, "Nazis Defend Wave of Terror."

10 *Newspapers were flooded:* "American Press Comment on Nazi Riots," *New York Times,* November 12, 1938.

11 *Germany hired:* Edmund Taylor, *The Strategy of Terror* (Boston: Houghton Mifflin, 1940), 70, 45.

similarly destroying: Lisa Sergio, "The Importance of Interpreting America," *American Library Association Bulletin* 35, no. 9 (October 1941), 486.

12 *On June 17, 1940:* Guido Enderis, "Ceremony Is Brief," *New York Times,* June 22, 1940.

After the armistice: "Berlin to Receive the Armistice Car," *New York Times,* June 22, 1940.

Once a nation: Loss, "Reading Between Enemy Lines," 818.

Libraries in occupied: Flora B. Ludington, "Books and the Sword — Symbols of Our Time," *American Library Association Bulletin* 37, no. 5 (May 1943), 151.

13 *H. G. Wells's Library:* "Events Connected with the Burning of the Books," 3, Council Records.

"There are two": Raoul de Roussy de Sales, *The Making of Tomorrow* (New York: Reynal & Hitchcock, 1942), 1.

14 *For eighteen hours:* Cabell Phillips, "War of the Air Waves," *New York Times,* December 28, 1941.

American expatriates: Lucas, *Axis Sally,* 58.

Germany's broadcasts: Phillips, "War of the Air Waves."

15 *"the destruction of":* "National Defense and the Library," *American Library Association Bulletin* 35, no. 1 (January 1941), 5.

In the words of one librarian: Emily Miller Danton, "Victory Begins at Home," *American Library Association Bulletin* 36, no. 9 (September 1941), 535.

"arise victoriously": Alfred Kantorowicz, "The Burned Books Still Live," *New York Times,* May 7, 1944.

2. $85 Worth of Clothes, but No Pajamas

17 *"In all phases":* "Keep Your Men Informed," *What the Soldier Thinks,* no. 7 (Washington, D.C.: U.S. War Department, 1944), 6–7 (quoting *Basic Field Manual 21-50,* p. 29).

Gallup poll: Hadley Cantril, "Impact of the War on the Nation's Viewpoint," *New York Times,* June 2, 1940.

"The most powerful": "To Defend America," *New York Times,* June 7, 1940.

18 *"Two worlds":* "Two Worlds," *Life,* December 23, 1940, p. 14.

With an army: John Alden Jamieson, *Books for the Army: The Army Library Service in the Second World War* (New York: Columbia University Press, 1950), 55.

President Roosevelt reminded: Charles Hurd, "Need of Men Vital," *New York Times,* August 3, 1940.

Under this legislation: "The Draft: How It Works," *Time,* September 23, 1940.

19   *In New York:* "Only Two Are Arrested, Though 991,000 Register," *New York Times,* October 17, 1940.

"*Land had to*": Doris Kearns Goodwin, *No Ordinary Time: Franklin and Eleanor Roosevelt; the Home Front in World War II* (New York: Simon & Schuster, 1994), 217.

The timing of: Meyer Berger, "American Soldier — One Year After," *New York Times,* November 23, 1941.

20   "*hell hole*": Francis A. O'Brien, *Battling for Saipan* (New York: Ballantine, 2003), 9–11.

"*You'll haul coal*": Marion Hargrove, *See Here, Private Hargrove* (New York: Pocket Books, 1942), 1, 3 (emphasis added).

21   a "*field uniform*": Frederick Simpich, "Around the Clock with Your Soldier Boy," *National Geographic,* July 1941, pp. 3, 23.

mop handle: Berger, "American Soldier."

At Fort McClellan: O'Brien, *Battling for Saipan,* 9–11.

"*troops carried wooden*": Dwight D. Eisenhower, *Crusade in Europe* (New York: Doubleday, 1948), 7.

Up at 6:00 a.m.: "Army Morale," *Life,* December 23, 1940, p. 55.

men would crawl: Alonzo G. Grace, *Educational Lessons from Wartime Training* (Washington, D.C.: American Council on Education, 1948), 16, 26–29.

22   "*You learned that*": James J. Fahey, *Pacific War Diary* (New York: Zebra Books, 1963), 5.

23   *most men preferred: What the Soldier Thinks: A Monthly Digest of War Department Studies on the Attitudes of American Troops,* vol. 1, no. 1 (Washington, D.C.: War Department, Morale Services Division, Army Service Forces, December 1943), 15; available at the website of the George C. Marshall Foundation, http://staging.gibsondesign.com/marshall/library /publications_soldier_thinks.html.

At Georgia's Fort Benning: "Army Morale," 55.

24   "*light and sinful*": *The Soldier's Pocket-Book* (Philadelphia: Presbyterian Board of Publication, 1861), 2.

"*soldiers in the field*": Homer B. Sprague, "Some Lessons of the War: An Old Soldier's Conclusions as to What It All Comes To," *Advocate of Peace* 77, no. 2 (February 1915), 41.

mélange of civilian: Vice Adm. Albert Gleaves, "Books and Reading for the Navy, and What They Have Meant in the War," *Bulletin of the American Library Association* 13, no. 3 (July 1919), 156.

25   *"made life worth"*: Maj. Thomas Marshall Spaulding, "Shall We Forget the
      Soldier?," *North American Review* 214, no. 788 (July 1921), 34–35.
      After World War I: Jamieson, *Books for the Army*, 15.
      "a valuable means": Col. Edward L. Munson, "Libraries and Reading as an
      Aid to Morale," *Bulletin of the American Library Association* 13, no. 3 (July
      1919), 135.
      As the nation: Letter from Edwin Ward to Julia Wright Merrill, January 6,
      1942, Victory Book Campaign Records, Manuscripts and Archives Division,
      New York Public Library, Astor, Lenox, and Tilden Foundations (hereinaf-
      ter VBC Records).

26   *Raymond L. Trautman*: Jamieson, *Books for the Army*, 20–23.

27   *wiped clean*: ALA Executive Board Meeting, October 6–8, 1941, document
      dated September 20, 1941; Memorandum for Colonel Watrous regarding the
      Report of Library Activities, VBC Records.
      "Books are available": Letter from Marie Loizeaux to Julius King dated Au-
      gust 30, 1941, VBC Records.
      1941 annual meeting: "Final Reports, Victory Book Campaign, 1942–1943,"
      VBC Records.

28   *Overcome by the*: Memorandum of Meeting in Washington, D.C., held on
      October 9, 1941, VBC Records.
      blueprint for the project: "Final Reports, Victory Book Campaign."
      "#1 in the field": Memorandum, "USO for National Defense, Inc.," VBC Rec-
      ords.

29   *"Before opening"*: Martha Boaz, *Fervent and Full of Gifts: The Life of Althea
      Warren* (New York: Scarecrow Press, 1961), 45–46.
      Warren later moved: "Biographical Information" for Althea Hester Warren,
      VBC Records.

30   *"Most of us"*: Boaz, *Fervent and Full of Gifts*, 95–96, 109.

3. A Landslide of Books

31   *"The soldier"*: Danton, "Victory Begins at Home," 535.
      "It is going": Boaz, *Fervent and Full of Gifts*, 97.

32   *National Transitads*: Letter from Myron T. Harshaw, Vice President of Na-
      tional Transitads, Inc., to Marie Loizeaux, December 30, 1941, and Safeway
      Bulletin, January 6, 1942; "Final Reports, Victory Book Campaign."
      Donations from: "Books Start to Pour In for Service Men; President and
      Mrs. Roosevelt Donate," *New York Times*, January 10, 1942.
      American troops began: Charles G. Bolte, *The New Veteran* (New York: Rey-
      nal & Hitchcock, 1945), 28–29.

33 *After being blessed:* "Books Start to Pour In."

"*Carrying the books*": "City Gives Books for Service Men," *New York Times,* January 13, 1942.

American Women's Voluntary: "Victory Book Campaign Program on the Steps of the New York Public Library," Advisory Committee Meeting, January 27, 1942, Report on the Progress of the Victory Book Campaign, VBC Records.

33 *Morley was a household name:* "Christopher Morley, Author, 66, Is Dead," *New York Times,* March 29, 1957.

34 *Morley's speech begins:* "Speech by Maurice Evans — The Gutenberg Address by Christopher Morley," January 21, 1942, VBC Records.

35 *By early 1942:* "8,000,000-Man Army: Stepping Up the Draft," *United States News,* May 22, 1942.

five largest cities: John Connor, "On to Victory with the Victory Book Campaign," *American Library Association Bulletin* 36, no. 9 (September 1942), 552.

Within two weeks: "100,000 Books Sent to Armed Services," *New York Times,* January 29, 1942.

"*Although we realized*": Meeting of Advisory Committee of the VBC, January 27, 1942, VBC Records.

36 "*Our library here*": Letter to the Wichita VBC from W. A. B., 2nd Lieut. Air Corps., Library Officer, March 5, 1942, VBC Records.

"*You have started*": Letter from W. B. to M. S., May 4, 1942, VBC Records.

"*Something's wrong*": Editorial, "Design for Giving," *Saturday Review of Literature,* February 7, 1942.

37 *the Office of Production:* "Aluminum Drive Set at 2,000 Planes," *New York Times,* July 12, 1941.

"*Enthusiastic householders*": Goodwin, *No Ordinary Time,* 258–60.

think twice: "Any Rags, Any Paper for Freedom Today?" *New York Times,* April 2, 1942.

38 "*not enough nonessential*": "Capitol Rounds up 318 Tons of Scrap," *New York Times,* July 3, 1942.

In two weeks: "Rubber Collection Extended 10 Days," *New York Times,* June 30, 1942; Goodwin, *No Ordinary Time,* 358.

"*workers stand ready*": "The President's Message," *New York Times,* January 7, 1942.

"*Life under a war*": Eugene S. Duffield and William F. Kerby, "The War Economy, Like Living in a Great Depression," *Wall Street Journal,* February 9, 1942.

General Motors: Goodwin, *No Ordinary Time,* 362, 357–59.

39 *Gone were:* Bennett Cerf, "Auto Curbs Bring New Book Demand," *New York Times,* January 3, 1943.

Even years after: Paul Fussell, *Wartime: Understanding and Behavior in the Second World War* (New York: Oxford University Press, 1989), 197–98.

"Whether or not": James M. Landis, "We Have Become a Team," *New York Times,* December 6, 1942.

When the Office: "Golf Ball Rush Causes Rationing," *New York Times,* December 19, 1941.

Women grabbed handfuls: "Girdles for the Duration," *New York Times,* January 11, 1942.

40 *"If it is news":* "Don't Be a Hoarder," *New York Times,* February 15, 1942.

"If you don't believe": "The President's Broadcast," *New York Times,* April 29, 1942.

Warren turned: "Victory Books Records, Publishers' Donations to the Victory Book Campaign," VBC Archives.

Pocket Books did: John Hersey, *Into the Valley: A Skirmish of the Marines* (New York: Pocket Books, 1943), 124.

41 *By early March:* "Report on Books Collected and Books Distributed," January 12 to March 1, 1942, VBC Records.

Newspapers had a: "A Symbol of Freedom," *Christian Science Monitor,* February 28, 1942.

The VBC did: "Report on Books Collected," VBC Records.

42 *"musn't be dirty":* "Wanted: Books for Fighters," *New York Times,* April 11, 1942.

early spring of 1942: "The President's Broadcast."

"Five years ago": Pyle, *Here Is Your War,* 226, 246, 255.

43 *"Monotony, monotony":* Pfc. H. Moldauer, "Monotony," *The Best from Yank, the Army Weekly* (New York: Armed Services Editions, No. 934 [1945]), 416.

"nine-tenths ordinary": Sgt. Walter Bernstein, "Infantry Battalion Sweats It Out in Italy," *The Best from Yank* (New York: Armed Services Edition, No. 934 [1945]), 115.

When a battle: Fussell, *Wartime,* 55, 278–79.

44 *"was difficult to":* E. B. Sledge, *With the Old Breed at Peleliu and Okinawa* (New York: Presidio Press, 2007), 108.

"suffers so deeply": Fussell, *Wartime,* 96.

War correspondent Ernie: Pyle, *Here Is Your War,* 49.

45 *"something worthwhile":* Letter from P. W. T., Chaplain, to John Connor, April 22, 1943, VBC Records.

In addition to: Christopher P. Loss, " 'The Most Wonderful Thing Has Happened to Me in the Army': Psychology, Citizenship, and American Higher Education in World War II," *Journal of American History* 92, no. 3 (December 2005), 874.

"When we read": Beverly Sigler Edwards, "The Therapeutic Value of Reading," *Elementary English* 39, no. 2 (February 1972), 215.

Many men who: Charles Bolte, *The New Veteran* (New York: Reynal & Hitchock, 1945), 14, 17.

46   *editorial Warren published:* Boaz, *Fervent and Full of Gifts,* 95–96.

Training camps' stores: Memorandum, to John Connor from H. D., June 23, 1942, VBC Records.

47   *"He was always":* Stan Elman, "John Michael Connor," *Special Libraries* (May/June 1979), 256.

By April 1942: "Book Drive Pushed for Service Men," *New York Times,* April 18, 1942.

"asked the cooperation": "Roosevelt Makes Victory Book Plea," *New York Times,* April 15, 1942.

48   *"We all know":* Letter to the American Booksellers Association from Franklin D. Roosevelt, April 23, 1942, Council Records.

Stories of citizens: "Book Drive Pushed," *New York Times;* "Wanted: Books for Fighters," *New York Times.*

49   *One Boy Scout:* "Final Reports, Victory Book Campaign," VBC Records.

Nearly nine million: "Report on Books Collected," VBC Records.

In the event: Letter from H. P., May 8, 1942, VBC Records.

last-minute collections: See generally Publicity 1942, Commencement Day Book Collections, VBC Records, Box 4, Folder 119.

50   *"Hunger, forced labor":* "Feast of the Book-Burners," *New York Times,* May 10, 1942.

Renowned for: "Winner for Novel Long in Business," *New York Times,* May 2, 1944.

Over the next: "Radio Today," *New York Times,* May 10, 1946.

"Justify the enemy": Stephen Vincent Benét, "They Burned the Books," *Saturday Review of Literature,* May 8, 1943.

51   "The Lorelei": A. Z. Foreman, "Heinrich Heine: The Lorelei (From German)," available at http://poemsintranslation.blogspot.com/2009/11/heinrich-heine-lorelei-from-german.html.

"with totalitarian": Benét, "They Burned the Books."

"This battle is": Benét, "They Burned the Books."

52   *"to let you know":* Letter from Pvt. S. C., to the ALA, December 11, 1942, VBC Records.

     "and I can assure": Letter from 1st Lt. S. F. S. to John Connor, May 24, 1943, VBC Records.

     a captain reported: Letter from Capt. S. B. to G. S., June 3, 1943, VBC Records.

53   *"the worst indictment":* Letter from Isabel DuBois to John Connor, August 25, 1942, VBC Records.

     "positive it is not": Letter from Charles Taft to Althea Warren, February 9, 1942, VBC Records.

54   *Between 1870:* Joanne E. Passet, "Men in a Feminized Profession: The Male Librarian, 1887–1921," *Libraries & Culture* 28, no. 4 (Fall 1993), 386.

     "#1 in the field": Memorandum, "USO for National Defense, Inc," VBC Records (emphasis added).

     "Taft began once again": Letter from John Connor to Althea Warren, August 14, 1942, Althea B. Warren Papers, Record Series 2/1/24-1, "Victory Book Campaign 1942," American Library Association Archives, University of Illinois.

     "How glad I am": Letter from Althea Warren to John Connor dated July 30, 1942, VBC Records.

55   *"any subject":* Memorandum for Colonel Corderman, December 28, 1942, VBC Records.

     turned to publishing companies: Publishers' Donations to the Victory Book Campaign, Box 2, Folder 2, VBC Records.

     Despite early setbacks: Jamieson, *Books for the Army,* 128–29.

56   *"late and tattered":* Bill Mauldin, *Up Front* (Cleveland, Ohio: World Publishing, 1945), 18.

     The 1942 reorganization: Jamieson, *Books for the Army,* 130–35, 141.

57   *"after a few more":* Sgt. Sanderson Vanderbilt, "Tough Shipment Ticket," *Yank, the Army Weekly* (British ed.), October 1, 1944, 9.

58   *"Even in good":* Jamieson, *Books for the Army,* 132–33.

     "war correspondents are": "A Message from the Editor of *The Saturday Evening Post,*" *Post Yarns* 5, no. 3 (1944).

4. New Weapons in the War of Ideas

59   *"The first couple":* Pyle, *Here Is Your War,* 4–5.

60   *"Too many people":* "Army to Purchase Books for Troops," *New York Sun,* May 12, 1943.

"American soldiers": "Public Campaign Fails, Army Will Buy Books," *New York Herald Tribune,* May 13, 1943.

a 1944 campaign: Minutes for Meeting, May 19, 1943, VBC Records.

"our warehouse": Letter from M. R. G. to Neola Carew, VBC Records.

"If libraries are": Letter from "Ward," Assistant to the Librarian of the Cleveland Public Library, to Neola Carew, September 8, 1943, VBC Records.

"Certainly the need": Letter to the Board of Directors of the Victory Book Campaign from L. C. B., September 2, 1943, VBC Records.

61   *"Dig a hole"*: Mauldin, *Up Front,* 143–44.

62   *"you could see"*: Sgt. Ralph Thompson, "A Report on Reading Overseas," *New York Times Book Review,* August 15, 1943.

"soldiers at the front": Mauldin, *Up Front,* 25.

fewer than two hundred thousand: Loss, "Reading Between Enemy Lines," 821.

However, the tides: Frank Adams, "Rationing Cuts Down Greatest Book Sales in History," *New York Times Book Review,* August 8, 1943.

63   *"was the most remarkable"*: "Books," *Time* (Pony Ed.), December 20, 1943, 33.

The concept for: Robert A. Ballou and Irene Rakosky, *A History of the Council on Books in Wartime, 1942–1943* (New York: Country Life Press, 1946), 1–3.

64   *Publishing was a second:* "Johnson, Ex-Head of Book Council," *New York Times,* February 28, 1958.

65   *"Books are weapons"*: Ballou and Rakosky, *A History of the Council on Books in Wartime,* 1–5.

"committee in search of": Ballou and Rakosky, *A History of the Council on Books in Wartime,* 1–5.

The essay began: "Books and the War," draft of essay, Council Records.

66   *"everyone who has"*: "The Literature of Power," speech by Honorable Adolf A. Berle Jr., May 12, 1945, New York Public Library.

"The book written": "U.S. Urged to Train Boys to Be Officers," *New York Times,* May 13, 1942.

After its Times Hall: Ballou and Rakosky, *A History of the Council on Books in Wartime,* 34–35.

67   *The program was first:* Script for "Assignment: USA.," Council Records.

69   Variety *reported:* Ballou and Rakosky, *A History of the Council on Books in Wartime,* 36.

NBC acquiesced: "NBC v. Boston," *Time* (Pony Ed.), April 17, 1944, 26.

70   *collaborated so wholeheartedly:* "Publishers to Back War Books Jointly," *New York Times,* December 1, 1942.

The book told: W. L. White, *They Were Expendable* (New York: Harcourt, Brace, 1942), v, 3–4.

71 *"Distinguished Service":* Orville Prescott, "Books of the Times," *New York Times,* December 18, 1942.

Hersey told of: John Hersey, *Into the Valley* (New York: Pocket Books, 1943), 66–71, 75.

In May 1943: "Willkie's Book Held 'Imperative,'" *New York Times,* May 7, 1943.

72 *This book argued:* Walter Lippmann, *U.S. Foreign Policy,* undated, Council Records; Lippmann, *U.S. Foreign Policy* (New York: Armed Services Editions, No. C-73 [1943]).

The fifth: Ballou and Rakosky, *A History of the Council on Books in Wartime,* 48.

"America of today": Lisa Sergio, "The Importance of Interpreting America," *American Library Association Bulletin* 35, no. 9 (October 1941), 487.

The sixth: Ballou and Rakosky, *A History of the Council on Books in Wartime,* 48.

73 *Snow, a war:* Edgar Snow, *People on Our Side* (New York: Random House, 1944).

Selection of a: Ballou and Rakosky, *A History of the Council on Books in Wartime,* 48.

Americans purchased: "The Year in Books," *Time* (Pony Ed.), December 20, 1943, 33.

74 *"I had best":* December 8, 1942, Exec. Meeting of the Council, Report of the Vice Chairman (John Farrar), Council Records.

After consulting with: Loss, "Reading Between Enemy Lines," 826.

5. Grab a Book, Joe, and Keep Goin'

75 *"I want to say":* V-mail Letter to the Council on Books in Wartime from "Pvt. W. R. W. & gang," Council Records.

In 1943: Austin Stevens, "Notes on Books and Authors," *New York Times Book Review,* January 17, 1943.

"We don't burn": "Praise the Lord and Pass the Ammunition; A Plea for Book Paper," *Chicago Daily News,* May 26, 1943.

But the government: "Council on Books in Wartime: Armed Services Editions," Memo dated April 11, 1943, p. 3, Council Archives.

76 *Even the longest:* Frank D. Adams, "As Popular as Pin-Up Girls," *New York Times Book Review,* April 30, 1944.

No book press: "Council on Books in Wartime: Armed Services Editions," Memo dated April 11, 1943, Council Records.

Thanks to their: "35,000,000 Books to Be Printed in Year in New Pocket Form for Forces Overseas," *New York Times,* May 18, 1943.

77 *"two up":* Jamieson, *Books for the Army,* 147.

One disadvantage: Loss, "Reading Between Enemy Lines," 828.

The council obliged: Minutes of Exec. Committee, September 14, 1943, Council Records.

Knowing that battle: Loss, "Reading Between Enemy Lines," 828.

78 *"small, light":* "Council on Books in Wartime: Armed Services Editions" memo, Council Records.

Book covers: Jamieson, *Books for the Army,* 151.

staples were favored: Adams, "As Popular as Pin-Up Girls."

79 *"the prices at":* Richard L. Simon, S. Spencer Scott, and Malcolm Johnson, "Armed Services Edition" report, September 1, 1943, Council Records.

the average cost: Adams, "As Popular as Pin-Up Girls."

5.9 cents per book: Jamieson, *Books for the Army,* 142, 293, n. 1.

At the project's: Minutes of Exec. Board, March 31, 1943, Council Records.

By the time: Jamieson, *Books for the Army,* 148–49; Ballou and Rakosky, *A History of the Council on Books in Wartime,* 74.

A three-part: Ballou and Rakosky: *A History of the Council on Books in Wartime,* 73–74.

The main consideration: Jamieson, *Books for the Army,* 152–53 (Table III).

80 *One of the:* Letter from Archibald G. Ogden to Sen. Robert A. Taft, July 8, 1944, Council Records.

These guidelines: William M. Leary Jr., "Books, Soldiers and Censorship During the Second World War," *American Quarterly* 20, no. 2, part 1 (Summer 1968), 238.

81 *"just about":* John Jamieson, "Armed Services Editions and G.I. Fan Mail," *Publishers Weekly,* July 12, 1947, p. 148.

F. Scott Fitzgerald's: Michael Merschel, "BookExpo America: Maureen Corrigan on How One Great Book Was Almost Forgotten," *Artsblog, Dallas Morning News,* http://artsblog.dallasnews.com/2014/05/bookexpo-america -maureen-corrigan-on-how-one-great-book-was-almost-forgotten.html/.

For authors, learning: "Armed Services Editions: Excerpts from Letters Received by the Center for the Book from Authors of Armed Services Editions," Library of Congress (prepared for February 17, 1983, Armed Services Editions 40th Anniversary Event).

82 *The books chosen:* Jamieson, *Books for the Army,* 155–56.

83 *Managing the production:* Ibid., 147, 150.

   One frustrated colonel: Minutes of the Exec. Committee, November 24, December 1, 1943, Council Records.

84 *"planned, organized":* Jamieson, *Books for the Army,* 149.

   "The books themselves": Malcolm Cowley, "Books by the Millions," *New Republic,* October 11, 1943, pp. 483–84.

85 *"a little unfair":* Letter to Malcolm Cowley from Archibald Ogden, October 18, 1943, Council Records.

   "editions are by": "Letters to the Editor," "The Armed Services Editions," *New Republic,* November 22, 1943, p. 720.

   "mountains of books": Adams, "As Popular as Pin-Up Girls."

86 *"moving, even heart-breaking":* "Armed Services Editions: Excerpts from Letters," Library of Congress.

87 *The Army immediately:* Minutes of the Exec. Committee Meetings, September 14, 1943; October 6, 1943; January 12, 1944; January 27, 1944, Council Records.

88 *"What the hell":* Letter from Charles Rawlings to Stanley Rinehart, June 5, 1944, Council Records.

89 *Lewis Gannett:* "Lewis Gannett, Book Critic, Dies," *New York Times,* February 4, 1966.

90 *"From hospitals":* Letter from Lewis Gannett to Philip Van Doren Stern (undated), Council Records.

   Palmer began: "Gretta Palmer, Author, 46, Dead," *New York Times,* August 16, 1953.

91 *"bad-tempered articles":* Letter from Gretta Palmer to the Editorial Board, November 30, 1944, Council Records.

6. Guts, Valor, and Extreme Bravery

92 *"I've just been":* Betty Smith, "Who Died?" *New York Times Magazine,* July 9, 1944.

93 *Germany faced:* Stephen E. Ambrose, *D-Day, June 6, 1944: The Climactic Battle of World War II* (New York: Simon & Schuster Paperbacks, 1994), 30.

   "Hello, Gang": Lucas, *Axis Sally,* 12, 73, 131.

94 *"Hello to the men":* Ambrose, *D-Day,* 55.

   The details for: Ibid., 120–21.

95 *One private recalled:* Ibid., 140.

   "The GI hitting": Ibid., 111.

   They crammed: Cornelius Ryan, *The Longest Day: June 6, 1944* (New York: Simon & Schuster Paperbacks, 1959), 180.

96   *"This is the first"*: A. J. Liebling, "A Reporter at Large, Cross-Channel Trip — I," *New Yorker,* July 1, 1944, pp. 39–40.

    "morale, given": Eisenhower, *Crusade in Europe,* 238.

    Eisenhower was known: Ryan, *The Longest Day,* 254.

    When the C-: Jamieson, *Books for the Army,* 158.

97   *"pil[ing] up"*: Minutes of the Exec. Committee, May 24, October 25, 1944, Council Records.

    "very few Armed": Jamieson, *Books for the Army,* 158.

98   *moon, tide:* Eisenhower, *Crusade in Europe,* 239.

    "Priests were": Ambrose, *D-Day,* 167, 170, 172, 182.

    The LCIs: Ibid, 183.

    "Them lucky bastards": Ryan, *The Longest Day,* 193.

99   *"I Double Dare"*: Ibid., 42, 71.

    "so many [were]": Letter from 2nd Lt. R. R. R. to Council on Books in Wartime, Council Records.

    "spread all over": Liebling, "A Reporter at Large: Cross-Channel Trip," 42.

    "Good evening": Ambrose, *D-Day,* 192.

100   *"much greater fighting"*: "Text of Roosevelt Talk on Rome," *New York Times,* June 6, 1944.

    president kept vigil: "President Kept Vigil on the News," *New York Times,* June 7, 1944; Lawrence Resner, "Country in Prayer," *New York Times,* June 7, 1944.

101   *"Almighty God"*: "Let Our Hearts Be Stout," *New York Times,* June 7, 1944.

102   *just another practice:* Ryan, *The Longest Day,* 203–4.

    near-certain death: Ambrose, *D-Day,* 326–27.

    Many men who: Ryan, *The Longest Day,* 199, 203–4, 227.

    In the first: "3,283 Killed and 12,600 Wounded U.S. Toll in Invasion, Bradley Says," *New York Times,* June 18, 1944; Ryan, *The Longest Day,* "A Note on Casualties."

    Eleven days: "3,283 Killed and 12,600 Wounded."

    "When we think": Sgt. Frank K. Turman, "Soldiers and GIs," *Yank, the Army Weekly* (British ed.), February 11, 1945, p. 18.

104   *"Inching back eastward"*: Letter from R. S. to Katherine Anne Porter, October 11, 1945, Katherine Anne Porter Papers, Special Collections, University of Maryland Libraries (hereinafter, Katherine Anne Porter Papers).

    "almost glad that I can say": Letter from B. V. to Katherine Anne Porter, May 6, 1945, Katherine Anne Porter Papers.

    "I had three": Letter to Joseph A. Barry from Katherine Anne Porter, January

17, 1948, Katherine Anne Porter Papers, c/o The Permissions Company, Inc., on behalf of the Katherine Anne Porter Foundation.

106 *"When I first":* V-Mail from Sgt. T. D. to Betty Smith, Betty Smith Papers, #03837, Southern Historical Collection, Wilson Library, University of North Carolina at Chapel Hill (hereinafter Betty Smith Papers).

"made [him] feel": Letter from B. P. C. to Betty Smith, October 20, 1944, Betty Smith Papers.

"a good letter": Letter to "Francis," from R. L. L., August 21, 1944, Betty Smith Papers.

"living my life": Letter from Cpl. M. M. to "Sirs," May 12, 1944, Council Records.

"nursing another literary seedling": Letter from F. S., Jr. to Betty Smith, March 19, 1945, Betty Smith Papers.

did not care for: Letter from L. M. to "Sirs," March 15, 1945, Betty Smith Papers.

"This is a fine": Letter from R. H. R. to Betty Smith, August 20, 1944, Betty Smith Papers.

Smith once estimated: Letter from Betty Smith to "Elizabeth," May 5, 1944, Betty Smith Papers.

108 *"Thanks — thanks — [for] your letter":* Letter from "Robinson" to Betty Smith, December 10, 1944, Betty Smith Papers.

"When I received [your] letter": Letter from L. W. to "Betty," undated, Betty Smith Papers.

"I am going to need another": Letter from L. W. to "Betty," February 18, 1945, Betty Smith Papers.

"You helped inspire me": Letter from J. W. P. to Betty Smith, April 11, 1945, Betty Smith Papers.

Months later: Letter from J. W. P. to Betty Smith, June 27, 1945, Betty Smith Papers.

"I think it's wonderful": Letter to "Elizabeth" from Betty Smith, May 5, 1944, Betty Smith Papers.

109 *"thanks for the joy":* Letter from J. C. E. to Rosemary Taylor, undated, "somewhere in New Guinea," Council Records.

"cooking without measuring": Letter from Capt. E. B. to Rosemary Taylor, July 17, 1944, Council Records.

110 *"resist the temptation":* Letter from B. B. to Rosemary Taylor, January 19, 1944, Council Records.

"remind[ed] them of": Jamieson, "Armed Services Editions and GI Fan Mail," 149.

111   *"Books are often"*: Letter from H. V. A. to Archibald Ogden, December 10, 1944, Council Records.

      "printed matter": Lieut. Col. Raymond L. Trautman, "Books and the Soldier," in *Books and Libraries in Wartime,* edited by Pierce Butler (Chicago: University of Chicago Press, 1945), 53.

7. Like Rain in the Desert

113   *"For days I've been hunting"*: Sgt. B. S. to the Armed Services Editions, Inc. (undated), Council Records.

114   *"a steaming, malarial"*: "Pacific Attack," *New York Times,* July 4, 1943.

      Incessant bombings: "Guadalcanal: A Crucial Battle," *New York Times,* October 18, 1942.

      "The nights are passed": T. Tillman Durdin, "It's Never Dull on Guadalcanal," *New York Times,* September 18, 1942.

115   *"worst defeat in a fair"*: Admiral Samuel Eliot Morison, "Guadalcanal — 1942," in *Battle: True Stories of Combat in World War II* (New York: Curtis Books, 1965), 181, 183–88.

      Pacific's most extreme: Sgt. Larry McManus, "Saipan Was Worse Than Tarawa," *Yank, the Army Weekly,* August 6, 1944, p. 22.

      "It was a case of": "We Take Saipan," *New York Times,* July 10, 1944.

      Over fifteen thousand: "American Losses on Saipan 15,053," *New York Times,* July 13, 1944.

116   *Within four days:* "Books March in Army's Front Lines — Even to Tiny Atolls of Pacific," *Christian Science Monitor,* March 13, 1945.

      "The morning after": Ballou and Rakosky, *A History of the Council on Books in Wartime,* 82–83.

      Turning to Stars: "Mail Call," *Stars and Stripes,* July 14, 1944.

117   *"not an uncommon sight"*: Letter from a field director for the American Red Cross, dated "Tuesday the 23rd," Council Records.

      "Soldiers carry your books": Letter from "a Major in the South Pacific," Council Records.

      "so popular that one is": B. T. C. to the "Armed Services Editions," October 17, 1944, Council Records.

      "From the Airborne": Letter "From an Army Hospital in England," Council Records.

118   *"Proof at last"*: Letter from 2nd Lt. R. R. R. to Council on Books in Wartime, January 30, 1945, Council Records.

      "I do not know who": Letter from Sgt. E. S. to the Council on Books in Wartime (undated), Council Records.

"*damned sincere thanks*": Letter from T. C. to the Council on Books in Wartime (undated), Council Records.

"*rain in the desert*": V-Mail from S. F. to the Armed Services Editions, July 17, 1944, Council Records.

"*six long tiresome*": Letter from J. C. to "Gentleman," undated, Council Records.

"*Since I have been*": Letter from J. B. to Chairman, January 4, 1945, Council Records.

119 "*gratifyingly pleased*": Letter from R. W. W. to the Armed Services Editions, July 21, 1944, Council Records.

"*worthy of a medal*": V-Mail from S. F. to the Armed Services Editions, July 17, 1944, Council Records.

"*For days I've been hunting*": Letter from Sgt. B. S. to the Armed Services Editions, Inc. (undated), Council Records.

"*You have no idea*": Letter from Pfc. J. M. N. to Sirs, July 8, 1944, Council Records.

120 "*would like to get hold of*": Letter from J. B. to the Chairman of the Council on Books in Wartime, January 4, 1945, Council Record.

a dictionary: "Editions for the Armed Services, Inc.," signed by entire unit (undated), Council Records.

"*requires little 'sales talk'*": Letter from Sgt. G. F. to Editions for the Armed Services, Inc., August 13, 1945, Council Records.

a request came in for more plays: Letter from D. B. to "Sirs," August 4, 1945, Council Records.

"*There is just one bit*": V-Mail from Sgt. H. H. to the Editions for the Armed Forces, December 21, 1944, Council Records.

not enough sports books: Letter from Cpl. W. C. G., July 9, 1944, Council Records.

"*My personal preference*": Letter from R. A. B. to the Editions for the Armed Services, Inc. (undated), Council Records.

121 "*recent history and people*": Letter from Pfc. D. M. L. to Philip Van Doren Stern, August 23, 1944, Council Records.

wife of an American POW: Letter from H. E. A. to the Editions for the Armed Services, Inc., September 25, 1944, Council Records.

A Navy nurse: Letter from E. G. to the Editions for the Armed Services, Inc. (undated), Council Records.

"*He says that I couldn't*": Letter from Dr. A. C. K. to Council on Books in Wartime, February 26, 1946, Council Records.

contractually obligated: Letter to M. P. S. from Philip Van Doren Stern, August 15, 1944; Minutes of the Executive Committee Meeting, January 24, 1945, Council Records.

122 *"Next month he will have":* Letter from W. A. to Editions for the Armed Services, Inc., September 16, 1945, Council Records.

"Being an ardent baseballer": Letter from K. W. R. to the Secretary of the Editions for the Armed Services, Inc., February 14, 1946, Council Records.

exceptions were made: Note to "Phil" handsigned (unreadable), (undated), Council Records.

123 *"The books that are most":* Letter from Pvt. D. S. to Editions for the Armed Services, Inc., March 23, 1945, Council Archives.

"fellas have a fever": Letter from B. N. to Editions for the Armed Services, Inc., September 7, 1945, Council Archives.

"If you've ever seen books": Paul Fussell, *Wartime,* 107.

Boston had banned: Neil Miller, *Banned in Boston: The Watch and Ward Society's Crusade Against Books, Burlesque, and the Social Evil* (Boston: Beacon Press, 2010).

"We're all looking forward": Excerpt from Letter from Capt. M. C., December 23, 1944, Council Records.

Eleanor Roosevelt had praised: "Boston Bans a Novel," *New York Times,* March 21, 1944.

124 *While* Forever Amber: Kathleen Winsor, *Forever Amber* (New York: Armed Services Editions, No. T-39 [1945]).

"objected to having to give": Minutes of the Executive Committee Meeting, October 11, 1944, Council Records.

125 "Forever Amber *and* Strange": Letter to Pvt. D. S. from Philip Van Doren Stern, April 1945, Council Records.

"Pay no attention": Letter from R. W. W. to the Armed Services Editions, July 21, 1944, Council Records.

"It's beginning to look": "Boston's Sons in Service Reading Those Awful Books," *Boston Traveler,* January 12, 1945.

man wrote from: Letter from Pvt. G. G. to Thomas Y. Crowell, Co., September 20, 1944, Council Records.

126 *"light ack ack battalion":* Letter from F. M. E. to Harper and Bros., September 21, 1944, Council Records.

127 *through heavy artillery fire:* Letter from L. D. J. to the Council on Books in Wartime (quoting a September 10, 1944, letter to L. D. J. from Pvt. C. T. J.), Council Records.

128 *"only to discover"*: Letter from Cpl. R. C. J. to The Macmillan Company, March 11, 1945, Council Records.

    "If it is your mission": Letter from M. S. T. to "Gentlemen," August 27, 1944, Council Records.

129 *"out here time hangs"*: Letter from M. S. T. to "Mr. Stern," September 27, Council Records.

    "many happy and contented": Letter from B. A. to the Editions for the Armed Services, Inc., June 26, 1945, Council Records.

130 *"to discover the names of"*: Letter from H. A. B. to the "Council on Books in Wartime (or whatever!)," May 11, 1944, Council Records.

131 *"there is no question of any"*: Letter from William Sloane to Private H. A. B., July 18, 1944, Council Records.

    "Don't you think": Letter from E. J. to the Council on Books in Wartime, March 12, 1945, Council Records.

132 *"Next to penicillin"*: Ballou and Rakosky, *A History of the Council on Books in Wartime*, 81.

    "bet dollars to GI Spam": Letter from "Sidney" from "somewhere at sea" (undated), Council Records.

8. Censorship and FDR's F---th T--m

133 *"If it is to be left"*: "Army Censor," *Lynchburg (VA) Daily Advance,* June 22, 1944.

    As accolades for: Jamieson, *Books for the Army*, 213.

134 *After the original law:* C. P. Trussell, "Both Sides Press Bids for 1944 Service Vote," *New York Times,* November 21, 1943.

    "the Services are unable": "The Nation: Votes for Soldiers," *Time* (Pony Ed.), January 17, 1944, p. 1.

    As this legislation began: Leary, "Books, Soldiers and Censorship"; William S. White, *The Taft Story* (New York: Harper & Row, 1954), 43–45; Joseph B. Treaster, "Charles P. Taft, Former Mayor of Cincinnati," *New York Times,* June 25, 1983.

135 *Acknowledging that it:* 90 Cong. Rec. 2404-2410 (1944).

    A February 1944 poll: "What They Think," *Time* (Pony Ed.), February 7, 1944, p. 25.

    "bobtailed ballot": 90 Cong. Rec. 2621–22 (1944).

136 *"In order to get a ballot"*: Ibid., 2637–38.

    "wholly inadequate": Leary, "Books, Soldiers and Censorship," 240.

    if those in the services wanted: 58 Stat. 141 (Title III at Sec. 303(a) ["Official

War Ballot"]); Title III at Sec. 306 (providing that the states would furnish lists of candidates).

"magazine . . . newspaper": See 58 Stat. 136, Title V, §§ 22(2)(b), 24 (April 1, 1944).

137 *"uses the broadest terms"*: War Department Memorandum, April 27, 1944, "Subject: Restrictions in new 'Federal Voting Law' on dissemination to members of the armed forces of political argument or political propaganda," 3, Council Records.

"law is quite clear": "Draft Letter to Be Sent to Publishers," April 28, 1944, Council Records.

"I hope you didn't send the": Letter to Philip Van Doren Stern from "Dick," Simon & Schuster, May 1, 1944, Council Records.

138 *Army . . . opposed editing:* Letter to Philip Van Doren Stern from Ray Trautman, June 7, 1944, Council Records.

"almost certainly result in": Letter to Philip Van Doren Stern from Randall Jacobs, June 7, 1944, Council Records.

While many critics: Rose Gladney, "A Letter from Lillian Smith: 'Old Seeds Bearing a Heavy Crop,'" *Southern Changes* 12, no. 4 (1990).

"selling literature containing": "Book Ban Is Put to Test," *New York Times,* April 7, 1944.

"four scenes of sexual": *Commonwealth v. Isenstadt,* 318 Mass. 543–47 (September 17, 1943).

139 *Beginning in May 1944:* "'Strange Fruit' Barred by Mails Then Admitted at Sender's Risk," *New York Times,* May 16, 1944.

140 *"increasing tendency on the part"*: "Resolution Proposed and Passed at Meeting of Executive Committee Meeting, May 24, 1944," Council Records.

the council drafted a press release: "For Immediate Release" (undated), first sentence beginning: "The Council on Books in Wartime, in a resolution sent today to the President, Postmaster-General, Secretaries of War and the Navy, Speaker of the House of Representatives, and the President of the Senate, protested the restriction on book distribution to the armed forces under the Soldiers' Vote Act," Council Records.

141 *"vigorous efforts on behalf"*: Letter to the Council on Books in Wartime from Mari Sandoz, June 27, 1944, Council Records.

"It looks as though": Leary, "Books, Soldiers and Censorship," 241.

In late May 1944: Letter to "Editor" from Archibald G. Ogden, June 15, 1944, Council Records.

142 *"Censorship for political"*: "A Silly Censorship," *Syracuse (NY) Post-Standard,* June 20, 1944.

"*since every voter*": Dorothy Thompson, "Amendment by Taft Deprives Soldiers of Some of Best Books," *Columbia (SC) State*, July 16, 1944.

"*almost any book except*": "Army Censor," *Lynchburg (VA) Daily Advance*, June 22, 1944.

"*One would think*": "Books in Wartime: Unwarranted Censorship Is Practiced," *San Antonio (TX) News*, June 22, 1944.

143 "*Congress in its wisdom*": "Insulating Servicemen," *Chicago Sun*, June 23, 1944.

"*If this is 'political'*": "Book Censors See Shadows," *Rochester (NY) Times Union*, July 18, 1944.

"*excellent discussion of how*": "Queer Censorship," *Monroe (MI) News*, June 23, 1944.

144 "*It shows somebody*": "Armed Services Editions, Excerpts from Letters Received by the Center for the Book from Authors," Library of Congress.

These textbooks: "Army Withdraws 6 History Texts," *New York Times*, July 5, 1944.

A few days later: "The Next Forty Years," *Time*, July 10, 1944, p. 32.

145 "*likely to be saved*": Norman Cousins, "Censoritis," *Saturday Review of Literature*, July 1, 1944, p. 12.

On July 3 and 5: Letters from Archibald Ogden to Alfred McIntyre, July 10, 1944; Archibald Ogden to Bernard De Voto, July 12, 1944, Council Records.

"*all of it [was] sympathetic*": Letter from Archibald Ogden to Senator Robert A. Taft, July 8, 1944, Council Records.

Trautman soon informed: Letter from Archibald Ogden to Alfred McIntyre, July 10, 1944, Council Records.

146 "*reported that the Army had*": Draft of Minutes of the Executive Committee Meeting, July 19, 1944, Council Records.

"*no one can question*": Letter from Sen. Robert A. Taft to Archibald Ogden, July 14, 1944, Council Records.

On July 20, Senator Taft: Ballou and Rakosky, *A History of the Council on Books in Wartime*, 23–24.

The group met: "Note to City Desks," Council Records.

sponsor amendments to the act: Ballou and Rakosky, *A History of the Council on Books in Wartime*, 24.

147 "*Leave it out when in doubt*": "Note to City Desks," Council Records.

"*the general principle*": "Statement by Senator Robert A. Taft of Ohio," Council Records.

148 "*were out of touch*": Letter to Radio Commentators from Alan Green, August 3, 1944, Council Records.

"Senator Taft apparently": Statement from "Lucas Headquarters" for "Immediate Release," Council Records.

Army continued to publicize: "Books, Soldiers and Censorship," 243–44.

149 *"not to shut off from members":* "Dissemination of Information to the Armed Forces," a Report by Mr. Green, August 15, 1944, Council Records.

With uncharacteristic speed: C. P. Trussell, "Senate Acts to Kill Army Reading Curb," *New York Times,* August 16, 1944; "The Day in Washington," *New York Times,* August 17, 1944.

By August 24, 1944: "For Immediate Release," August 24, 1944, Council Records.

150 *"it is a refreshing example":* Letter from Archibald G. Ogden to Mari Sandoz, August 21, 1944, Council Records.

relatively slim margin: "About the Election," *Yank, the Army Weekly* (British ed.), November 19, 1944, p. 3; "Franklin D. Roosevelt," *Yank, the Army Weekly* (British ed.), April 27, 1945, p. 10.

"No change of address": "The Presidency," *Time* (Pony Ed.), December 11, 1944, p. 5.

9. Germany's Surrender and the Godforsaken Islands

151 *"There were people":* Joseph Heller, *Catch-22* (New York: Simon & Schuster, 2011), 19–20.

152 *"shot to pieces":* John B. Hench, *Books as Weapons* (Ithaca, NY: Cornell University Press, 2010), 29–31.

Knowing of the emaciated: Ballou and Rakosky, *A History of the Council on Books in Wartime,* 83–93, Appendix D (listing books published in Overseas Editions).

154 *"a crate of ASE's mounted":* Letter from T. C. to the Council (undated), Council Records.

155 *"cheek by jowl":* Valerie Holman, *Print for Victory* (London: British Library, 2008), 30.

paper rationing further: Iain Stevenson, *Book Makers* (London: British Library, 2010), 115–18.

Although Britain organized: Holman, *Print for Victory,* 42–43.

"stroll into the mess": Letter from B. F. D. to the Council, December 20, 1944, Council Records.

156 *"Humour was always":* Letter from W. G. J. to "Sirs," April 25, 1944, Council Records.

157 *"those in the services;"* Louis Golding, *Store of Ladies* (London: Bear, Hudson Ltd., 1946) (Bear Pocket Book), interior front cover.

lifted until 1949: Stevenson, *Book Makers,* 117.

But on April 12, 1945: Arthur Krock, "End Comes Suddenly at Warm Springs," *New York Times,* April 13, 1945.

"It wasn't like just": Gene Currivan, "Generals and GI's Mourn Late Chief," *New York Times,* April 14, 1945.

158 *despite the collapse:* Sgt. Mack Morriss, "Berlin Death Battle," *Yank, the Army Weekly,* June 15, 1945.

"flags of freedom fly": "The Messages, Here and at Home, Proclaiming the End of the War in Europe: President Truman," *Yank, The Army Weekly* (British ed.), May 18, 1945.

articles created a false: "News from Home," *Yank, the Army Weekly* (British ed.), September 10, 1944; "News from Home," *Yank, the Army Weekly* (British ed.), August 27, 1944.

On May 10, the Army: Sidney Shalett, "Army to Return 3,100,000 in Year; 400,000 Will Remain in Europe," *New York Times,* May 10, 1945.

Only a minority: Hanson W. Baldwin, "Army Shift to Pacific Next Big War Problem," *New York Times,* May 6, 1945.

159 *"Relief period in the Pacific":* Pfc. Justin Gray, "Pacific Combat," *Yank, the Army Weekly* (British ed.), June 15, 1945.

"Just like that old favorite:" S/Sgt. Jas. V. Coon, "So-Called Rest," *Yank, the Army Weekly* (British ed.), December 17, 1944.

"Those who are to be": Ibid.

bitterest battle: "4,000 Marine[s] Dead on Iwo Indicated," *New York Times,* March 16, 1945.

160 *American casualties exceeded:* Cyril J. O'Brien, "Iwo Jima Retrospective," available at http://www.military.com/NewContent/0,13190,NI_Iwo_Jima2,00.html.

"hand-to-hand fighting": Warren Moscow, "Marines and 77th Division Drive Near Naha and Shuri," *New York Times,* May 12, 1945.

"Home alive in '45": Fussell, *Wartime,* 257.

"set in jungle glades": Maj. Frederick Simpich Jr., AUS, "At Ease in the South Seas," *National Geographic* (January 1944), 79.

Guadalcanal was unrecognizable: Sgt. Barrett McGurn, "Guadalcanal Goes Garrison," *Yank, the Army Weekly,* August 27, 1944.

Across the Mariana Islands: Ernie Pyle, *Last Chapter* (New York: Henry Holt, 1946), 18.

161 *Tokyo Rose, a persona:* Russell Warren Howe, *The Hunt for 'Tokyo Rose'* (Lanham, Md.: Madison Books, 1990), 28–32, 71.

"Well, you boys in Moresby": "By Any Other Name," *Time* (Pony Ed.) April 10, 1944, 31.

"*In these South Sea isles*": Maj. Simpich, "At Ease in the South Seas," 80.

"*with little to do*": "Boston's Sons in Service Reading Those Awful Books," *Boston Traveler*, January 12, 1945.

162 "*a soldier with a monthly pay*": Col. Trautman speech, Feb 1, 1945, Council Records.

163 "*many hours of precious*": Letter from N. J. P. to the Editions for the Armed Services, Inc., May 27, 1945, Council Records.

164 *At a 1945 meeting:* Minutes of Exec. Committee, January 11, 1945, Council Records.

"the *most important*": Minutes of Exec. Committee, January 24, 1945 (emphasis added), Council Records.

"*never seems to be enough*": Letter from R. A. L. "To Those Who Can Do It," attached to letter to Isabel DuBois dated April 19, 1945, Council Records.

"*You see . . . my kid brother*": Letter from V. B. T. to "Sirs," Council Records.

165 *In early 1945 Philip:* Minutes of the Exec. Committee, January 11, 1945, Council Records.

"*If enough funds were*": Minutes of Exec. Committee, May 2, 1945, June 20, 1945, Council Records.

166 "*scraping the bottom*": Minutes of the Exec. Committee, December 13, 1944, Council Records.

"*even if the adage*": Austin Stevens, "Books and Authors," *New York Times Book Review,* December 13, 1942; Austin Stevens, "Notes on Books and Authors," *New York Times Book Review,* January 17, 1943.

Stern offered a compromise: Minutes of the Exec. Committee, December 13, 1944, Council Records.

167 *loathed titles:* Letter from Isabel DuBois to Mr. Stern, June 9, 1945, Council Records.

"*not any of them have*": Letter from Isabel DuBois to Mr. Stern, June 12, 1945, Council Records.

"*a huge issue of a triviality*": Memorandum to P. V. D. S. from L. U., June 11, 1945, Council Records.

avoid "selected": Letter from Philip Van Doren Stern to Isabel Du Bois, June 19, 1945, Council Records.

168 "*should be taken as a complaint*": Letter from Isabel Du Bois to Mr. Stern, June 29, 1945, Council Records.

"*no longer print any books*": Letter to Bureau of Navy Personnel from H. Stahley Thompson, February 15, 1946; Letter to Miss Du Bois from H. Stahley Thompson, February 15, 1946, Council Records.

169 *"When one is far from home":* Copy of Letter from Major E. V. P. to Henry Hough, September 14, 1945, Council Records.

10. Peace at Last

170 *"My old division":* Bill Mauldin, *Up Front,* 197.

"Home had faded": Robert Case, "Through to Murmansk," in *Battle: The True Stories of Combat in World War II* (New York: Doubleday & Company, 1965), 38.

171 *As late as 1940:* Loss, "'The Most Wonderful Thing,'" 867.

172 *provided information:* Darrell Huff and Frances Huff, *Twenty Careers of Tomorrow* (New York: Armed Services Edition, No. 1002 [1946]); Minutes of Exec. Committee, April 25, 1945, Council Records.

how to choose a vocation: William G. Campbell and James H. Bedford, *You and Your Future Job* (New York: Armed Services Edition, No. 1081 [1946]); John F. Wharton, *The Theory and Practice of Earning a Living* (New York: Armed Services Edition, No. 1105 [1946]).

172 *Sulfanilamide, a substance:* Pyle, *Here Is Your War,* 75.

inspired many servicemen to go: Letter from Colonel L. C. W. to Arthur Train, February 29, 1944, Arthur Train Correspondence 1944–1945, Archives of Charles Scribner's Sons, Author Files I, Box 181, Folder 11; Manuscripts Division, Department of Rare Books and Special Collections, Princeton University Library.

173 *"death, plus rain":* Letter from Pvt. G. G. to Thomas Y. Crowell, Co., September 20, 1944, Council Records.

sheets cut from a paper bag: Letter from R. C. to W. W. Norton, October 10, 1944, Council Records.

"the most intensive bombardment": Hanson W. Baldwin, "1,000 Plane Blows Daily Is Prospect for Japan," *New York Times,* June 3, 1945.

174 *B-29s daily dropped:* Warren Moscow, "B-29's Rain Pamphlets on Japan; Surrender Talk Seen Taking Root," *New York Times,* June 4, 1945.

"will smash the enemy": "Premier Sees War Decided in Japan," *New York Times,* June 9, 1945.

Japan's grip on the Philippines: Lindesay Parrott, "'41 Congress Sits in the Philippines," *New York Times,* June 10, 1945.

"There was a terrific": "The War Ends," *Life* (Overseas Service ed.), August 20, 1945, p. 6.

Four square miles: W. H. Lawrence, "Visit to Hiroshima Proves It World's Most-Damaged City," *New York Times,* September 5, 1945.

175 *"they may expect a rain"*: "Text of Statements by Truman, Stimson, on Development of Atomic Bomb," *New York Times,* August 7, 1945.

"desire for an early": "Japan Keeps People in Dark on Nature of New Scourge," *New York Times,* August 8, 1945.

Seventy-five hours: "The War Ends," *Life,* 7.

"we shall use the atomic": "The President's Report," *New York Times,* August 10, 1945.

five agonizing days: Alexander Feinberg, "All City 'Lets Go,'" *New York Times,* August 15, 1945.

Around the world: "Victory Reports Around the World," *Life,* August 20, 1945, 16B–16C.

176 *On September 2, 1945:* "Truman's Nephew in Crew," *New York Times,* September 2, 1945.

The Army estimated: Joseph A. Loftus, "Says Army Speeds Discharge Rate," *New York Times,* September 13, 1945.

177 *remained a need for ASEs:* Minutes of Exec. Committee, August 22, September 12, 1945, Council Records.

"it would be short sighted": Minutes of Exec. Committee, September 12, 1945, 2, Council Records.

In December 1945: Jamieson, *Books for the Army,* 156.

178 *But as the size of the Army:* Ibid.

179 *Midway through the contract:* "Notice of Special Meeting of Directors of Editions for the Armed Services, Inc," January 15, 1947, Malcolm Johnson Papers, private collection of Molly Guptill Manning.

180 *"followed me through combat"*: Letter from Capt. B. V. B. to the Secretary of the Council on Books in Wartime, January 10, 1946, Council Records.

11. Damned Average Raisers

181 *"We have taught our youth"*: H. Doc. No. 344, House of Representatives, 78th Con., 1st Sess. (December 13, 1943), 5, "Message from the President of the United States Transmitting Preliminary Report of the Armed Forces Committee on Post-War Educational Opportunities for Service Personnel," dated October 27, 1943.

"political consequences": Glenn C. Altschuler and Stuart M. Blumin, *The GI Bill* (New York: Oxford University Press, 2009), 43.

182 *pressing matter of national:* Loss, "'The Most Wonderful Thing,'" 886.

"This prevailing tendency": Charles G. Bolte, *The New Veteran* (New York: Reynal & Hitchcock, 1945), 140.

"a future of ditch digging": Loss, "'The Most Wonderful Thing,'" 887.

"*cheaper to keep men*": "Hershey Sees a Million or Two Out of Armed Forces After Reich Falls," *New York Times,* August 22, 1944.

183 "*This plan would be quite*": "Replies to General Hershey," *Yank, the Army Weekly* (British ed.), September 10, 1944, p. 19.

"*During the war*": H. Doc. No. 361, House of Representatives, 78th Con., 1st Sess., "Message from the President of the United States Transmitting a Request for Passage of Legislation to Grant to All Veterans of Our Armed Forces Mustering-Out Pay, A Uniform System of Allowances for Unemployed Veterans; Also Legislation to Amend the Federal Old-Age Survivors' Insurance Law to Include All Veterans of the Present War," November 23, 1943.

184 "*Nothing . . . would be more*": H. Doc. No. 344, House of Representatives, 78th Con., 1st Sess., "Message from the President of the United States Transmitting Preliminary Report of the Armed Forces Committee."

In 1940 the average worker: Goodwin, *No Ordinary Time,* 513.

"*the political sex*": Altschuler and Blumin, *The GI Bill,* 54, 60.

185 "*emphatic notice*": Cong. Rec. Sen. Vol. 153, Pt. 17, at 24453 (September 17, 2007) (quoting Roosevelt).

As of February 1, 1945: Stanley Frank, "The G.I.'s Reject Education," *Saturday Evening Post,* August 18, 1945, p. 20.

"*understatement of the decade*": Altschuler and Blumin, *The GI Bill,* 78.

"*has no patience for*": Frank, "The G.I.'s Reject Education," 20, 101–2.

"*I would rather have had*": Pvt. G. H., "Bill of Rights," in "Mail Call," *Yank, the Army Weekly* (British ed.), February 18, 1945, pp. 18–19.

Congress enhanced the law: "Discharged Veterans," *Monthly Labor Review* 62, no. 4 (April 1946), 595.

186 *pocket-sized booklet: Going Back to Civilian Life,* WD Pamphlet 21–4 (Washington, D.C.: U.S. Government Printing Office, 1945).

Librarians once again rose: Margaret Fulmer, "For the Returning Service Man," *American Library Association Bulletin* 39, no. 6 (June 1945), 197–200.

187 *Between August 1945:* Altschuler and Blumin, *The GI Bill,* 83, 95.

turned out in droves: Suzanne Mettler, *Soldiers to Citizens* (New York: Oxford University Press, 2005), 62.

Over the course: Loss, "'The Most Wonderful Thing,'" 887, 889.

Damned Average Raisers: Altschuler and Blumin, *The GI Bill,* 95.

188 "*one priceless quality*": Mettler, *Soldiers to Citizens,* 71.

"*heartening sign*": Altschuler and Blumin, *The GI Bill,* 95.

"*Legalized segregation denied*": Loss, "'The Most Wonderful Thing,'" 889.

189 "*back to the kitchen*": Mettler, *Soldiers to Citizens,* 147–48.

190 *"If 'Editions for the Armed Services'"*: Bruce Bliven, "Books for Soldiers," *New Republic*, April 9, 1945.

"the best read army": Clip Boutell, "Authors Are Like People," *New York Post*, April 19, 1945.

"I found that a lot of them": "Armed Services Editions Excerpts from Letters Received by the Center for the Book from Authors," Library of Congress.

191 *Before the war:* David Paul Nord, Joan Shelley Rubin, and Michael Schudson, eds., *A History of the Book in America*, vol. 5 (Chapel Hill: University of North Carolina Press, 2009), 42–45.

Afterword

193 *more than 100 million:* Jonathan Rose, *The Holocaust and the Book* (Amherst: University of Massachusetts Press, 2001), 1.

Index

ILLUSTRATION CREDITS

Frontispiece: Library of Congress, Prints and Photographs Division. *Book burning:* Mary Evans Picture Library / Süddeutsche Zeitung Photo. *Library rally:* Manuscripts and Archives Division, New York Public Library, Astor, Lenox and Tilden Foundations. *Althea Warren:* Manuscripts and Archives Division, New York Public Library, Astor, Lenox and Tilden Foundations. *Kate Smith:* © Corbis. *Eleanor Roosevelt:* © Corbis. *Give More Books:* Author's collection. *Bus passes:* Author's collection. *Penn Station girl:* © Corbis. *Shakespeare:* © Corbis. *Malcolm Johnson:* Author's collection. *Porter front and back covers:* Author's collection. *Chicago Cubs:* Author's collection. *Strange Fruit:* Courtesy of the collection of Brian Anderson. *Forever Amber:* Author's collection. *A Tree Grows in Brooklyn:* Author's collection. *Chicken Every Sunday:* Author's collection. *Betty Smith:* Author's collection. *Soldier in traction:* U.S. Army Pictorial Service. *Soldier in LST:* © Corbis. *Mobile library in Italy:* © Corbis. *Sholund letter:* Edgar Sholund correspondence, 1945, Council on Books in Wartime Records, Box 32, "Letters from Servicemen J–Z" folders, 20th Century Public Policy Records, Seeley G. Mudd Manuscript Library, Department of Rare Books and Special Collections, Princeton University Library.